WRITING
&
SELLING
YOUR
MYSTERY
NOVEL

REVISED & EXPANDED

**WRITER'S DIGEST
BOOKS**

WRITER'S DIGEST
BOOKS

An imprint of Penguin Random House LLC
penguinrandomhouse.com

Copyright © 2016 by Hallie Ephron
Penguin supports copyright. Copyright fuels creativity, encourages diverse voices, promotes free speech, and creates a vibrant culture. Thank you for buying an authorized edition of this book and for complying with copyright laws by not reproducing, scanning, or distributing any part of it in any form without permission. You are supporting writers and allowing Penguin to continue to publish books for every reader.

ISBN 978-1-4403-4716-0

Printed in the United States of America

Edited by Rachel Randall
Designed by Claudean Wheeler
Cover illustrations by Shutterstock.com: Benguhan
and Shutterstock.com: DeCe

ACKNOWLEDGMENTS

I owe a huge debt of gratitude to the many crime fiction writers who have shared with me their writing process and given me a healthy distrust of the notion that there's any "one way" to write a terrific crime novel. Sadly, I've also learned that there is no formula for catapulting a novel onto the bestseller lists. Thanks to the many authors whose works I've quoted in this book in order to demonstrate where to set the bar.

Thanks to my agent, Gail Hochman, and to my lucky stars that she represents me. To editor Rachel Randall for her on-point suggestions and for ably shepherding this book through to publication. To Writer's Digest's publisher, Phil Sexton, for going to bat for this new edition. To Melanie Rigney and Barbara Kuroff, former editors at Writer's Digest Books, who sat through a mystery writing class I taught and asked me afterward if I'd consider writing a how-to book on mystery writing.

Special thanks to Sara Paretsky, a modern master and lodestar in the mystery community, for graciously agreeing to write the foreword to this book and for doing a smashing job.

And loving thanks to my husband, Jerry Touger.

ABOUT THE AUTHOR

Hallie Ephron is the *New York Times* best-selling author of suspense and mystery novels. Her novels have been called "deliciously creepy" (*Publishers Weekly*), "gripping" (*The Boston Globe*), and "snaky and unsettling" (*Seattle Times*). She is a four-time finalist for the Mary Higgins Clark Award, recognizing excellence in suspense. Her novel *Never Tell a Lie* was turned into a movie for the Lifetime Movie Network. She wrote an On Crime book review column for *The Boston Globe* for more than ten years and won the Ellen Nehr Award for Excellence in Mystery Reviewing. The first edition of *Writing and Selling Your Mystery Novel* was an Edgar Award finalist. Hallie is a popular speaker and teaches writing at conferences nationally and internationally.

SUSPENSE NOVELS BY HALLIE EPHRON:

You'll Never Know, Dear
Night Night, Sleep Tight
There Was an Old Woman
Come and Find Me
Never Tell a Lie

BOOKS ABOUT WRITING BY HALLIE EPHRON:

Writing and Selling Your Mystery Novel
Writing Your First Novel

THE PETER ZAK MYSTERY NOVELS BY G.H. EPHRON,
CO-AUTHORED WITH DONALD DAVIDOFF:

Guilt
Obsessed
Delusion
Addiction
Amnesia

FIND HALLIE EPHRON AT:

Website: HallieEphron.com
Facebook: www.facebook.com/hallie.ephron
Twitter: @HallieEphron
Blog: Jungle Red Writers (www.jungleredwriters.com)

TABLE OF CONTENTS

PART III

REVISING

PART IV

PUBLISHING YOUR MYSTERY NOVEL

FOREWORD

Sara Paretsky

"Begin at the beginning," the King said, very gravely, "and go on till you come to the end: then stop."

This excellent advice, from the King of Hearts in *Alice in Wonderland,* is all we need to write a novel. Even better, the King is presiding over a trial—to determine the guilt of the Knave of Hearts for stealing a plate of tarts made by the Queen of Hearts. Would-be crime writers can see how a master handles courtroom drama, and how an innocent victim, railroaded by the courts, extricates herself.

So—what could be easier? You've got a killer idea, and you've been told since first grade that you were a good writer. Just sit in that chair, turn on the machine, begin at the beginning, and—wait, you say you don't know what the beginning is?

There are three difficult parts to a novel: the beginning, the middle, and the end. They each present different challenges, but knowing where and how to begin may be the hardest.

Choosing to start a novel is like standing on a mountain. It's a clear day, and as you turn around, you see one interesting destination after another: a beautiful valley, a remote village, a fascinating ruin.

You decide on your destination and start down the mountain. The next thing you know, you're wading through bogs and getting tangled in brambles, you have no idea whether you're heading in the right direction, and you seriously question whether the goal is desirable. At some point, disheartened, you climb back up and start again. Or you become totally disheartened and call for the Coast Guard to bail you out.

I have published eighteen novels, and only one of them, my fourth, flowed smoothly from beginning to end. My discarded drafts run as long as 150 pages. I've fallen in love with characters who disappeared from the final draft. I have scenarios that don't work out, and one 250-page draft that couldn't be salvaged.

In other words, there is no easy way to write a novel. There are, however, ways to make it easier. That's what Hallie Ephron's *Writing and Selling Your Mystery Novel* will do for you. This is an invaluable volume for novices, but experienced writers can learn from it as well—I took away at least one important tip.

It's not a paint-by-numbers exercise, but Ephron steps you through everything, from how to get your characters on and off the stage, how to create believable dialogue, how changes in dialogue change the tone of your work, how to make plots work.

Ephron also offers strategies for the part of the job that everyone finds hardest: keeping your butt in the chair. Find a place that's yours to work in, and go there faithfully. You may have a gift equal to that of Dickens or Brontë, but none of us will ever know it if you don't put yourself in that chair and write until you come to the end. So, my sister and brother writers, get yourself to your special work space—that attic, or the curtained-off corner of your kitchen, or your bed, if you like to write like Edith Wharton. Stick this book next to your computer or legal pad or paper bags (if you write like Jean Rhys), and get going.

INTRODUCTION

"In order to become even sort of good at it, you have to be willing to be bad at it for a long time"

—David Owen in *The New Yorker* (March 7, 2016)

■ ■ ■

I came across the above quote as I was getting ready to revise the 2005 edition of this book. The "it" that Mr. Owen is talking about is playing bridge, but he might as well have been talking about writing a crime novel, another game with a steep learning curve. Almost everyone's first efforts stink.

This discovery was particularly painful for me. I'd always gotten straight As in English, and I'd read a million crime novels, so it was easy to underestimate the task at hand. How hard could it be? After all, I wasn't trying to write great literature, just a gripping page-turner. I hoped my characters would be nearly as vibrant as Ruth Rendell's, my dialogue almost as snappy as Elmore Leonard's, and my plots twisty like Agatha Christie's. I was not prepared for the reality. The aforementioned stink.

Learning my craft was a long hard slog. It took me about six years to write a mystery novel that I felt was good enough to send to potential agents, and I have two manuscripts and a ton of short stories—all of them unpublished and un-publishable—in the drawer to show for it.

Writing a mystery novel is not for the faint of heart. Juggler, conjurer, and herder of cats—those are all in the job description. Be prepared to keep three or four intertwined plots spinning. Get ready to master the art of misdirection so readers will ogle the red herrings you've sprinkled throughout the story while ignoring the clues in plain sight. Don't be surprised when you find yourself trying to corral characters who refuse to do what you want them to.

And it gets even more complicated. There is no recipe for success. Ask for advice from ten successful writers and they'll swear by ten different approaches. That's because, just like you, every one of them has a unique assortment of strengths and weaknesses. Maybe your dialogue sings but your descriptions are pallid. Maybe you have a grand time coming up with plot twists and writing slam-bang action scenes but your characters tend to be flat, without emotional insight. Maybe you write complex, interesting female characters but your men are cardboard cutouts. Your first draft will reflect whatever strengths and weaknesses you bring to the table.

I'm often asked: Can *anyone* learn to write a saleable mystery novel? My answer is no. A few are so naturally talented that they can turn out a masterpiece while barely breaking a sweat. At the other extreme are writers who, even after decades of striving, still churn out work that's destined to circle the drain. But most of us fall in between, and no one can tell at the outset who will succeed and who will fail.

Aspiring writers don't necessarily fail because they lack raw talent. Often they lack the stamina and patience needed to finish a first draft. Or they're too thin-skinned to hear criticism and haven't got the resilience to revise, revise, revise. Or they fold after the first few rejections and never reach the finish line.

This book presents a writing process that capitalizes on your strengths and shores up your weaknesses. Throughout, you'll find a range of strategies that have worked for successful mystery writers, along with invitations to try them and see what works for you.

There is no guarantee of success, so persevering is up to you. Only one thing is certain: If you never finish a first draft, you'll never know if you can get to "good enough."

So here's my first piece of sage advice to anyone about to embark on writing a mystery novel: *Just hold your nose and write.*

WHAT IS A MYSTERY NOVEL?

At the heart of a mystery novel is at least one **puzzle**, if not several. Something bad happens—often a murder—and the novel takes the reader and the protagonist on a journey of discovery to figure out the answers to questions like *What's really going on? Who did it?* and *Why?*

Here are a few examples of puzzles that have kicked mystery novels into gear:

PUZZLE	BOOK
How was an elderly American man killed on a train en route to Istanbul?	*Murder on the Orient Express* by Agatha Christie
Who murdered Miles Archer, the partner of private investigator Sam Spade?	*The Maltese Falcon* by Dashiell Hammett
What happened to Nick Dunne's wife, Amy?	*Gone Girl* by Gillian Flynn

Mystery novels have a protagonist who *needs* to unravel the puzzle. Often the protagonist plays the part of *sleuth*. The story unfolds with *twists and turns,* and the reader and sleuth are led astray by *red herrings*. Every character has *secrets*.

Early on, the nefarious goings-on seem to be about one thing, but in the end, they often turn out to be about something else entirely. This is absolutely the case in the three examples above. (Warning: Spoilers ahead!):

- Every passenger on the Orient Express had a motive to kill the wealthy American.
- Miles Archer's murder was staged to get Sam Spade to investigate the theft of a valuable icon.
- Amy isn't dead; she's trying to frame Nick.

To make the plot work, the writer comes up with a string of events and reflects them in a series of fun house mirrors. The main story gets intertwined with subplots and complicated by characters who may or may not have something to hide and who usually have their own goals that conflict with the protagonist's. When the truth is revealed, the reader should be surprised but not gobsmacked by its outlandishness.

Think of that moment in the movie *The Sixth Sense* when you realize the main character is dead. If you're like me, your jaw dropped. Then you watched the movie again just to see how the filmmaker pulled it off.

That's how you want readers to feel when they finish reading your mystery novel: completely surprised, realizing that they should have seen it coming, and wanting to read the novel over to see how you pulled it off.

Genre Conventions
People categorize mystery novels as *genre fiction*, meaning that these stories contain certain conventions that readers know and expect. As the author of a book that will be marketed as a mystery, it behooves you to know those conventions,

too. Not because you are duty bound to adhere to them but because you should know when you're swimming against the tide.

Here's a short list of what readers expect to find in a crime novel:

- There's a crime—bad things happen and there's usually at least one murder.
- At least part of the story is told from the point of view of the sleuth.
- The author "plays fair"—the reader knows everything that any point-of-view character knows.
- By the end of the novel, the reader knows who did it and why; all is explained, and loose ends are tied up.
- The reader feels satisfied that *some form of justice* has triumphed in the end.

Does that mean that a mystery author has to write within the confines of these genre conventions? Not at all. Plenty of books marketed as mystery novels have no murders in them. Plenty of authors leave plot strands dangling, especially when they're writing a series and plan to pick up the pieces in a future series novel. And authors may take readers to the dark side, where justice, in the traditional sense, is not served.

Here's the governing rule of the genre, which isn't really a rule at all: *Write a good enough book and you can break any rule and get away with it.*

Subcategories

The label *mystery novel* covers a lot of turf. A straight **mystery** is a whodunit or whydunit or howdunit with a main character who investigates. If the book is a tension-filled page-turner that keeps the reader on edge, wondering what's going to happen next, the publisher might market it as **suspense**. If the book is an adrenaline-filled race to keep the bad guy from striking again, the publisher might call it a **thriller**. Many novels incorporate all three elements: mystery, suspense, and thriller. **Crime novel** is a blanket term that papers over these differences.

In addition, here are a host of mystery subgenres.

- **COZY:** Also referred to as a "traditional mystery," these novels are written with a light touch and an element of fun. The setting is a small community, and the protagonist is an amateur sleuth. Sex and violence occur, for the most part, offstage. Agatha Christie invented the category, and her Miss Marple remains the quintessential cozy protagonist. Other classic cozy series include Diane Mott Davidson's Goldy Schulz series, which features a small-town caterer and recipes; Carolyn Hart's Death on Demand series with mystery bookseller Annie Laurance; and Alexander McCall Smith's No. 1 Ladies' Detective Agency novels set in Botswana.

- **POLICE PROCEDURAL:** The protagonist is in law enforcement; the investigation involves police procedure. Wilkie Collins's *The Moonstone*, with its Scotland Yard detective, is credited as one of the earliest. The books that excel in this subgenre are usually anchored in a gritty urban setting. For example, Ed McBain's (a.k.a. Evan Hunter) 87th Precinct novels are set in New York City, Joseph Wambaugh's novels are set in Los Angeles, Ian Rankin's Inspector Rebus novels are set in Edinburgh, and Louise Penny's Chief Inspector Armand Gamache novels are set in Quebec.

- **PRIVATE INVESTIGATOR:** The main character is a private investigator. This subgenre was perfected by the greats Dashiell Hammett (Sam Spade) and Raymond Chandler (Philip Marlowe). Modern exemplars and their detectives include Sue Grafton (Kinsey Millhone), Robert B. Parker (Spenser), James Lee Burke (Dave Robicheaux), Sara Paretsky (V I Warshawski), and Walter Mosley (Easy Rawlins).

- **HISTORICAL:** The story is set in an earlier historical era. A classic is Josephine Tey's *The Daughter of Time*, in which a present-day police inspector unravels the murder of Richard III's young nephews. Other examples are Anne Perry's Victorian crime novels, featuring Thomas and Charlotte Pitt; Laurie R. King's novels, featuring Sherlock Holmes and his young wife, Mary Russell; Jacqueline Winspear's Maisie Dobbs series; and Susan Elia MacNeal's Maggie Hope series.

- **LEGAL:** The legal system is the playing field, and an attorney is a main player. Believable courtroom drama is the centerpiece. Masters of the form include Scott Turow (*Presumed Innocent*), William Landay (*Defending Jacob*), and Lisa Scottoline (Rosato & Associates series). British author John Mortimer's Rumpole of the Bailey series did a brilliant comedic turn on the genre.

- **PSYCHOLOGICAL SUSPENSE:** These novels are often standalones that have as their engine the dark impulses that drive the human psyche. They often break genre conventions. Some of today's best include Tana French (*The Woods*), Gillian Flynn (*Gone Girl*), Jennifer McMahon (*Island of Lost Girls*), and Megan Abbott (*The End of Everything*).

- **ROMANTIC SUSPENSE:** The best ones balance nail-biting suspense with romance. The In Death series by Nora Roberts, writing as J.D. Robb, features a married couple; Sandra Brown does a great job, too, mixing suspense and romance in works like *Friction*. For a classic, reread Daphne du Maurier's *Rebecca*.

There are plenty of other subgenres, like **political thrillers** (Steve Berry, Barry Eisler, Brad Thor, David Baldacci), **spy thrillers** (John le Carré, Graham Greene, Alex Berenson, Tom Clancy), and **Westerns** (Tony Hillerman, Craig Johnson, C.J. Box).

Series and Standalones

A **series** mystery novel features a mystery that gets solved within the context of each book and a cast of repeating characters whose stories continue from book to book. A **standalone** is written as a one-off, and the plot and the characters are intended for a single novel without a plan for a prequel or sequel.

At the outset, it's a good idea to decide whether the book you're about to write is the first of a series or a standalone. This will affect many of the decisions you make—not the least of which is whether you can bump off your main character.

In any established series, every plot has to be good, but it's the repeating character whom readers come back for. Time spent up front developing your protagonist for a series debut pays off in the long run.

There are a host of reasons to go the series route. First, you don't have to keep starting over. You create a rich set of repeating characters in book one, each with a backstory and issues; situate them in a richly textured setting; and continue to develop them book to book. From a business standpoint, too, there's somewhat less pressure to come out of the gate with a bestseller. With the help of a supportive publisher, you have time to build an audience. Early books are more likely to stay in print because each new series entry energizes sales of the previous ones.

By the third or fourth book, the downside of a series becomes clear. You have to find a fresh way to reintroduce the ensemble characters in each book without boring those who've read the previous books. At the same time, you have to give new readers a taste of each character's past without spoiling the earlier stories. You have to keep coming up with new catastrophes and life-changing crises to throw at the main characters. And most publishers want their series authors to deliver at least a book a year.

In the happy event that you pen a successful series, you may find after five or six series novels that writing a standalone and working on a broader canvas seem very appealing. Dennis Lehane published five successful Patrick Kenzie/Angela Gennaro novels before hitting it big with *Mystic River*. Harlan Coben had seven Myron Bolitar sports agent series novels under his belt before hitting a standalone bestseller, *Tell No One,* out of the park. Laura Lippman alternates between writing Tess Monaghan novels and standalones.

On the other hand, Sue Grafton looks as if she's going to get all the way to *Z* with her best-selling Kinsey Millhone series novels.

WHAT MAKES A MYSTERY NOVEL POPULAR?

First let's take the high road: Whether it's hard-boiled or soft, and regardless of whether there's a murder in the book at all, mystery novels that find a strong audience give readers something more than an edge-of-the-seat ride. Often they examine serious themes and social issues. Truth, culpability, love, racism, corruption, power, redemption—weighty matters such as these are at the core of the best mystery fiction. The most compelling mysteries have unforgettable characters who undergo a transformation. On top of that, the mystery has to be a fun read and a page-turner with a satisfying ending that leaves the reader wide-eyed in amazement, thinking: *I should have seen that coming.*

Now the low road: From a commercial marketing standpoint, it doesn't hurt to have a gimmick. This is particularly true when you or your agent is submitting your manuscript to publishers. Editors like books they can figure out how to pitch and promote to their own sales force, booksellers, and readers. So it can be advantageous if your book has a hook, some unique feature you can communicate in ten seconds.

A hook can be anything from your protagonist's occupation to a particularly intriguing setting or backdrop to an added bonus beyond the mystery in the mystery.

Here are some examples of authors and their series hooks:

AUTHORS AND THEIR SERIES	HOOK
Rita Mae Brown's Sneaky Pie series	The cats solve the crimes.
Alan Bradley's Flavia de Luce series	The sleuth is a cheeky eleven-year-old in pigtails.
Rhys Bowen's Royal Spyness series	A failed royal, penniless and thirty-forth in line to the throne, solves crimes.
Laura Childs's Tea Shop mysteries	The novels feature the owner of a teahouse in Charleston.
Katherine Hall Page's Faith Fairchild mysteries	These culinary mysteries include recipes.
Barbara Ross's Maine Clambake series	The sleuth's family owns a clambake company in scenic coastal Maine.

AUTHORS AND THEIR SERIES	HOOK
Charlaine Harris's Southern Vampire (True Blood) series	The characters are vampires, werewolves, shape-shifters, and faeries, and the books are narrated by a telepath.
Carolyn Harte's Bailey Ruth Raeburn series	The sleuth is a ghost, an emissary from Heaven's Department of Good Intentions, who keeps breaking "rules."

A hook is by no means essential. There are plenty of star performers who deliver, year in and year out, bestsellers that are nothing more than good old-fashioned crime fiction with a professional or semiprofessional sleuth. These include Michael Connelly, Janet Evanovich, Sue Grafton, Carl Hiaasen, William Kent Krueger, Steve Hamilton, Linwood Barclay, and, of course, James Patterson. These authors tell great stories with great style, and any gimmicks are incidental to their long-term success.

TUNING YOUR EAR: A READING LIST

Some authors find it difficult to read mystery fiction while they're writing their own. When I tried to write after reading my first Robert B. Parker novel, my characters started trading banter that sounded suspiciously like Spenser and Hawk. *Delete. Delete. Delete.* As you get more secure in your voice, this tends to become less of a problem.

That's a good thing, because boy, oh boy, can you learn from the masters. Reading good mystery fiction tunes your ear. Books by Elmore Leonard are lessons in dialogue. Books by Jeffery Deaver are lessons in suspense. Read the titans of mystery fiction to see what makes readers respond. Read the Edgar Award winners to learn the definition of quality. Read first mystery novels that turned into bestsellers to see what some writers have been able to do, right out of the gate. And don't forget the classics that define the genre.

Here's a short reading list to get you started.

Novels that Set the Standard

- PLOT

  - *An Unsuitable Job for a Woman* by P.D. James
  - *The Chill* by Ross Macdonald
  - *Presumed Innocent* by Scott Turow

- **CHARACTER**

  - *Gone Girl* by Gillian Flynn
  - *Devil in a Blue Dress* by Walter Mosley
  - *The No. 1 Ladies' Detective Agency* by Alexander McCall Smith

- **DIALOGUE**

  - *High Five* by Janet Evanovich
  - *LaBrava* by Elmore Leonard
  - *Looking for Rachel Wallace* by Robert B. Parker

- **SETTING AND DESCRIPTION**

  - *Farewell, My Lovely* by Raymond Chandler
  - *Coyote Waits* by Tony Hillerman
  - *Mystic River* by Dennis Lehane

- **ACTION**

  - *The Hard Way* by Lee Child
  - *Final Jeopardy* by Linda Fairstein
  - *The Day of the Jackal* by Frederick Forsyth

- **SUSPENSE**

  - *Where Are the Children* by Mary Higgins Clark
  - *Indemnity Only* by Sara Paretsky
  - *Tell No One* by Harlan Coben
  - *The One I Left Behind* by Jennifer McMahon

Debut Novels that Became Blockbusters

- *The Black Echo* by Michael Connelly
- *When the Bough Breaks* by Jonathan Kellerman
- *The Girl on the Train* by Paula Hawkins

Classics that Define the Genre

- *The Moonstone* (1868) by Wilkie Collins
- *The Hound of the Baskervilles* (1901) by Sir Arthur Conan Doyle

- *The Circular Staircase* (1908) by Mary Roberts Rinehart
- *The Roman Hat Mystery* (1929) by Ellery Queen
- *The Maltese Falcon* (1930) by Dashiell Hammett
- *The Murder at the Vicarage* (1930) by Agatha Christie
- *The Nine Tailors* (1934) by Dorothy L. Sayers
- *Fer-de-Lance* (1934) by Rex Stout
- *Death in Ecstasy* (1936) by Ngaio Marsh
- *The Big Sleep* (1939) by Raymond Chandler
- *I the Jury* (1947) by Mickey Spillane
- *Brat Farrar* (1949) by Josephine Tey
- *The Talented Mr. Ripley* (1955) by Patricia Highsmith
- *The Laughing Policeman* (1968) by Maj Sjöwall and Per Wahlöö
- *Indemnity Only* (1982) by Sara Paretsky
- *Twice Shy* (1982) by Dick Francis

NESTING INSTRUCTIONS

Virginia Woolf said it most eloquently: "A woman must have money and a room of her own if she is going to write." In today's equal-opportunity environment, that adage applies to men as well.

If you're going to write, I have two pieces of advice:

- Set up a space for writing.
- Don't quit your day job unless you have an independent source of income.

When I started writing, I held on to my day job but reduced my hours so I'd have time to write. I set up my computer at the end of my bedroom and worked there with spotty results. I'd start writing and end up straightening my underwear drawer.

When my daughters outgrew the small enclosed sunporch that had been their playroom, I turned that space into my office. I found that once I had a place dedicated to writing, I'd go in there and write. If I was in my office, everyone in the house knew I was working and to leave me alone.

If you don't have a spare room, then at least set up a separate space that no one else uses. Get a folding screen to close yourself off, and to communicate to friends and family: DO NOT DISTURB. Then set a schedule.

Every writer has a different capacity for churning out pages. Robert B. Parker, who was known to publish three books in a year and still manage to take six months off from writing, once said that he didn't quit until he'd written ten pages each day. He wrote five days a week. At that clip, and because he did very little revision, he was able to finish a novel in six weeks.

Parker's pace leaves the rest of us in the dust. I work every day, seven days a week, except when I'm on vacation or on break between books. My self-imposed, daily minimum is 500 words—that's barely a page and a half. Not a whole lot. But write 500 words a day, every day, and in six months you've got yourself a completed first draft.

Set a minimum goal for each day, placing the bar slightly above what you know you can do without breaking a sweat. Then stick to it. Set up a writing schedule that suits your biorhythms. I get up at 7 A.M., make myself a cup of coffee, and start writing. By lunchtime, my spark and creativity for the day are sapped, and I'm pretty much useless as far as writing a first draft goes—though I can still revise and research.

Be sure you have everything you need right there in your office. A computer connected to the Internet has nearly eliminated the need for those reference books that were once indispensable, not to mention trips to the library. The encyclopedia, dictionary, Bible, thesaurus, Bartlett's *Familiar Quotations*, and *The Elements of Style* (Strunk and White), and more are available in searchable format on Bartleby.com. Even so, I own physical copies of each. In addition, I have several handbooks on English usage, guides to forensics and crime scene investigations, a collection of books about writing, plus my favorite books by my favorite writers.

Here are a few other essentials for creating a space conducive to writing:

- a comfortable desk chair with good back support
- a generous, well-lit work surface
- an electric pencil sharpener (I love this contraption, and though I rarely write in pencil, there's something very comforting about having a container full of sharpened pencils.)
- a computer with an Internet connection
- a reliable printer
- a phone (Yes, it's a source of interruption, but you won't have to leave the room to answer it.)

Finally, my office wouldn't be complete without paper fortunes stuck to my wall, saved from years of eating Chinese takeout because I was writing all day instead of preparing dinner. I read them whenever I get discouraged. My favorite is at least a decade old and completely faded:

You will succeed in a far out profession.

HOW THIS BOOK WORKS

"Do you promise that your detectives shall well and truly detect the crimes presented to them, using those wits which it may please you to bestow upon them and not placing reliance on Divine Revelation, Feminine Intuition, Mumbo-Jumbo, Jiggery-Pokery, Coincidence or the Act of God?"

—Membership oath of The Detection Club, founded in 1928; past presidents include Dorothy L. Sayers and Agatha Christie

■ ■ ■

This book is designed to be interactive. It's loaded with examples for you to read and analyze, **Now You Try** exercises to do on the spot, and **On Your Own** end-of-chapter activities for follow-up. The more you do, the more you'll get out of it.

You'll notice that some exercises and activities have numbers to the right of the title. This number indicates that the exercise or activity has a downloadable version, located at www.writersdigest.com/writing-and-selling-your-mystery-novel-revised. Simply go to the website, locate the exercise number, and click the link to download.

The book divides the writing process into five parts:

1. **PART I, PLANNING:** Beginning with a premise, this section provides a step-by-step guide to the process of planning a mystery novel. As you complete each chapter, you'll be instructed to go to the **BLUEPRINT** at the end of Part I. Completing the blueprint is integral to the planning process. By

the time you finish the Planning section, you'll have a completed blueprint and be ready to write.

2. **PART II, WRITING:** From compelling opening scene to climax to final coda, this section guides you through the writing process. It discusses writing scenes, introducing characters, writing the investigation, and creating suspense and action. It also suggests techniques to keep the reader turning the pages.

3. **PART III, REVISING:** This section provides a range of techniques for restructuring and polishing your novel so it shines in an editor's slush pile. The chapters guide you through the revision process, first flying at high altitude and examining big issues such as pacing and characterization, then flying low, examining scenes, sentences, and phrases.

4. **PART IV, PUBLISHING:** This section provides tips on publishing your novel. It walks you through the exciting and somewhat overwhelming array of choices open to an author. Are you aiming for a traditional publisher, or will you self-publish? Do you need an agent? Discover the path that's right for you.

5. **APPENDIX OF RESOURCES:** Here you'll find information about organizations, conferences, and other resources for mystery writers.

PART I

PLANNING

"Having a set of rules to follow as guidelines for writing a mystery makes sense for beginners, just as beginning artists learn the rules for color and perspective. Rules are fine until you get a feel for your own style and are skilled enough to stretch the limits of your writing. Certain rules, like playing fair with the reader, will always make sense."

—Rhys Bowen

Getting started writing a mystery novel can feel overwhelming. Where to begin? Lore has it that fiction writers are either *planners* (they write a detailed outline or synopsis first) or *pantsers* (they just write, flying by the seat of their pants). But in my experience, many of us are hybrids, combining planning and pantsing in whatever proportions work best for the demands of the current project.

You may need to think about your story for weeks until it's sufficiently gelled to write an outline. Or maybe you'll prefer to write a synopsis, a bloodless overview of what you're going to write before you try to bring it to life on the page. Or you may prefer to jump in and write a chunk to get to know your characters and the situation before you try to wrap your arms around the big picture. Or perhaps you are among the rare and fortunate few who can write straight through from start to finish, barely pausing to take a breath.

Whatever method works for you, keep in mind that a mystery novel is complex and must be meticulously wrought. So I recommend that at some point, either early on or after you're well into a first draft, that you pick your head up out of the weeds and think your story through.

To help you build that big picture, turn to the end of this section and look over the **Blueprint for Planning a Mystery Novel**. It's a place to record your planning ideas as they evolve. At the end of each chapter in Part I, you'll be invited to go to the blueprint and complete another section.

No one follows a plan to the letter. Changes may be needed when a character you thought would play a minor role starts doing pirouettes, or when a plot point critical to your solution stretches credibility to the breaking point. But by getting down the basics and really thinking through your story and your characters, you give yourself a solid foundation.

CHAPTER 1

THE PREMISE

"Anyone who ever waited for the great inspiration to strike is still waiting to write her first book or short story. I start with an idea, of course; something that intrigues me. Then I start asking myself three questions: Suppose, what if, and why?"

—Mary Higgins Clark

■ ■ ■

I used to think that I couldn't write fiction because I'm not very good at making things up. Where would I find ideas?

Then I stumbled across a terrific idea at a yard sale.

It was at a Victorian house with gingerbread-trimmed gables and leaded glass windows. I was peppering the homeowner (a complete stranger) with questions about their recent renovations, and she asked me if I wanted to go inside the house and have a look around. Of course I did.

I was wandering through the house when I thought, *Suppose a woman goes to a yard sale. What if somehow she manages to talk her way into the house? And what if she never comes out?*

I ran home and started writing. The book, *Never Tell a Lie*, starts with a yard sale at a Victorian house and ended up being a finalist for the Mary Higgins Clark Award. It was also made into a movie for the Lifetime Movie Network.

Turns out intriguing ideas are all around you. Learn to tune in and pay attention when your brain perks up and says, *Oh, that's interesting.*

WHERE TO FIND IDEAS

Here are just a few places to find ideas:

- books (No, you can't steal the main idea of a book—that's plagiarism—but you can build on an image, a situation, or a line of dialogue.)
- conversations—your own or overheard
- news and magazine stories
- something that happened to someone you know
- your own experience
- your dreams

Whenever I trip over a story idea, I jot it down and stash it in a folder labeled COMPOST. By now, the folder is bulging with clippings and handwritten notes. Here are some ideas culled from the news:

- A Toyota salesman tries to investigate terrorists on the Internet and gets arrested for terrorism.
- Severed feet, still inside shoes, keep washing up on a beach.
- A man tries to stage his own disappearance by murdering a look-alike he finds on the Internet.
- A woman finds a bullet in the pork butt she's cooking.
- A young man who writes his sexual fantasies in a personal journal is charged with creating child pornography.

Start your own compost file, and save ideas that intrigue you.

MAKING THE LEAP FROM IDEA TO PREMISE

A **premise** is the basic proposition behind the book. Transforming an idea into a well-articulated premise is the first step of writing a mystery novel.

Here's an example of a premise developed from one of the ideas in my compost heap.

IDEA FROM THE NEWS	MYSTERY NOVEL PREMISE USING *SUPPOSE* AND *WHAT IF*
A young man who writes his fantasies in a personal journal is charged with making child pornography.	**Suppose** a troubled young man writes violent, explicit sexual fantasies in his journal and shares his journal with his therapist. And **what if** a series of violent crimes then occur that closely mirror the details of his fantasies?

The words *suppose* and *what if* anchor a well-articulated premise. A premise written in this format shows you where you're going. It keeps you on track throughout the writing process, and it can be useful when you're pitching your book to agents, editors, and, ultimately, booksellers and readers.

Once the premise is articulated, it suggests all kinds of plot possibilities. Did the young man commit the crimes? Did his therapist? Did the therapist share the man's journal with someone else, or was the journal stolen? Or maybe the young man copied those fantasies from another source. The story could explore issues of culpability and privacy. And on and on and on ...

With a good idea and a premise in hand, you're off and running.

✎ NOW YOU TRY: PREMISE WRITING
1.1

Practice turning an idea into a premise. Clip articles from the newspaper that appeal to you and contain the germ of an idea for a mystery novel. Jot down each idea in the left column below. In the right column, transform it into a premise using *suppose* and *what if*.

IDEA FROM THE NEWS	MYSTERY NOVEL PREMISE USING SUPPOSE AND WHAT IF

⬇ Download a printable version of this worksheet at www.writersdigest.com/writing-and-selling-your-mystery-novel-revised.

USING REAL EVENTS AND PEOPLE

Some real events and real people are too bizarre for fiction. For instance, there's a news story in my compost heap about a highway toll collector who received a call from a friend, warning her to be on the lookout for a 2003 white Chevy Silverado driven by a shooting suspect on the lam. Moments later (!) that Silverado drove through her toll lane. If you put that story in a book, readers would cry foul because it seems so unbelievable. *But it really happened,* says you. *So what?* says the reader. Reality is no excuse. Plenty of things happen in real life that don't pass the sniff test in a work of fiction.

A well-constructed fictional world isn't necessarily realistic, but it must be believable.

MARKET-DRIVEN IDEAS

Does your idea have to be marketable? Sure, what you're writing about has to be interesting to more than you and a few geeky professional colleagues. On the other hand, it's hard to predict what readers will find interesting. Can you imagine a book about the physics of icebergs appealing to a large audience? That's the focus of Peter Høeg's best-selling suspense novel *Smilla's Sense of Snow.* Dan Brown's *The Da Vinci Code* combines an international murder mystery with a minute analysis of esoterica culled from two thousand years of Western history. B.A. Shapiro's *The Art Forger* is loaded with gory details about how to make a painting look old. These authors make arcane content interesting by writing about it in a compelling way, and they tap into the mystery reader's appetite for learning new things.

Should you try to follow trends and write what's hot in the marketplace right now? I don't recommend it. Readers are notoriously fickle, and what appeals to the crowd this year may be considered humdrum three years from now, when, if you're lucky, your book hits the shelves. By then, readers will be looking for something new and fresh.

Because writing a novel is really hard and takes a long time, my advice to you is this: *Write your passion.* Write what you care deeply about. Write about what interests and intrigues you. You'll be more likely to finish a novel if you care about what you're writing, and only a finished novel stands a chance of being published.

ON YOUR OWN: FINDING IDEAS

1. **BECOME AN OBSERVER.** The world around you is full of inspiration. Watch what goes on while you're riding a bus, drinking at a bar, or waiting at an airport. Listen to conversations. Notice what people wear, their mannerisms. Take notes.

2. **BE PREPARED WHEN IDEAS STRIKE.** Carry a pad and pen in your pocket, and keep them by your bed, too. You think you'll remember, but you won't.

3. **MAKE A FOLDER OF IDEAS.** Clip and save intriguing stories from newspapers and magazines. Throw in other ideas that inspire you.

4. **CARRY A VOICE RECORDER.** Do you get your best ideas while driving? I do. Keep a voice recorder handy so you'll be able to capture those ideas without causing an accident.

➡ **COMPLETE THE PREMISE SECTION OF THE BLUEPRINT AT THE END OF PART I.**

CHAPTER 2

THE MYSTERY SLEUTH

"A really good detective never gets married."

—Raymond Chandler, *Raymond Chandler Speaking*

■ ■ ■

An editor once told me that when she reads a manuscript, especially the first of a new series, she's looking primarily for a compelling protagonist who will anchor the story. Readers need to care about what happened to that character *before the book opens* and what's going to happen to that character *after the book ends.* The journey of solving the mystery should be *transformational* so that by the end the protagonist has changed in some fundamental way.

So what kind of character makes readers care? It goes without saying that the character must be fully realized and complex, not a cipher or a cliché. She needs to be sympathetic, if not entirely likeable. But perfect? No way. Moral, intellectually infallible, physically flawless characters are boring. Readers are far more taken with a character who is flawed in interesting ways. Michael Connelly's detective, Harry Bosch, is a haunted, emotionally bruised former cop who makes mistakes and steps on toes as he pursues justice. V I Warshawski, Sara Paretsky's private investigator, is tough, principled, and has a temper that gets her in trouble.

Harry Bosch and V I Warshawski are typical hard-boiled mystery protagonists: unattached and childless. Unencumbered protagonists live relatively uncomplicated lives. They can have romantic liaisons. They can go anywhere, anytime, without having to call Grandma or a babysitter. Every time they rush headlong into danger, the reader isn't worrying about their orphaned child or widowed spouse.

On the other hand, some of the most popular mystery series feature main characters with plenty of personal baggage. Precious Ramotswe of Alexander McCall Smith's *The No. 1 Ladies' Detective Agency* gets married and adopts a child. Katherine Hall Page's Faith Fairchild is a caterer married to a clergyman and has two young children.

Start creating your protagonist by getting to know him thoroughly, more intimately than you know your best friend. You don't need to tell the reader whether your character sleeps naked (V I Warshawski does), but *you* should know.

How does your character approach an investigation? Is it going to be with bumbling and brute force, intellectual finesse and cunning, or cool professionalism and emotional detachment? Does he charge into an interrogation hurling threats and accusations, or lurk in a corner waiting for the suspect to make a gaffe?

What motivates your protagonist to solve this particular crime? Even if investigation is part of her everyday job, she must have some inner driving force that makes her willing to take risks and face danger in order to ferret out the villain.

Though you'll never tell readers even half of what you decide, knowing your protagonist inside and out enables you to pick the telling details that make your character jump off the page.

DEVELOPING YOUR PROTAGONIST'S DARK PAST

Mystery fiction is riddled with protagonists who have been variously tortured by their authors. They've suffered physical or emotional abuse, been addicted to drugs or alcohol, been falsely convicted of a crime, lost a loved one … the litany of woe goes on.

There's a reason why mystery authors give their main characters tortured backstories: That dark past can be used to motivate the character in the present. A detective who investigates sex crimes may have survived a brutal rape. A police officer investigating police corruption may be haunted by his father's removal from the force under suspicion of misconduct. A character who grew up in a cult will go great lengths to see that an abusive cult leader is brought to justice.

When your protagonist has a dark past, it raises the stakes. Each time out, the sleuth not only solves a crime but also takes a personal journey and gets a chance to *get it right this time.* Redemption is a powerful motivator.

DETERMINING YOUR SLEUTH'S EXPERIENCE LEVEL

If you or I were to trip over a dead body, we'd likely call the cops, end of story. But a three-hundred-page mystery novel requires that the main character get mixed up in the investigation. You have to create a setup that makes this situation believable. This certainly isn't a problem if investigating crimes is part of your main character's day job, but it's more challenging if your protagonist is an ordinary guy or gal who would normally leave detecting to the pros.

Mystery readers are willing to go along with all kinds of amateur sleuths as long as the character would logically have access to the investigation or has a compelling, credible reason for getting involved. For example:

- The amateur sleuth possesses special expertise or inside knowledge that the police need.
- The amateur sleuth is married to the homicide detective.
- The police investigators are corrupt or incompetent.
- The police suspect the wrong person, and the sleuth can't convince them to redirect their investigation.
- The police don't believe a crime has been committed.

Below is a short list of sleuths' professions from published mystery novels. Amateurs are on the left, people who possess some expertise that police might logically need are in the middle, and the pros are on the right.

AMATEUR SLEUTHS	⟵———————⟶	PROFESSIONAL SLEUTHS
Actor	Archaeologist	Bail bond agent
Artist	Attorney	Crime scene investigator
Cabbie	Clergy	Expert witness
Caterer	Judge	Federal agent
Bookstore owner	Museum curator	Investigative reporter
College professor	Physician	Medical examiner
Horse trainer	Psychologist	Military police officer
Librarian	Scientist	Police officer or detective
Wedding planner	Thief	Private investigator

When you pick a profession for your protagonist, keep in mind that the less likely your sleuth is to trip over a dead body, the more you'll have to work to establish a believable, compelling reason for your character to investigate the crime.

RESEARCHING YOUR CHARACTER

A credible main character gets you to that "look, Ma, no hands" moment in a mystery when the reader thinks, *Wow, this really could happen.*

The more you know the world your protagonist inhabits, the easier it will be to write her convincingly. Dashiell Hammett worked as a detective for the Pinkerton Agency in the years before he created his fictional PI, Sam Spade. Aaron Elkins was an anthropologist before he created fictional forensic anthropologist Gideon Oliver. Lisa Scottoline, Scott Turow, and John Grisham were all practicing attorneys before they wrote their first legal thrillers.

Tear the illusion of authenticity and you stop the reader in his tracks. For instance, suppose you're reading a mystery novel about a judge presiding over a murder case. The judge runs into the jury foreman at a cocktail party, and they chat about the case. If you're like me, you stop reading. Judges don't chat, even casually, with jury members during a trial.

If you give your protagonist a profession you haven't experienced firsthand, be prepared to do the research necessary to make your character ring true. Here are some ways to find out what you need to know:

- **INTERVIEWS:** Talk to someone who's in your protagonist's profession. Bring along a digital recorder, and be prepared with questions.
- **TAGALONGS:** Convince someone who shares your protagonist's profession to let you hang around for a few hours or days. Ride along with a cop. Get a criminal attorney to let you spend a day observing. Take notes.
- **CITIZEN'S POLICE ACADEMY:** Many communities have programs designed to acquaint citizens with the inner workings of their local police department. The training often includes ride-alongs and firearms instruction. Check if any are offered in your area. If you go, make friends with the officers you meet so you can follow up with questions that arise as you write.

Find Experts

You will find that people are surprisingly willing to share their specialized knowledge. The trick is finding them.

- **CHECK OUT WHO YOU KNOW:** You may already know someone who has the knowledge you seek. If you're writing a police procedural, you might be as lucky as I am and have a state trooper living next door—he tries to answer my questions, or puts me in touch with other experts, and once he let me sit in his cruiser so I'd get the full sensory experience of sitting behind the cage barrier in the backseat.
- **ASK YOUR FRIENDS:** Maybe you know someone who knows someone who … You'll be surprised by how few "degrees of separation" there are between you and that lawyer, doll maker, or forensic psychologist you seek.
- **GO WHERE YOUR CHARACTER WOULD HANG OUT:** Visit places where your character would inhabit and make friends.
- **MINE THE INTERNET:** Many websites are hosted by experts in various fields and post both the person's credentials and their contact information. Identify the right person and get in touch. You can also connect via Facebook and LinkedIn, or join an online group where you can post queries.

CRAFTING A REALISTIC PROTAGONIST

Creating a main character who feels real is a tall order. As you imagine yours, take the following qualities into consideration.

Appearance: Conveying and Hiding

Physical appearance determines how other characters respond to your protagonist. Even if you never give the reader a detailed description, you need to know what your character looks like. Does he resemble an active-duty Marine, an over-the-hill prizefighter, or a used-car salesman? Does she look like a hotshot attorney, a beauty queen who's all glam and gams, or an insecure mouse who's learned it's safer not to say what she thinks?

Personally, I prefer a main character who feels like a real person. But a protagonist who's a little larger-than-life isn't a bad thing. As Janet Evanovich once said of Stephanie Plum: "I wanted a heroine with big hair." Jack Reacher stands 6'5"— an inch taller than his creator, Lee Child. Brilliant, vengeful computer hacker Lisbeth Salander (*The Girl with the Dragon Tattoo*) has "hair as short as a fuse," a pierced nose and eyebrows, "a wasp tattoo about an inch long on her neck, a tattooed loop around the biceps for her left arm and another around her left ankle."

Characters who aren't what they seem at first blush intrigue readers. For example, a character who looks like the proverbial "dumb blonde" might turn out to have a Ph.D. in chemistry. Or a character who blusters like a tough hard-boiled cop might turn out to be an old softie who rescues puppies. The pleasure for the reader comes in peeling away the layers. First, they experience surprise at discovering hidden aspects of the character. Second, they're delighted when other characters are fooled by the character's outward appearance.

Take Jane Marple, for example. Here's how Agatha Christie described her in the "The Tuesday Night Club," the 1927 short story in which she was first introduced:

> Miss Marple wore a black brocade dress, very much pinched in around the waist. Mechlin lace was arranged in a cascade down the front of the bodice. She had on black lace mittens, and a black lace cap surmounted the piled-up masses of her snowy hair. She was knitting, something white and fleecy. Her pale blue eyes, benignant and kindly, surveyed her nephew and her nephew's guests with gentle pleasure.

Outwardly, Miss Marple seems an unassuming, possibly ditzy old woman. But the white hair, old-fashioned getup, and knitting are pure camouflage for a sharp, logical intellect and a mind that is engaged and observing at every moment. The pleasure for the reader comes when a pompous police detective dismisses her as a dithery spinster—and then gets his comeuppance when she discerns the clues he missed.

Christie creates a gap between who Miss Marple is and who she appears to be.

MISS JANE MARPLE		
Who she appears to be:	THE GAP	Who she really is:
Dithery		Logical
Naive		Wordly
Unobservant		Sharp

Think about which aspects of your main character's appearance are a genuine reflection of character and which ones form a misleading façade. Create a disconnect between your character's physical presence and true capabilities. Then **mine the gap**: Through plot and action, reveal who your character really is.

✎ **NOW YOU TRY: APPEARANCE—WHAT TO CONVEY, WHAT TO HIDE**　　2.1

List the qualities you want others to readily infer from your character's appearance; list other qualities you want readers to discover as they get to know him.

QUALITIES APPARENT TO OTHERS	QUALITIES HIDDEN AT FIRST

⬇ Download a printable version of this worksheet at www.writersdigest.com/writing-and-selling-your-mystery-novel-revised.

✎ NOW YOU TRY: APPEARANCE—GET DOWN THE BASICS   2.2

Crystallize your character's features. Take all those ideas floating around in your head and get them in writing. Here's a list to get you started:

Gender:

Age:

Build:

Most striking feature:

Hair color, and if it's natural:

Hairstyle:

Wears what to work:

Wears what to a formal affair:

Wears what to sleep:

Facial hair, tattoos, body piercing, scars:

Ethnicity, and from what physical features others could guess it:

Mannerisms, gestures:

Health problems:

What actor or actress you would cast in the role:

⬇ Download a printable version of this worksheet at www.writersdigest.com/ writing-and-selling-your-mystery-novel-revised.

Disequilibrium: Present Status and Ambition

Disequilibrium makes for interesting characters and exciting plots. For instance, in the opening of Hank Phillippi Ryan's *The Other Woman*, reporter Jane Ryland has lost her job for refusing to reveal a source. The novel is as much about Jane regaining her reputation as it is about finding a serial killer.

The right disparity between who your character is and who he aspires to be in the future can provide a compelling source of motivation in your plot. A character who is pursuing a promotion from desk sergeant to homicide detective might be willing to take risks to prove herself. A character who's just discovered that her husband cheated on her might be readily deceived by a woman's false claims that her husband abused her.

Think about who your character is when your story opens and what your character aspires to be in the future; use that disequilibrium to drive your plot.

List your character's present status and aspirations for the future. Identify the disparities that you can take advantage of in building your plot.

	PRESENT STATUS	ASPIRATIONS
Profession/Job		
Accomplishments		
Income Level		
Current Residence		
Reputation		
Romantic Attachments		
Children		
Lifetime Achievement		

⬇ Download a printable version of this worksheet at www.writersdigest.com/writing-and-selling-your-mystery-novel-revised.

Background

Your character's background influences the way he responds to events and other characters. For example, S.J. Rozan's PI Lydia Chin is an American-born Chinese woman whose overprotective mother worked in a sweatshop while Lydia was growing up. So of course Lydia wants to help a young, up-and-coming Chinese fashion designer whose sketches are being held for ransom in *Mandarin Plaid*. Michael Connelly's detective Harry Bosch is a former foster child. In *City of Bones*, when buried bones turn out to be those of a foster child, of course he ignores orders from higher-ups to stop wasting his time trying to find the boy's killer. In *Gone Girl*, Amy Dunne's parents are psychiatrists who idealized their daughter in a series of best-selling Amazing Amy books. So why wouldn't Amy grow up to be a psychopathic narcissist who assumes she can get away with murder?

You can make your character an only child who is used to being the center of attention or the third of nine siblings who's learned early on how to get that coveted turkey wing. You can make her the only child of a concert violinist who has traveled the world or the oldest daughter of an unemployed alcoholic who has never been out of Schenectady.

Knowing where your character comes from can help you create a complex, consistent human being. There are no right and wrong choices, but the background you invent should mesh with the direction you want your story to take. If aspects of your character's background are personally meaningful to you, you'll be able to reach within yourself and your past experiences to guide your character's reactions.

NOW YOU TRY: BACKGROUND DECISIONS   2.4

Determine these aspects of your character's background.

Birth order:

_____

Parents (occupations, education, and income):

_____

Siblings:

_____

Hometown:

_____

Childhood home (apartment, ranch house, mansion, etc.):

_____

Education:

_____

Dream profession:

_____

How and when the character lost his or her virginity:

_____

Past trauma or formative event:

_____

Keepsake from the past and what it represents:

⬇ Download a printable version of this worksheet at www.writersdigest.com/
writing-and-selling-your-mystery-novel-revised.

Talents and Skills

Talents and skills give your character texture. Take Robert B. Parker's PI Spenser, for example. He's a large, powerfully built man who enjoys weight lifting and jogging. He also loves to cook. Laura Lippman's tough-minded private investigator Tess Monaghan is a reporter with a passion for rowing.

It helps if you're familiar with the talents and skills with which you endow your protagonist, but it's not essential. Parker never boxed, but he did lift weights for years, and he was modest about his cooking prowess. Like her character, Laura Lippman was a hotshot reporter at a Baltimore daily newspaper and belonged to a rowing club.

Are there things your character has to do that he hates? Is he a reporter who dreads making cold calls? A police officer who hates target practice? Contradictions make for interesting characters.

Think about what your character is good at. Is he physical or cerebral? An artist or an engineer? Are all her strengths obvious to others, or are some hidden? You can use your character's strengths to help shape your plot. Use hidden strengths to surprise the reader.

✏ NOW YOU TRY: TALENTS AND SKILLS   2.5

What are your protagonist's talents and skills? Here's a list to get you started.

Most obvious skill:

Hidden skill:

Most obvious weakness:

Hidden weakness:

_____

Talent:

_____

Things he or she hates to do:

_____

⬇ Download a printable version of this worksheet at www.writersdigest.com/
writing-and-selling-your-mystery-novel-revised.

Personality

Humor, anger, fear, love—what triggers these reactions in your character's emotional core? Is he fearless while climbing mountains but terrified by cockroaches? Does he have lots of buddies but no close friends? Does he like puns but hate practical jokes?

The more you define your character's personality, the more you'll know how he'll react in the routine and extreme situations you're going to throw him into. You'll know what will make him persevere in the face of grave danger and apparently insurmountable obstacles, what kinds of pressure would make him buckle, and what would cause him to crack.

✎ NOW YOU TRY: PERSONALITY TRAITS   2.6

Answer each of these questions for your character:

_____

What is your character frightened by?

_____

What angers your character?

_____

What does your character find humorous?

_____

What does your character hate to be teased about?

_____

What qualities does your character find attractive in others?

What qualities does your character find annoying in others?

What is your character's capacity for physical violence?

What is your character's capacity for intimacy?

Who are your character's heroes and role models?

What nervous tics and obsessive behaviors does your character have?

What swear words does your character use when annoyed? Which ones does he use when he's angry? Outraged?

⬇ Download a printable version of this worksheet at www.writersdigest.com/ writing-and-selling-your-mystery-novel-revised.

Demeanor While Under Duress

The nature of a mystery novel is such that your character will be tested. He'll be insulted, lied to, bullied, humiliated, cheated, threatened, and injured. He'll see other people duped, scapegoated, and hurt. Characters, like real people, show their mettle in do-or-die situations.

A news story a while back reported an armed confrontation among a group of young men on the subway. Many terrified passengers witnessed it, but only one got up and made his way through the train, warning others. What would your character have done?

Think about how your character reacts under duress. Does she trade insult for insult or turn the other cheek? Does he go off half-cocked or simmer until he explodes? Does he throw a punch, draw a firearm, or call 9-1-1?

Jot down what your protagonist would do in each of these situations:

Gets a bad haircut:	
Is enjoying a steak dinner when the woman at a nearby table lights a cigar:	
Gets shortchanged at the supermarket:	
Discovers a pair of condoms in the purse or pocket of his significant other:	
Hits a dog while driving, hurrying to the airport to catch a plane:	
Gets propositioned by a beautiful woman or a handsome man:	
Breaks down at two in the morning on a deserted road:	
Finds a diamond ring on a park bench:	
Discovers that a best friend has been embezzling funds from a charity:	
Discovers that a close relative is a child molester:	

⬇ Download a printable version of this worksheet at www.writersdigest.com/writing-and-selling-your-mystery-novel-revised.

Tastes and Preferences

This is the fun stuff. Tastes and preferences provide you with the grace notes you need to express your character's personality and flesh out his daily life. Dorothy L. Sayers's Lord Peter Wimsey is a wine connoisseur. Rex Stout's Nero Wolfe breeds orchids.

Think about your character's tastes and preferences. Is she likely to sit in a bar nursing a Budweiser, or would she prefer a glass of vintage merlot? At home alone at night, is she likely to turn on the tube, read a book, or talk on the phone? Is she likely to wear vintage clothing snagged from a thrift store or hang around in sweats and sneakers? Does he frequent a local diner or a gourmet French bistro? Does he have a passion for great pizza or great cigars? Details like these make your character come alive.

✎ NOW YOU TRY: TASTES AND PREFERENCES   2.8

Use this list of questions to flesh out your character's tastes and preferences.

What is your character's favorite place to eat out?

What does your character eat for dinner, alone on a weeknight?

What does your character usually order at a bar?

What book or magazine is on the bedside table?

What music does your character listen to in the car?

What is your character's favorite thing to do on a quiet Saturday afternoon?

What is your character's favorite thing to do on a Saturday night?

What is your character's idea of the perfect vacation?

What is your character's favorite place to hang out?

What does your character have a weakness for?

What does your character collect?

What is your character's political affiliation?

Is your character an activist for a cause?

⬇ Download a printable version of this worksheet at www.writersdigest.com/ writing-and-selling-your-mystery-novel-revised.

Personality traits exist across a spectrum. Draw an X to show where your character belongs on each continuum:

Cautious   <1----2----3----4----5----6----7----8----9----10>   Impulsive

Aloof   <1----2----3----4----5----6----7----8----9----10>   Gregarious

Analytical   <1----2----3----4----5----6----7----8----9----10>   Emotional

Anxious   <1----2----3----4----5----6----7----8----9----10>   Easygoing

Charming   <1----2----3----4----5----6----7----8----9----10>   Abrasive

Cocky   <1----2----3----4----5----6----7----8----9----10>   Insecure

Fastidious   <1----2----3----4----5----6----7----8----9----10>   Unfussy

Honest   <1----2----3----4----5----6----7----8----9----10>   Deceitful

Optimistic   <1----2----3----4----5----6----7----8----9----10>   Pessimistic

Lethargic   <1----2----3----4----5----6----7----8----9----10>   Energetic

Rigid   <1----2----3----4----5----6----7----8----9----10>   Flexible

Sensitive   <1----2----3----4----5----6----7----8----9----10>   Thick-Skinned

Stubborn   <1----2----3----4----5----6----7----8----9----10>   Accommodating

Vain   <1----2----3----4----5----6----7----8----9----10>   Modest

Define any other personality traits that are important to your character below:

_____   <1----2----3----4----5----6----7----8----9----10>   _____

_____   <1----2----3----4----5----6----7----8----9----10>   _____

_____   <1----2----3----4----5----6----7----8----9----10>   _____

⬇ Download a printable version of this worksheet at www.writersdigest.com/writing-and-selling-your-mystery-novel-revised.

Honesty or Deceitfulness

Mystery novels are fueled by lies. Characters tell them to each other and to themselves. But one of the so-called rules in mystery writing is that viewpoint characters should "play fair" with the reader. In other words, they shouldn't lie to the reader or withhold information.

Agatha Christie mangled that rule in 1926 with *The Murder of Roger Ackroyd*. (Spoiler alert ahead!) Dr. James Sheppard, the novel's narrator and Poirot's assistant, turns out to be the killer. Dr. Sheppard doesn't outright lie for the book's nearly three hundred pages, but he obfuscates and omits, fooling Poirot and pulling the wool over readers' eyes.

Christie played fast and loose with her readers, but it hardly mattered: The members of the British-based Crime Writers' Association named the book the best crime novel ever written.

Dr. Sheppard is an **unreliable narrator**. Modern best-selling crime novels are full of them. Nick and Amy Dunne both lie to readers in *Gone Girl*. Rusty Sabich, the attorney accused of killing his mistress in Scott Turow's *Presumed Innocent,* never reveals to the reader whether he's innocent. Rachel in Paula Hawkins's *The Girl on the Train* is drunk throughout the story so her memory can't be trusted.

NOW YOU TRY: WHY YOUR CHARACTER MIGHT LIE 2.10

Put a check mark beside every reason you can imagine for why your protagonist might lie:

____ to hide a secret

____ to avoid facing the truth

____ to protect a loved one

____ to even a score or wreak revenge on an enemy

____ for personal gain

____ because he doesn't know what the truth is (has amnesia, wasn't there, misinterprets something he heard or saw, was intoxicated or stoned or unconscious, believes a lie someone else told …)

____ because he's a pathological liar

____ other reasons: _____

⬇ Download a printable version of this worksheet at www.writersdigest.com/writing-and-selling-your-mystery-novel-revised.

Naming Names

Now that you know your protagonist inside and out, pick a name that fits. Mystery authors usually pick catchy, easy-to-remember names for their protagonists that suggest, by sound or meaning, something about their characters.

Janet Evanovich says she picked the name Stephanie Plum for her bounty hunter protagonist because of the way *Stephanie* rolls off the tongue, and because she likes the juicy ripeness of *Plum*. And besides, Evanovich says, there were lots of Stephanies when she was growing up in blue-collar New Jersey, and Stephanie Plum is the quintessential "Jersey girl."

Think about the names Dashiell Hammett picked for two of his best-known mystery sleuths: *Sam Spade* and *Nick Charles*. Even if you didn't know, you'd probably be able to guess which one is a hard-boiled, edgy, steely-nerved San Francisco detective and which one is the dapper Manhattan man about town.

The name *Sam Spade*, with its single syllables and repeated sibilance, sounds like a tough guy who *calls a spade a spade*. Sam is a working-class, no-nonsense first name. (Trivia: Sam was Hammett's real first name.) *Nick Charles* has a softer, more casual sound. We can easily imagine some Manhattan society matron pronouncing the last name *Chawles*. Still, *Nick* echoes the character's Greek-American background—he changed his unpronounceable last name to Charles when he retired from his job as a PI to manage his wife's sizable fortune.

So what's a good name for your protagonist? You've fleshed him out, decided what he looks like, and determined his preferences, profession, locale, and so on. Now you're ready to choose a name that fits.

NOW YOU TRY: NAME YOUR PROTAGONIST   2.11

1. Think about what you want your character's name to convey. Strength? Vulnerability? Age? Ethnicity? Personality? Social class? Occupation? List at least four characteristics you want the name to suggest.

_____

_____

_____

_____

2. Now make a list of first and last names that meet your criteria:

FIRST NAMES	LAST NAMES

Pick the combination you like best.

3. Search the Internet for the full name you picked (using quotes) to see how common it is and if it's already been used in a book.

⬇ Download a printable version of this worksheet at www.writersdigest.com/writing-and-selling-your-mystery-novel-revised.

 ## ON YOUR OWN: PLANNING YOUR PROTAGONIST   2.12

1. Write a five-minute, one-paragraph biography of your protagonist that could actually appear in the novel.

2. List four of the most significant, formative events in your main character's life. Briefly describe the impact each event has had on your protagonist.

EVENT	IMPACT
1.	1.

2.	2.
3.	3.
4.	4.

3. Write a one-page, first-person monologue in your character's voice, talking about one of the events you listed in step two.

⬇ Download a printable version of this worksheet at www.writersdigest.com/writing-and-selling-your-mystery-novel-revised.

➔ **COMPLETE THE PROTAGONIST SECTION OF THE BLUEPRINT AT THE END OF PART I.**

CHAPTER 3

THE CRIME AND THE VICTIM'S SECRETS

"Everybody counts or nobody counts. That's it. It means I bust my ass to make the case whether it's a prostitute or the mayor's wife."

—Detective Harry Bosch, in Michael Connelly's *The Last Coyote*

■ ■ ■

At the center of every mystery is a crime. Someone does something bad, and someone else—a victim—gets hurt or killed. The search for the culprit forms the backbone of the novel. Even if you don't yet know who did it, a good place to start planning your story is with the **crime scenario.** Decide who gets hurt, how, and where.

THE CRIME

The crime might take place when the novel opens, or it might occur later, after the story is well underway. It might have happened in the past. There are no rules about who gets killed or how, but readers expecting a more soft-boiled tale want their violence offstage and will be very unhappy if you bump off cats, dogs, or children. Readers expecting a more hard-boiled tale have stronger stomachs. You can't please everyone, so decide what audience you're writing for.

Make the Crime Matter to the Protagonist

Heads up! When planning your novel, the single most important thing to figure out is this: why your protagonist *needs* to solve this crime.

Whether the crime is big (it threatens the future of humanity) or small (it threatens a good person's reputation), it has to matter to the sleuth. There should be something about this crime or these victims that touches this particular protagonist in a profound and personal way. In other words, there has to be something *at stake*, and the more personal the stakes, the better.

Here are some of the plot devices that make the crime matter to the protagonist:

- The victim is the protagonist's friend, colleague, lover, or relative.
- The *next* likely victim is the protagonist's friend, colleague, lover, or relative.
- The protagonist may be the next victim.
- The protagonist is accused of the crime.
- The protagonist identifies with the innocent person accused of the crime.
- The protagonist identifies with the victim.
- The protagonist or a loved one suffered a similar crime.

Come up with a crime, and a reason the crime matters to your protagonist. Create the connection that links victim to protagonist, and use that motivation to propel your story forward.

THE VICTIM

How much you need to know about the victim depends on the story you're telling. You may need to know very little—only what put that character in harm's way. For instance, a novel about a museum heist in which a guard is killed may linger for only a few sentences on the victim: wrong place, wrong time, just doing his job, and the story moves on. But what if it turns out that this museum guard knew the robbers? Maybe he was an accessory or an unwilling pawn. Or maybe the sleuth is his sister, or his brother was one of the robbers. Suddenly, understanding the victim becomes important to the plot, and the writer needs to flesh him out.

More often than not, the victim *is* essential to the story. For instance, in Scott Turow's *Presumed Innocent*, deputy chief prosecutor Rusty Sabich is asked to investigate the rape and murder of one of his colleagues, Carolyn Polhemus.

Through dialogue and flashbacks, the reader learns that the victim was a strong, sensuous, magnetic woman who made her share of friends and enemies. We also learn a secret: She was Sabich's former lover. When his relationship to the victim is discovered, Sabich becomes the prime suspect.

The Victim's Secrets

The revelation of secrets twists the plot and propels a mystery novel forward. Everyone has secrets, including the victim.

Here's an example of a crime scenario with a list of possible victim's secrets. As you read the list, think about how each victim's secret suggests a different path for investigators.

CRIME SCENARIO	VICTIM'S SECRETS
Lorinda Lewis, a thirty-year-old bank teller, is carjacked in front of her home. A short time later, she's killed when she's thrown onto the Hollywood Freeway.	• Suppose she was about to expose a scheme to embezzle money from the bank. • Suppose she was having an affair with her boss. • Suppose she had a night job as a stripper and was being stalked. • Suppose she was a drug addict. • Suppose she had a sister who looked just like her. • Suppose she was a compulsive gambler. • Suppose her boyfriend was a drug dealer. • Suppose she was an adopted child who'd just made contact with her birth mother.

Don't pick a secret that you don't want to write about. If your victim's secret was that she was a stripper, you'll have to research and write about stripping and strip clubs. If she was embezzling money from the bank, you'll have to learn the technical details of the crime. So pick secrets that interest you and will take you where you want to spend your time.

How many secrets can a victim have in one novel? Two or three, maybe even four. Some secrets will turn out to be red herrings that make innocent suspects appear guilty. At least one secret will turn out to be a genuine clue to the villain's true identity.

 **NOW YOU TRY: THE VICTIM'S SECRETS**   3.1

Write your own crime scenario on the following page. Brainstorm six possible victim's secrets. Think about which ones will work best in your novel.

YOUR CRIME SCENARIO: WHO GETS HURT, HOW, AND WHERE	THE VICTIM'S SECRETS
	1.
	2.
	3.
	4.
	5.
	6.

⬇ Download a printable version of this worksheet at www.writersdigest.com/writing-and-selling-your-mystery-novel-revised.

 ## ON YOUR OWN: THE CRIME AND THE VICTIM'S SECRETS

1. Create a simple scenario for each crime in your novel: Who gets hurt? How? Where?
2. Why does your protagonist *need* to solve this crime?
3. Plan your victim(s). Create a thumbnail sketch, including:

   - name
   - age
   - gender
   - occupation
   - appearance (a few physically distinguishing characteristics)
   - significant personality traits (smart or stupid, generous or selfish, well liked or despised, etc.)
   - a few telling details (something she owns or does, a favorite expression, etc.) that define the victim
   - what it is about the character that puts her in harm's way
   - what secret(s) the victim is hiding

➡ COMPLETE THE CRIME SECTION OF THE BLUEPRINT AT THE END OF PART I.

CHAPTER 4

THE VILLAIN

"I do empathise with people who are driven by dreadful impulses. I think to be driven to want to kill must be such a terrible burden. I try, and I think I succeed, in making my readers feel sorry for my psychopaths, because I do."

—Ruth Rendell

■ ■ ■

As any mystery reader knows, today's villain is no Snidely Whiplash, standing in broad daylight, twirling his moustache and sneering. Any character who looks that nefarious will almost certainly turn out to be innocent.

Readers are delighted when the bad guy was hiding in plain sight, an innocuous-looking character who cleverly conceals his true self, luring trusting victims and then snaring them in a death trap. But "the butler did it" won't wash in a modern mystery. Minor characters who are part of the wallpaper for the first twenty-eight chapters can't be promoted to villain status at the end just to surprise the reader. And you can't give a character a personality transplant in the final chapter. Disbelief will trump surprise unless you've left subtle clues along the way.

PLANNING AHEAD

Some writers know from the get-go which character is guilty. They start with the completed puzzle and work backwards, shaping the story pieces and fitting them together. Others happily write without knowing whodunit until the scene when the villain is unmasked. Then they rewrite, cleaning up the trail of red herrings and establishing subtle clues that make the solution work.

Do you need to know the bad guy's identity before you start writing? I do. I always think I know, but about half the time I turn out to be wrong. My friend and fellow author, Hank Phillippi Ryan, says she never knows the identity of the villain until she writes it. She's as surprised as her readers.

CREATING A VILLAIN WORTH PURSUING

You can't just throw all your suspects' names into a bowl and pick one to be your villain. For your novel to work, the villain must be special. Your sleuth deserves a worthy adversary—a smart, wily, dangerous creature who tests your protagonist's courage and detective prowess. Stupid, bumbling characters are good for comic relief, but they make lousy villains. The smarter and more invincible the villain, the harder your protagonist must work to find his vulnerability and the greater the achievement in bringing him to justice.

Must the villain be loathsome? Not at all. He can be chilling but charming, like Hannibal Lecter. She can be shrewd, gorgeous, and vulnerable, like Brigid O'Shaughnessy in *The Maltese Falcon*. (Who among us isn't a little bit conflicted when Sam Spade lets the police cuff her?) It's better when the reader can muster a little empathy for a complex, realistic bad guy who feels his crimes are justified.

So, in planning, try to wrap your arms around why your villain does what he does. What motivates him to kill? Consider the standard motives like greed, jealousy, or hatred. Then go a step further. Get inside your villain's head and see the crime from his perspective. To law enforcement, it might look like a murder motivated by greed. To the perpetrator, it might look like a means to a noble, even heroic, end.

Here's how a villain might justify a crime:

- righting a prior wrong
- revenge (the victim deserved to die)
- vigilante justice (the criminal justice system didn't work)
- protecting a loved one
- restoring order to the world
- God's will

Finally, think about what happened to make the villain the way he is. Was he born bad? Did he sour as a result of a past experience? If your villain bears a grudge against society, why? If she can't tolerate being jilted or ignored or teased or shortchanged, why? You need to know your villain's backstory, even if you never share it with your reader.

By understanding how the villain justifies the crime to himself, and by knowing the formative events in his life, you give yourself the material you need to get past a black-hatted caricature and to paint your villain in shades of gray.

Here's an example of the information you need to decide about your villain before you write.

CRIME SCENARIO	Who gets hurt, how, and where	Lorinda Lewis, a thirty-year-old bank teller, is carjacked, thrown from the car, and killed.
THUMBNAIL SKETCH OF VILLAIN	Basic information: name, age, job, physical description, family, background	Drew MacNee, bank manager, boyishly handsome; fiftyish; father of two teenage girls; married to the mousey but wealthy Melinda for twenty-five years; lifts weights and runs thirty miles a week; grew up the youngest and the only son with three older sisters in an affluent household and always got what he wanted.
MOTIVE	Ostensible reason for committing the murder	To keep Lorinda from revealing his many affairs with young, attractive bank tellers (including Lorinda).
MOTIVE	How the villain sees the crime	"Lorinda, that vengeful bitch, couldn't stand it when I dumped her; now she's out to destroy everything I've worked so hard for. I've got to stop her and protect my family."
LIFE TRIGGER(S)	Past experience that might explain why the villain commits this crime	When Drew was captain of his high school football team, he and his buddies raped a girl and were protected from prosecution by the coach and town officials.

✏ NOW YOU TRY: SPENDING TIME IN YOUR VILLAIN'S HEAD   4.1

Think about the villain in your mystery novel. Jot down your ideas.

Crime scenario:

_____

Thumbnail sketch of villain:

_____

Motive (ostensible reason for committing the crime):
_____

Motive (how the villain sees the crime):
_____

Life trigger(s):
_____

⬇ Download a printable version of this worksheet at www.writersdigest.com/
writing-and-selling-your-mystery-novel-revised.

MAKING THE CRIME FIT THE VILLAIN

There are many ways to kill off a victim. You can have him shot, stabbed, stran-
gled, poisoned, or pushed off a cliff. You can have her run over by a car or bashed
in the head with a fireplace poker. But murder is not a random event. The first
issue to consider is the following: *Would this particular villain have the expertise,
capabilities, and disposition to commit this particular crime?*

Here's an example: Suppose I'm writing about a surgeon who, up to page 302,
has been the soul of buttoned-down respectability. Suddenly, on page 303, he
leaps from a hospital laundry bin brandishing a machine-gun and mows down
his professional rival, another doctor who's competing with him for the open
hospital director position. Never mind that up to that point in the novel, this guy
has done nothing more than attend board meetings, get drunk and obnoxious
at a cocktail party, and perform heart surgery. Now, suddenly, he's the Termi-
nator? The behavior doesn't fit the character. If he stabbed, poisoned, or pushed
his rival off the hospital roof, the reader might swallow it. The author might get
away (barely) with the shooting if hints were dropped earlier that this surgeon
once served in military Special Forces.

Choose a modus operandi that your villain (and your suspects) might plausibly adopt, and establish that your villain has the capability and expertise required.
A murder by strangling, stabbing, or beating is more plausible if your villain is
strong and has a history of physical violence. If your villain plants an electroni-
cally activated, plastic explosive device, be prepared to establish how he learned
to make a sophisticated bomb and how he got access to the components. If a
woman shoots her husband with a .45 automatic, be prepared to show how she
learned to use firearms and that she's strong enough to handle the recoil of a .45.

The second issue to consider: *Is the rage factor appropriate?*

The more extreme the violence, the more likely the crime was motivated by hatred and rage. A robber shoots a victim once; an enraged husband pumps bullets into the man who raped his wife. A villain may administer a quick-working, deadly poison to a victim he wants out of the way, but a villain who hates his victim might pick a poison that's slow and painful, and then hang around to watch the victim die.

Adjust the violence quotient to match the amount of rage your villain has toward his victim.

✏ NOW YOU TRY: MAKE THE CRIME FIT THE VILLAIN   4.2

How would your villain kill his victim? Consider your villain's motive, strength, and expertise. Consider the rage factor. Check the methods that could fit.

____ asphyxiate by smoke inhalation

____ beat to death

____ bludgeon

____ bury alive

____ drown

____ hang

____ mow down with machine-gun fire

____ poison with cyanide

____ poison with an insulin overdose

____ push in front of a train

____ run down with a car

____ run over with heavy equipment

____ shoot with a pistol

____ slit throat

____ smother

____ stab once

____ stab multiple times

____ strangle

⬇ Download a printable version of this worksheet at www.writersdigest.com/writing-and-selling-your-mystery-novel-revised.

ON YOUR OWN: THE VILLAIN

1. Reread a favorite mystery novel, or read Scott Turow's *Presumed Innocent* or Agatha Christie's *And Then There Were None (Ten Little Indians)*. Pay special attention to the villain. Think about how the author creates a bad guy who is somewhat sympathetic and three-dimensional, and how the villain rationalizes the crime.

2. Brainstorm your villain and jot down your ideas: family background, physical appearance, education, formative events, and so on.

3. Pick a plausible modus operandi for your villain, taking into account your villain's capabilities, expertise, and relationship to the victim.

➡ **COMPLETE THE VILLAIN SECTION OF THE BLUEPRINT AT THE END OF PART I.**

CHAPTER 5

INNOCENT SUSPECTS

"Everybody has something to conceal."

—Sam Spade in Dashiell Hammett's *The Maltese Falcon*

■■■

"I've called you all together ..." announces the great Hercule Poirot as he rearranges Staffordshire figurines on a marble mantle into perfect symmetry before turning his beady-eyed attention on the suspects gathered around in the drawing room. With great drama, he lays out the case against suspect number one, only to reveal his innocence. He does the same with suspect number two, and so on around the room until, somewhere around suspect number five Poirot spins around and confronts anew one of the earlier suspects and reveals him to be, ta-dah, the killer.

Modern mysteries are rarely so heavy-handed, but the basic bait-and-switch principle still applies. There's a passel of suspects, each with a motive for murder, each with a secret or two. Attention moves from one suspect to the next until the villain is revealed. For the solution to surprise the reader—and **credible surprise** is what readers crave—then either the most obvious suspect is not the killer, or the crime is not what it appears to be.

How many suspects do you need? At least two (plus the true villain) will keep the reader guessing. More than five and it starts to feel like a parlor game.

DETERMINING THE SUSPECTS' SECRETS

Create a cast of innocent suspects who have secrets. Secrets have the power to make characters look guilty or reveal their innocence.

A secret can be something the suspect doesn't know. For instance, a suspect might not know that her husband was once married to the victim. Or a suspect might not be aware that she's the prime beneficiary of her murdered aunt's estate.

A secret can be something the suspect knows and lies about to cover up.

Or the secret can even be that the suspect doesn't exist. A clever villain might plant evidence implicating someone who's dead or whose identity was entirely fabricated.

Here are some examples of suspects' secrets and lies:

SECRET	LIE
A suspect is on the run from an abusive ex-boyfriend.	She lies about her true identity to keep her ex-boyfriend from finding her.
A suspect was robbing a bank across town when the murder happened.	He says he was with his girlfriend at the time of the murder; he's lying to avoid being arrested for the heist.
A suspect thinks her brother is guilty.	She says her brother was with her at the time of the murder to protect him.

MAKING INNOCENT SUSPECTS LOOK GUILTY

Virtually any character in your novel can be made to look suspicious. Here's a rule of thumb that's familiar to any mystery reader: The guiltier a character looks at the beginning of the story, the more likely he will turn out to be innocent.

Here are some devices that you can use to cast the shadow of guilt on innocent characters:

- **OBVIOUS MOTIVE:** The character inherits the estate, or was having an affair with the victim's husband, or was being blackmailed by the victim, or had been jilted by the victim.
- **A VANISHING ACT:** The character is nowhere to be found when investigators come to question him after the murder.
- **STONEWALLING:** The character can't remember or refuses to tell the police where she was at the time of the murder.
- **CONTRADICTORY BEHAVIOR:** A character who claims to be clueless about guns has an NRA membership card in his wallet.
- **EAVESDROPPER:** The character is overheard telling the victim, "Drop dead."

- **ENMITY BETWEEN THE CHARACTER AND THE VICTIM:** The two are cut-throat business rivals, were engaged in a nasty lawsuit, or are in love with the same person.
- **OVEREAGERNESS TO ANSWER QUESTIONS:** The character goes to investigators and provides bushels of information that implicate others ... but not all of it turns out to be true.
- **ROTTEN REP:** The character is known to be a swindler or a compulsive liar.
- **GUILT BY ASSOCIATION:** The character hangs out with other unsavory characters or is married to someone who hated the victim.
- **PREVIOUSLY SUSPECTED:** The character was questioned in a similar homicide investigation; someone else was convicted, but now investigators wonder.
- **PREVIOUSLY CONVICTED:** The character was convicted of a similar crime, though he claims he was innocent.
- **SKELETONS IN THE CLOSET:** No one knows it, but the character was once a compulsive gambler, alcoholic, drug addict, pedophile, or embezzler.
- **CRACKS IN THE VENEER:** A flawlessly beautiful, kind, or generous character is seen kicking a dog, slapping a child, or grinding a delicate trinket under his heel.

PLANNING A SUSPECT

A good way to prepare for bringing a suspect to life on the page is to create a thumbnail sketch. Use unexpected contrasts to keep your suspects from turning into clichés. A jealous, bleached-blond, Armani-wearing wife might once have been a Peace Corps volunteer who still sponsors Bolivian orphans. A rigid, controlling bank manager might love to share knock-knock jokes with his five-year-old daughter. Contrasts like these make characters feel human.

A thumbnail sketch of a suspect should include the following:

- **BASIC INFORMATION:** The suspect's name, relationship to the victim, age, gender, any distinguishing physical characteristics, anything significant about his personality or past, a few telling details (something he owns or does, a favorite expression, etc.) that define him, and quirky contrasts to make him unique.
- **MOTIVE:** Why this character might have committed the murder.

- **LIE(S):** The lie(s) this character tells.
- **SECRET(S):** The secret that makes this character look guilty; the secret that demonstrates this character's innocence.

Here's an example of a thumbnail sketch of a suspect:

> **CRIME SCENARIO:** Martha Collicott, a wealthy, elderly widow, is strangled in her bed.
>
> **SUSPECT:** Terry Blaine
>
> **THUMBNAIL SKETCH:**
> **Basic Information**
> He's Martha's nephew, twenty years old, unemployed, handsome, fair-haired college dropout; bright but an underachiever; was always Martha's favorite nephew; drives a vintage Corvette and wears $200 sneakers; no regular address (says he's "staying with friends"). He's the only one who cried at Martha's funeral.
>
> **Motive**
> He inherits Aunt Martha's money.
>
> **Lie**
> He says he was at a friend's house, alone, watching television at the time of the murder.
>
> **Secrets**
> **Secret that makes him look guilty:** Terry is a compulsive gambler, deeply in debt, and being threatened by loan sharks; he needs Aunt Martha's money to save himself.
> **Secret that demonstrates innocence:** Terry was dealing drugs at the time of the murder.

✎ NOW YOU TRY: THE SUSPECT'S SECRETS   5.1

For one innocent suspect in your novel, come up with the following:

Suspect's name:
_____

Basic information:
_____

Motive:
_____

Lie(s):

_____

Secrets:

_____

⬇ Download a printable version of this worksheet at www.writersdigest.com/
writing-and-selling-your-mystery-novel-revised.

✐ ON YOUR OWN: INNOCENT SUSPECTS   5.2

1. Watch a crime show such as *NCIS* or *Law and Order*. List the characters
   who become suspects, and note the secrets revealed about each one. Notice that sometimes the secret makes a suspect appear to be guilty; other
   times the secret demonstrates a suspect's innocence.

Suspect:	Secrets:
Suspect:	Secrets:
Suspect:	Secrets:

2. Write a one-paragraph description of each innocent suspect in your novel.
3. Pick one innocent suspect in your novel. Brainstorm a list of possible secrets the suspect might be hiding.
4. Write a one-paragraph first-person monologue in the voice of the suspect
   you picked in step three, talking about the secret he's hiding.

➡ **COMPLETE THE INNOCENT SUSPECTS SECTION OF THE BLUEPRINT AT THE
END OF PART I.**

CHAPTER 6

THE SUPPORTING CAST

"Without Goodwin's badgering, Wolfe would surely starve, collapse under the weight of his own sloth ..."

—Loren D. Estleman, from the introduction to the 1992 Bantam
paperback edition of *Fer-de-Lance* by Rex Stout

■ ■ ■

Sir Arthur Conan Doyle gave Sherlock Holmes a full panoply of supporting characters. There was Dr. Watson, the quintessential sidekick, to provide Holmes with a sounding board; Scottish landlady Mrs. Hudson to cook and clean and fuss over Holmes; Scotland Yard detective Inspector Lestrade to provide a foil for Holmes's intuitive brilliance, as well as access to official investigations; the Baker Street Irregulars to sneak around where Holmes can't and ferret out information; and Mycroft Holmes, his politically powerful older brother, to provide financial and strategic support.

Likewise, your cast of supporting characters should reflect what your protagonist *needs*. For instance, an amateur sleuth needs a friend or relative with access to inside information: a police officer, private investigator, or reporter fits the bill. A character who is arrogant and full of himself needs a character to keep him from taking himself too seriously, maybe an acerbic co-worker or his mother. You might want to show a hard-boiled police detective's softer side by giving him kids or a pregnant wife.

THE SIDEKICK

The most important supporting character is the sidekick. Many mystery protagonists have one. Rex Stout's obese, lazy, brilliant Nero Wolfe has Archie Goodwin—a slim wisecracking ladies' man. Robert B. Parker's literate, poetry-quoting Spenser has black, street-smart, tough-talking Hawk. Harlan Coben's former basketball star turned sports agent, Myron Bolitar, has a rich, blond, preppy friend, Windsor Horne Lockwood III. Tess Gerritsen's medical examiner, Dr. Maura Isles, plays a cool, self-contained, and logical counterpoint to Detective Rizzoli's hot-tempered passionate impulsivity (they're each other's sidekicks).

Dr. Watson, a married medical doctor, romantic and sentimental, says of Holmes in "A Scandal in Bohemia": "All emotions … were abhorrent to his cold, precise, but admirably balanced mind. He was, I take it, the most perfect reasoning and observing mind that the world has ever seen."

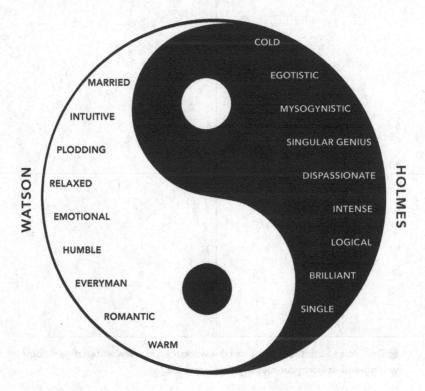

See a pattern? It's the old **"opposites attract"** setup. Mystery protagonists and their sidekicks are a study in contrasts. Sidekicks are the yin to the protagonists' yang. The contrast puts the protagonist's characteristics into relief.

So the place to start in creating a sidekick is the profile you developed of your sleuth in chapter two. Think about how the sidekick's traits can mirror those of the protagonist.

✎ NOW YOU TRY: TRAITS FOR A SIDEKICK   6.1

Make a list of your protagonist's characteristics; list the opposites you could give to a sidekick. Circle the ones you like best.

PROTAGONIST	SIDEKICK
1.	1.
2.	2.
3.	3.
4.	4.
5.	5.
6.	6.
7.	7.
8.	8.
9.	9.
10.	10.

⬇ Download a printable version of this worksheet at www.writersdigest.com/writing-and-selling-your-mystery-novel-revised.

THE ADVERSARY

Every protagonist/mystery sleuth needs an adversary, too. This is not the villain but a good-guy character who drives your protagonist nuts, pushes his buttons, torments him, puts obstacles in his path, and is generally a pain in the patoot. She might be an overprotective relative or a know-it-all co-worker. Or she might be a police officer or detective who "ain't got no respect" for the protagonist. She might be a boss who's a micromanager or a flirt.

Sherlock Holmes's adversary is Inspector Lestrade, who has much disdain for Holmes's investigative techniques. In the same vein, Kathy Reichs's forensic anthropologist, Temperance Brennan, has a tormentor in the person of Montreal police detective sergeant Luc Claudel. Their sparring is an ongoing element in her books. In *Monday Mourning,* Brennan finds out Claudel is going to be working with her on the case. She describes him this way:

> Though a good cop, Luc Claudel has the patience of a firecracker, the sensitivity of Vlad the Impaler, and a persistent skepticism as to the value of forensic anthropology.

Then she adds:

> Snappy dresser, though.

Conflict is the spice that makes characters come alive, and an adversary can cause the protagonist all kinds of interesting problems and complicate your story by throwing up roadblocks to the investigation.

An adversary may simply be thickheaded—for example, a superior officer who remains stubbornly unconvinced and takes the protagonist off the case. Or an adversary may be deliberately obstructive. For example, a bureaucrat's elected boss might quash an investigation that threatens political cronies, or a senior reporter may fail to pass along information because he doesn't want a junior reporter to get the scoop.

In developing an adversary, remember that he or she should be a character who is positioned to thwart, annoy, and generally get in your protagonist's way. With an adversary in the story, the protagonist gets lots of opportunity to argue, struggle, and show her mettle and ingenuity.

Think about the characters you have planned for your novel. Which ones can act as adversaries? List the possibilities below, and brainstorm how each character can complicate your character's life or obstruct the investigation.

POTENTIAL ADVERSARY	COMPLICATIONS AND OBSTRUCTIONS

⬇ Download a printable version of this worksheet at www.writersdigest.com/ writing-and-selling-your-mystery-novel-revised.

THE SUPPORTING CAST

The supporting character can include anyone in your protagonist's life: a relative, a friend, a neighbor, a co-worker, or a professional colleague; the local librarian, waitress, or town mayor; even a pet pooch. Maybe this character will get ensnared in the plot and land in mortal danger. He might even take a turn as a suspect.

Supporting characters come with baggage, so pick yours carefully. If you give your protagonist young kids, you'll have to deal with arranging for child care. A significant other? Be prepared to handle the inevitable attraction to that sexy suspect. A pet St. Bernard? He'll have to be walked—twice a day. And your readers will worry about the dog, even if you don't.

Supporting characters give your character a life, but each one should also play a critical role in the story. Here are some of the roles the supporting characters can play:

- sounding board
- possessor of special expertise
- provider of access to inside information
- bodyguard or tough guy
- caretaker or worry wart
- drudge
- mentor
- mole
- money bags
- influential cutter of red tape
- love interest

Supporting characters might start out as stereotypes: a devoted wife, a nagging mother-in-law, a bumbling assistant, a macho cop, or a slimy lawyer. They can be typecast during the planning phase. But when you start writing, you'll want to push past the stereotypes and flesh out supporting characters, turning them into human beings who do things that surprise you. You don't want supporting characters to hog the spotlight, but cardboard cutouts shouldn't be clogging up your story either.

NAMING SUPPORTING CHARACTERS

Give each supporting character a name to match the persona, and be careful to pick names that help the reader remember who's who.

Nicknames are easy to remember, especially when they provide a snapshot reminder of the character's personality (Spike, Godiva, Flash) or appearance (Red, Curly, Smokey). Giving the character a name inspired by his ethnicity (Zito, Sasha, Kwan) makes it memorable, too. Avoid the dull and boring (Bob Miller) as well as the weirdly exotic (Dacron).

It's not easy for readers to keep all your characters straight, so help them out:

- Don't give a character two first names like William Thomas, Stanley Raymond, or Susan Frances.
- Vary the number of syllables in character names—it's harder to confuse a Jane with a Stephanie than it is to confuse a Bob with a Hank.

- Pick names that don't sound alike. If your protagonist's sister is Leanna, don't name her best friend Lillian or Donna.
- Pick names that start with different first letters. Keep track so you don't end up with a Mary, a Melinda, *and* a Michelle.

Names are hard to come up with when you need them. An obvious source for inspiration is your local telephone directory. And there are lots of websites with baby names and others that serve up surnames by ethnicity. On Social Security's "Popular Names by Decade" website, you can look up the decade in which the character was born and find out which names were popular then.

Whenever I discover a name I like, I add it to a list I keep on my computer. My list begins with Cecilia Spoon, a name I once found in a local paper. Perhaps it's a bit too Dickensian, but I know one day I'll find a home for it.

Create a list of "keeper" names, and add to it whenever you find one you like.

 ON YOUR OWN: THE SUPPORTING CAST

1. Name and profile your sidekick(s).
   - name
   - occupation
   - major roles vis-à-vis your protagonist (sounding board, love interest, etc.)
   - personality
   - background
   - strengths and weaknesses
2. Name and profile your adversary:
   - name
   - position of power that enables this character to obstruct your sleuth
   - relationship between your protagonist and this adversary
3. Make a list of the other supporting characters your story needs. For each one, create a brief profile that includes these elements:
   - name
   - role in the story
   - brief description (including age, gender, appearance, personality, and anything else you feel is important about this character)

➔ **COMPLETE THE SUPPORTING CAST SECTION OF THE BLUEPRINT AT THE END OF PART I.**

CHAPTER 7

THE WEB OF CHARACTERS WITH COMPETING GOALS

"When two characters with opposing agendas meet, you have built-in tension."

—James Scott Bell, *Plot & Structure*

■■■

The fuel of a page-turner is conflict, and you build in conflict by giving your characters **competing goals**. Once you've assembled your cast of characters, it's time to think about them in relationship to one another. How is each one going to help or hinder your protagonist in reaching his goal?

To get some perspective on this, create a **character web** (see the next page).

Write your protagonist's name and his goal in the web's center. On the outer end of each web spoke, write the other characters' names. For each spoke, draw an arrow that indicates whether that character is pulling for or against the protagonist reaching his goal.

Characters who pull in opposite directions add tension to the story. Even more interesting is when a character is pulling in *two directions at once*. In the character web example above, the villain obstructs, the sidekick assists, while the adversary both obstructs and assists. For example, the sleuth's boss (adversary)

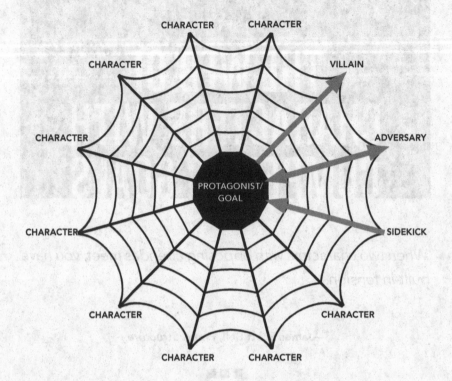

might theoretically want the protagonist to find the killer, but at the same time he needs to protect a personal secret that could come out as a result.

For an example of a more complete character web, below are brief descriptions of the main characters in Dashiell Hammett's *The Maltese Falcon*.

The cast includes:

- **SAM SPADE (PROTAGONIST):** PI; his goal is to bring his partner's killer to justice; in order to do so, he has to find a priceless artifact, the Maltese falcon
- **BRIGID O'SHAUGHNESSY** (a.k.a. Miss Wonderly): hires Spade and Archer to find a sister whom Archer is killed looking for; she really wants Spade to find the Maltese falcon (she doesn't have a sister); she does not want him to find out who killed Miles Archer
- **JOEL CAIRO:** a thief who wants the Maltese falcon
- **IVA ARCHER:** Miles Archer's widow, who was having an affair with Spade
- **EFFIE PERRINE:** Spade's loyal secretary
- **SGT. POLHAUS:** an honest cop who is investigating Archer's murder

WRITING & SELLING YOUR MYSTERY NOVEL

The diagram below illustrates the web created by these characters and their conflicting goals. Brigid O'Shaughnessy, for example, wants Spade to find the Maltese Falcon for her, but she does not want him to find out who killed Archer.

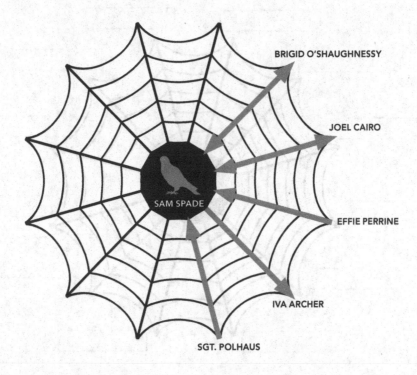

1. List your characters and their goals. (Keep going until you run out of characters.)

Protagonist/goal(s): _____

Character/goal(s): _____

Character/goal(s): _____

Character/goal(s): _____

Character/goal(s): _____

Character/goal(s): _____

2. In the web diagram below, write your protagonist's name and her goal in the center; write the other character names in the other blocks. Draw arrows to show which characters are helping the protagonist, obstructing her, or both.

3. Assess. Have you built in enough conflict and enough tension? Think about how you can add more.

⬇ Download a printable version of this worksheet at www.writersdigest.com/ writing-and-selling-your-mystery-novel-revised.

➔ **COMPLETE THE CHARACTER WEB SECTION OF THE BLUEPRINT AT THE END OF PART I.**

CHAPTER 8
SETTING

> "My books begin with a place, the feeling I want to set a book there, whether it's an empty stretch of beach or a community of people."
>
> **—P.D. James in an interview with Salon.com**

■■■

It's been said that a vivid setting is like another main character in the novel, and sometimes it is. At the very least, your setting has to be credible and fit your story's plot, characters, theme, and emotional tone.

Setting includes these dimensions:

- **WHEN:** year and season
- **WHERE:** geographic locale, exteriors, and interiors
- **CONTEXT:** activities and institutions that provide the primary backdrop

I began writing *There Was an Old Woman* with a mental image of Mina Yetner, a ninety-one-year-old woman sitting on her back porch, gazing across a salt marsh, over an expanse of water to the Manhattan skyline. So I set her house in the Bronx, where there really is a community with modest old houses that fit the bill. When Mina was little she lived there and watched the great skyscrapers go up. I learned about a B-25 bomber that crashed into the seventy-ninth floor of the Empire State Building on a fogbound morning in 1945, so I decided that Mina's first job had been working in the Empire State Building. She was one of the few remaining survivors of a fire that followed the crash. Those details of time and place worked perfectly with my story.

Pick your settings carefully, because whatever you choose both constrains and enriches your story's possibilities. Before you start writing, make a list of possible whens and wheres for potential scenes. Then research and explore the dramatic possibilities. If you can, pay a visit to each place. Take pictures and take notes. If you can't visit, then find photographs and written descriptions and talk to people who've been there. When it's time to write, you'll be able to use real details and add plausible fictional touches.

WHEN: THE YEAR

When your novel takes place—in the present, the past, the future, or even a made-up time in a fantasy universe—has a major impact on all aspects of the book. It affects what characters wear, what they worry about, what their homes are like, how they get around, the products they use, the music they listen to, and so on. It also constrains the kind of crime investigation that can take place. Laurie R. King's protagonist, Mary Russell, apprentice and then wife to Sherlock Holmes in early-twentieth-century London, relies on old-fashioned observation and deduction. Kinsey Millhone is in a 1980s time warp, so Sue Grafton never has to work her plots around cell phones or DNA evidence. Kathy Reichs sets her Temperance Brennan series in the present, so she has all the trappings of modern forensic science at her disposal. Give the investigators in your novel the tools appropriate to their time period.

Setting your story in a particular historical time frame allows you to intertwine your story with concurrent events. The Great Depression, the Roaring Twenties, World War II—virtually any time period can provide a rich historical context with real individuals and events you can use as part of your story.

Set your story in the present and you can include current events. The downside is that current events can quickly make your story seem dated. Remember, even for writers with a contract in hand for their new book, it often takes two years from the time they begin writing until the book is published. What seems like a major news story when you're writing your novel may be a big yawn a year later. So only include current events that matter to your story.

Some events might feel too big to be left out of any story set in the fictional present. I was in the middle of writing a novel set in the present when 9/11 terrorist attacks took place. My paranoid villain would have been profoundly affected by the news. I considered putting the event into the book, but decided not to. I was convinced that readers weren't ready to read about those events in a crime novel meant to entertain. Moreover, I wasn't emotionally equipped to write about it.

Make a conscious, reasoned decision on whether to include concurrent events in your novel. Weigh the pros and cons, the advantages and limitations, and most of all trust your instincts.

✏️ **NOW YOU TRY: INCLUDING CONCURRENT EVENTS** 8.1

Make a list of the events that are concurrent with your novel's time frame. List reasons in favor of including or excluding those events.

YEAR:		
CONCURRENT EVENT	REASONS TO INCLUDE THE EVENT	REASONS TO EXCLUDE THE EVENT

⬇ Download a printable version of this worksheet at www.writersdigest.com/writing-and-selling-your-mystery-novel-revised.

WHEN: THE SEASON

You can exploit the season in which your story takes place in several ways. Extreme weather—hurricanes, monsoons, blizzards—can create a dramatic backdrop. In this example from Raymond Chandler's short story "Red Wind," a description of Southern California Santa Ana winds provides a powerful way to open the first scene:

> There was a desert wind blowing that night. It was one of those hot, dry, Santa Anas that come down through the mountain passes and curl your hair and make your nerves jump and your skin itch. On nights like that, every booze party ends

in a fight. Meek, little wives feel the edge of the carving knife and study their husbands' necks. Anything can happen.

The Santa Anas most often arise in the fall and winter.

The season—or seasons, if your novel's time frame is long enough—you pick creates multiple story possibilities. In winter, an ice storm in Vermont can shut down roads and delay a medical examiner trying to reach a crime scene. A summer heat wave in Kansas City can leave elderly shut-ins dead, one of whom turns out to have been murdered. Soaking spring rains can turn roads to mud, send hillsides sliding into houses, and leave your protagonist stranded by the side of the road and chilled to the bone.

Be aware of the nuisance factor in the season you pick. Set your story in a New England winter and your characters will be forced to bundle up and de-ice their car windshields whenever they go out. If you want your character to take a pleasant stroll and come across a body washed up at the edge of a creek, make sure that the weather would be warm enough at that time of year for strolling and that creeks wouldn't be dried to a trickle. You can't have a character skulking about in pools of darkness between the streetlights at eight o'clock on a July evening—the sun wouldn't have set.

Whatever time period and season you choose to set your story, spend some time planning how you'll put those choices to work in your story.

✏ NOW YOU TRY: MAKING THE MOST OF "WHEN"   8.2

Write down the year(s) and season(s) you've chosen to set your novel. Brainstorm a list of how your choices can affect your story in terms of investigational techniques, concurrent events, weather, and so on.

YEAR/SEASON	HOW YOUR CHOICE AFFECTS YOUR STORY

⬇ Download a printable version of this worksheet at www.writersdigest.com/writing-and-selling-your-mystery-novel-revised.

WHERE: GEOGRAPHIC LOCALE

The geographic locale where you set your novel provides you with a range of possible dramatic landscapes in which to bring your story to life. A small town presents as many possibilities as a big city. The quiet Kentish village of St. Mary Meade serves as the perfect backdrop for Agatha Christie's Miss Marple series. Venice, with its mist-shrouded canals and palazzos, makes a rich backdrop for Donna Leon's Commissario Guido Brunetti novels.

Readers love local color, and the audience for most mystery series grows from its geographic location. On the other hand, exotic locations entice readers who yearn for the unknown. What matters is that you know your setting, bring it to life on the page, and take advantage of the opportunities your setting presents.

Let the geographic locale shape your characters' behavior. New Yorkers avoid eye contact with strangers, while Texans say "howdy" to everyone. A Milwaukee police officer might have a passion for bratwurst; one of Chicago's finest might be an aficionado of Red Hots.

Here are some ways your characters might reflect the geographic locale you pick:

- how they talk—word choice, speech patterns, and dialect
- what they wear
- what they eat and drink
- how they get places
- how they treat strangers
- what sports teams they root for

Here's an example from Laura Lippman's *The Sugar House*. Through the details Lippman chooses, she makes Baltimore come alive.

> Sour beef day dawned clear and mild in Baltimore.
> Other cities have their spaghetti dinners and potluck at the local parish, bull roasts and barbecues, bake sales and fish fries. Baltimore had all those things, too, and more. But in the waning, decadent days of autumn, there came a time when sour beef was the only thing to eat, and Locust Point was the only place to eat it.

Like so many mystery writers, Lippman writes about her series setting so vividly because she lives there. If you set your novel where you've lived, you can use your insider's knowledge. If you set your story somewhere you've never lived, leave yourself time during the planning stages to visit and research the locale thoroughly.

WHERE: EXTERIORS

Once you've picked your geographic locale, think about the exteriors you can use to set scenes. If you're using real exteriors, make them as accurate as possible. Readers don't like it when your character drives the wrong way up a one-way street or when a well-known restaurant is unwittingly relocated to a new neighborhood.

You can finesse the details by creating a fictional neighborhood that echoes the features of a real one. Dennis Lehane set *Mystic River* in a fictitious blue-collar Boston neighborhood he called "East Buckingham," but its details will ring true to anyone familiar with the Boston suburbs of Charlestown, Southie, Brighton, or Dorchester (where Lehane grew up).

> They all lived in East Buckingham, just west of downtown, a neighborhood of cramped corner stores, small playgrounds, and butcher shops where meat, still pink with blood, hung in the windows. The bars had Irish names and Dodge Darts by the curbs. Women wore handkerchiefs tied off at the backs of their skulls and carried mock leather snap purses for their cigarettes.

A few pages later, Lehane sets a scene in another semifictional locale he calls the Flats:

> Jimmy looked at the Flats spread out before him as he and the old man walked under the deep shade of the tracks and neared the place were Crescent bottomed out and the freight trains rumbled past the old, ratty drive-in and the Penitentiary Channel beyond, and he knew—deep, deep in his chest—that they'd never see Dave Boyle again.

Made-up exteriors like East Buckingham and the Flats work fine as long as the details are vivid and ring true. An adobe hacienda in the middle of Boston won't wash, nor will cobblestone streets in Los Angeles. Some writers draw maps of the exteriors they invent to keep themselves oriented and their story consistent.

WHERE: INTERIORS

Your novel may have as many as a dozen interior settings. One recurring interior will probably be your protagonist's home.

Here are two kitchens described in my novel *There Was an Old Woman*. My goal was not only to create vivid interiors but to *show* the reader the contrast between the two women who inhabit these spaces.

Evie's mother's kitchen:

Evie turned instead and entered the kitchen. She threaded her way around piles of newspapers and loaded paper bags and plastic garbage bags. The sink was overflowing with dishes, and the faucet was dripping. Evie reached over and turned it off. Pushed open the red-and-white gingham curtains that were gray and crusty with dust, and opened the windows. On the sill, a row of African violets were brown and withered.

Evie's neighbor's kitchen:

Now Evie looked around in awe at the spotless kitchen with its black-and-white checkerboard tiled floor, two-basin porcelain-over-cast-iron sink standing on legs, and a pair of pale-green metal base cabinets with a matching rolltop bread box sitting on a white enamel countertop. Spatulas and spoons hung from hooks on the wall, all with wooden handles painted that same green. The utensils had the patina of old tools, used for so long that they bore the imprint of their owner's hand. Evie felt as if she'd stepped into a 1920s time warp.

Each time you bring an interior setting to the page, decide what you want to show the reader about the character who inhabits that space. If your character is anal and methodical, you might choose steel-and-glass furniture and a Mondrian print on the wall. If your character is absentminded and careless, his desk might be adrift in paperwork and the rug frayed at the edges. If your character is cheerful and optimistic, her home would probably be freshly painted and filled with bright colors. If he's morose and brooding, maybe the windows are shrouded with dusty, green velvet drapes.

In your mind, transport yourself to your character's home. Is it a mansion, apartment, mountaintop cabin, or homeless shelter? Is it filled with fine antiques, battered items salvaged from yard sales and thrift stores, minimalist designer furniture, or unopened storage boxes? Is there a big-screen TV or a vintage radio? Does the kitchen have all the latest gadgets or just a microwave for reheating takeout? Each choice should be a reflection of your character's personality and where he is at this juncture in life.

Other interiors relate to your protagonist's job. If your protagonist is an attorney, you'll probably write scenes that take place in a jail and a courtroom. If your protagonist is a medical examiner, you'll need an autopsy room and a morgue. Most novels featuring a homicide detective have scenes that take place in squad cars and police stations.

Have at the ready some interiors where your protagonist goes to relax. Sue Grafton's Kinsey Millhone often finds refuge at a dingy local tavern serving Hungarian food cooked up by Rosie, a colorful recurring character.

It's fun to use real interiors to set scenes. Local readers enjoy finding places they recognize. A good rule of thumb is: It's okay to use a real place if nothing terrible happens there. If your characters are meeting for a relaxing meal, you can use a real restaurant; if your character is going to get food poisoning after eating there, you should use a made-up place. You don't want to make enemies out of restaurant owners, and you certainly don't want to get sued.

NOW YOU TRY: MAKING THE MOST OF "WHERE" 8.3

Pick a geographic location and list all the interior and exterior settings where you've chosen to set your novel. List the aspects of setting that you'll be able to use to your advantage in the story.

GEOGRAPHIC LOCALE	ASPECTS YOU CAN USE IN YOUR STORY

INTERIOR SETTINGS	ASPECTS YOU CAN USE IN YOUR STORY

EXTERIOR SETTINGS	ASPECTS YOU CAN USE IN YOUR STORY

⊕ Download a printable version of this worksheet at www.writersdigest.com/
writing-and-selling-your-mystery-novel-revised.

CONTEXT: ACTIVITIES AND INSTITUTIONS

The activities and institutions that provide the backdrop to your story are another dimension of setting. Most mysteries have the context in which the sleuth operates, plus the context in which the crime occurred. For example, the most common context for a mystery is law enforcement—the main characters are police detectives; the activities are basic interrogation and investigation; and the institutions are those that make up the criminal justice system, from police departments to jails to courtrooms. Still, each police procedural has an added context: the backdrop for the crime. For example, if the police are investigating art theft, their investigations might take them into artists' studios, art museums, galleries, or auction houses. If you're writing an amateur sleuth, the backdrop becomes your sleuth's day job and the world your sleuth inhabits.

The backdrop you pick for your book is an important factor in marketing your novel. A mystery set in a medical examiner's office featuring graphic autopsies is going to repel the more squeamish reader. A mystery set at a bird sanctuary featuring a birder who witnesses a crime while tracking down a red-footed falcon probably won't appeal to readers who like their mysteries fast paced and hard-boiled.

Here are some examples of backdrops that have been used in mystery novels:

ACTIVITIES	INSTITUTIONS
Art collecting	Museums, auction houses, art galleries
Medical research	Hospitals, universities, private labs
Gambling	Race tracks, casinos
Smuggling endangered species	U.S. Fish and Wildlife Services, U.S. Customs
Drug dealing	Organized crime, street gangs
Golfing	The PGA tour, country clubs, golf courses

Pick a backdrop you know intimately or one that interests you enough so you won't mind doing the research necessary to make it come alive.

Here are some of the aspects of backdrop to research in advance:

- **COSTUME:** the formal or informal dress codes that determine what people wear; how clothing indicates status
- **JARGON:** the special terms and expressions that are widely used
- **EQUIPMENT:** special equipment and tools, and how they operate; safety precautions
- **PECKING ORDER:** the high- and low-status jobs, and how people at various levels recognize and treat one another
- **SCHEDULE:** the events that happen in a typical day or night, week, or month
- **BEHAVIOR:** the written and unwritten codes that influence how people behave in typical and extreme situations; what boundaries they're not supposed to cross

---

✎ NOW YOU TRY: MAKING THE MOST OF THE BACKDROP 8.4

Write down the institutions and activities that provide a backdrop for your mystery novel. Make a list of the questions you need to answer in order to write a convincing backdrop.

BACKDROP: INSTITUTIONS AND ACTIVITIES	QUESTIONS TO BE RESEARCHED

⬇ Download a printable version of this worksheet at www.writersdigest.com/writing-and-selling-your-mystery-novel-revised.

PERSONAL SPACES THAT REVEAL CHARACTER

The details of a character's personal spaces—his office, car, kitchen, bedroom—offer you rich opportunities to demonstrate the character's personality and quirks. Here's Stephanie Plum looking in her refrigerator in Janet Evanovich's first series novel, *One for the Money*. The details are pungent and priceless.

> ... I shuffled into the kitchen and stood in front of the refrigerator, hoping the refrigerator fairies had visited during the night. I opened the door and stared at the empty shelves, noting that food hadn't magically cloned itself from the smudges in the butter keeper and the shriveled flotsam at the bottom of the crisper. Half a jar of mayo, a bottle of beer, whole-wheat bread covered with blue mold, a head of iceberg lettuce, shrink-wrapped in brown slime and plastic, and a box of hamster nuggets stood between me and starvation. I wondered if nine in the morning was too early to drink beer.

Open a character's refrigerator for the reader and you might find:

- six-packs of vitamin water
- stacked matching plastic containers of leftovers, each labeled with the contents and date
- so much food that the milk leaps out at whoever opens the door
- medications
- nothing but a powerful stench
- DVDs
- bundles of cash

Your character's car is also ripe with possibilities. Janet Evanovich's Stephanie Plum drives a convertible Miata. Michael Connelly's Lincoln Lawyer rides around in a Lincoln Town Car that doubles as his office. His chauffeur is a client who can't pay his legal bill.

✎ NOW YOU TRY: IMAGINING A PERSONAL SPACE   8.5

Think about your character's bathroom and jot down the details that make this personal space unique:

What's in the medicine cabinet?	

What's in the trash?	
What's on the sink?	
Does the faucet drip?	
Do the drains drain?	
Are the towels hanging and folded?	
How does the room smell?	
What kinds of hair products are there?	
Is it clean where you can see?	
Is it clean where you can't see?	

⬇ Download a printable version of this worksheet at www.writersdigest.com/writing-and-selling-your-mystery-novel-revised.

MAKING A SETTING FEEL CREDIBLE

As a writer, your goal is not to re-create a completely accurate place and time—leave that to history books and travel guides. The last thing you want to do is bog down your story with pages of descriptive detail, no matter how evocative. Aim, instead, for *credibility*.

Whether a setting is real or imaginary, you need to know it inside and out before you start writing so you can create a credible sense of place. Put pink flamingos on suburban lawns in Chicago and you'll blow your cover as a Floridian.

Plausibility is what counts. With a few strokes of physical and sensory descriptions—a few *telling details*—you can to bring a particular setting to life.

That's where research comes in. How much research you have to do depends on how familiar you are with the setting you've chosen to write about and what resources you can access. I spent hours behind the scenes with a curator of the New-York Historical Society so I could plausibly provide a work setting for Evie Ferrante in *There Was an Old Woman*. To write Ivy Rose, the pregnant protagonist of *Never Tell a Lie*, all I had to do was remember what it was like when I was on leave from work, waiting to give birth to my first child.

Susan Elia MacNeal writes the Maggie Hope series set in Europe during World War II. Research informs this description of the interior of No. 10 Downing Street in *Mr. Churchill's Secretary*.

> Maggie Hope walked up the steps, past the guards and knocked. The door opened, and she was led by one of the tall, uniformed guards past the infamous glossy black door with its brass lion-head knocker, and through the main entrance hall. She passed through, barely noticing the Benson of Whitehaven grandfather clock, the chest from the Duke of Wellington, and the portrait of Sir George Downing. Then continued up the grant cantilever staircase. From there they took a few turns down a warren of corridors and narrow winding passageways to the typists' office, ripe with the scent of floor polish and cigarette smoke.

Susan says that for settings in her books, "I try to visit the actual site if at all possible. However, for that paragraph, I couldn't actually go to No. 10 Downing Street—which is not open to the public—so I relied on books." She found copies of out-of-print books like *10 Downing Street: The Illustrated History* from Amazon and took a virtual tour of No. 10 online on a U.K. government-hosted website.

Even if your story takes place in a made-up time or place, the details have to feel believable and consistent. Draw maps of your locations, jot down the distances, and note the prominent geographic features. Refer to your notes as you write, adding to the map as you embellish the fictional place with realistic detail.

GETTING THE INFORMATION YOU NEED

Here are some suggestions for researching your setting:

- **GO THERE:** Pay a visit to the places where your mystery is set. Go as an *active observer*, not as a tourist or resident.

  - Look at the people: Who's there, how do they look, what are they doing?

- Look around and identify the props that define the place.
- Use all your senses: Are there distinctive sounds and smells?
- Check out the local newspaper.
- Collect maps, tourist guides, and postcards.
- Bring a tape recorder, a notebook, and a camera; capture the details.

- **TALK TO PEOPLE WHO HAVE BEEN THERE:** If you're writing a police procedural set in a big city, talk to big-city cops; if you're writing a cozy set in a New England inn, interview a New England innkeeper. Don't know any innkeepers? Call or e-mail a couple of inns and plead your case. Many people are delighted to share their knowledge and expertise.
- **READ DIARIES AND LETTERS:** First-person accounts and memoirs are a rich source of information for the writer, especially if the setting is historical. There's no better source for domestic detail, for example. Find them in libraries, in historical society archives, and on the Internet.
- **FIND NEWSPAPER ACCOUNTS:** Your library can give you access to newspaper archives where you may find photographs and stories to give you visual detail.
- **SEARCH THE INTERNET:** The Internet is full of images and descriptions of real places, as well as links to people with special interests and special expertise. Remember, though, much of what's out there has not been vetted. Verify any facts that you want to include in your novel.
- **READ BOOKS:** With so much information available online, it's easy to forget about books and libraries. For rich descriptions and photographs, check out travel guides and coffee table books that contain photo essays about a particular place. Buy them at bookstores or borrow them from the library, where you'll find the writer's best friend, the librarian. At Google Books or at online bookstores, you may be able to search inside the book and find what you need
- **BE METHODICAL:** Impose a method on your information gathering. Some people copy facts onto index cards; others use spreadsheets or text files. Be sure to capture the information *as well as its source.*

1. Compile a list of questions you need to research to create a convincing setting.
2. Visit as many of your novel's settings as you can; take along a notebook, a camera, and a digital recorder. Spend at least an hour observing and taking notes or recording.
3. Research the settings you can't visit. Consult books, magazines, newspapers, and the Internet, or interview people who have been there. Be methodical; record facts and their sources.
4. Write a five-minute, half-page description of your protagonist's home or office or car that could actually appear in the novel.

⟶ COMPLETE THE SETTING SECTION OF THE BLUEPRINT AT THE END OF PART I.

CHAPTER 9

STAKING OUT THE PLOT

"An outline is crucial. It saves so much time. When you write suspense, you have to know where you're going because you have to drop little hints along the way. With the outline, I always know where the story is going.

—John Grisham

"I do a very minimal synopsis before I start, and I know where I end up, I know sort of stations along the way, but I give myself freedom to kind of just discover things as I go along."

—Louis Bayard

"I just dive in and hope the book comes out at the other end. And as I get to the character, slowly the plot develops like a Polaroid."

—Tana French

■■■

A great mystery plot is like a thrilling ride on a roller coaster. The cars go shooting out of the starting gate. Then there's a slow, steep climb before a deep plunge. There's a brief respite before the ride gathers speed, going fast and then faster, rising to a hairpin turn and an even steeper drop. You barely catch your breath and the ride gains speed again, rising to yet another twist and plunge. There's a final twist and a heart-stopping plunge, and then you coast back to the platform, exhilarated and ready to ride again.

In more mundane terms, a mystery novel is comprised of groupings of **scenes** that can be thought of as **acts**, sandwiched between a dramatic opening that sets up the novel at the beginning and a coda that explains all at the end.

During each act, tension rises to dramatic climaxes and plot twists. At or near the end of the last act, there's a slam-bang dramatic finale in which the protagonist is in jeopardy and the truth revealed. At the end, loose ends are tied up and the world is safe from evil once more.

THE SHAPE OF A MYSTERY PLOT

The graphic below shows the big picture: the typical three-act structure of a mystery novel.

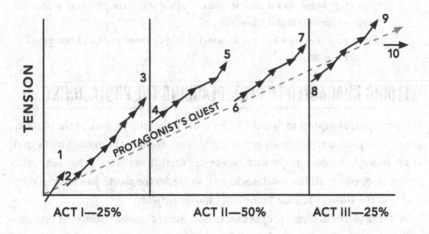

Tension rises as the story moves forward through three acts. The short arrows are meant to suggest that each act is made up of scenes—though in fact there are many more scenes than are shown, and tension rises and falls among them. The dashed line represents the protagonist's quest.

Briefly, this is how a plot might unfold over the three acts:

ACT I

1. The act begins with a dramatic opening, the incident that sets the story in motion.
2. The story continues: The protagonist, the main characters, and the setting are developed along with the main problem of the story and the initial goal.
3. The act ends with a major plot twist, usually a revelation and a reversal that sets back or derails the investigation.

ACT II

4. Throughout the act, complications mount (roadblocks, more danger, the stakes grow higher and more personal); secrets are revealed; and past events are revealed.
5. At the midpoint, a major plot twist occurs.
6. Through the second half, there are more complications, the stakes rise, and the clock ticks.
7. The act ends with another major reversal; the protagonist hits the wall and seems utterly defeated.

ACT III

8. The protagonist rebounds from the reversal at the end of Act II.
9. The story builds to a dramatic climax during which the protagonist faces off against the villain and triumphs.
10. A final few scenes serve as a coda, tidying up loose ends and bringing the story to a close.

WELDING CHARACTER TO PLOT: PLAGUING THE PROTAGONIST

The **protagonist's quest** to find the killer unifies a mystery novel. In the plot diagram, this quest is represented by the dashed line. In Act I the protagonist's goal is set, though the goal might shift before the final shoes drop. What keeps the reader hooked are all the **roadblocks** and **setbacks** the sleuth has to overcome and how the **stakes** increase as the story moves forward.

Drama works in direct proportion to how miserable you make your protagonist. Here are some ways to plague him:

- **DISCOMFORT:** The hungrier, thirstier, colder (or hotter), achier, and generally more pissed off he becomes, the more heroic the quest. Give him a scraped knee, sprained ankle, dislocated finger, bloody nose, broken arm, or gunshot wound, and show how he pushes past pain and disability in order to continue his pursuit. Make sure the reader knows he feels the pain, but be careful about letting him bitch and moan too much about it—no one likes a whiny hero.

- **INNER DEMONS:** If you're going to throw your character into a snake-filled pit, establish beforehand that she's terrified of snakes. If your character is an alcoholic trying to stop drinking, make her quest for the killer take her into bars.
- **MISHAPS:** Throw obstacles at your character to slow him down. His car can break down, or he can be set upon by thugs who turn out to be protecting the villain, or his car can roll over and end up in a ditch after being nudged off the highway by a semi. Maybe your character learns something damaging about one of the suspects, but she can't get anyone to listen to her. After each setback, the sleuth comes back stronger and more determined.
- **MODULATING THE MISERY:** Begin with minor woes and build as the story progresses to its final climax. From time to time, things should improve. Then, just when it looks as if your protagonist is out of the woods, let the next disaster strike.
- **RAISING THE STAKES AND MAKING IT PERSONAL:** On top of all those plagues, keep raising the stakes so your protagonist's need to bring the killer to justice gets stronger. For example, an innocent character is about to be convicted of the crime. Or maybe the protagonist or a loved one is in jeopardy. Or a villain threatens to escalate his attacks, and your protagonist is the only one who can stop him.

Reaching the end goal should feel heroic, worth all the pain and misery your protagonist had to overcome along the way.

✎ NOW YOU TRY: YOUR SLEUTH'S QUEST 9.1

In a sentence or two, describe your sleuth's quest. What does she want or need to achieve before the novel ends? Where does the quest start, and where does it end? Then make a list of plagues—potential setbacks, roadblocks, and other forms of misery you might throw in her way. Finally, decide how you're going to raise the stakes.

Your Sleuth's Quest

Plagues	How the Stakes Are Raised

⬇ Download a printable version of this worksheet at www.writersdigest.com/writing-and-selling-your-mystery-novel-revised.

A DRAMATIC OPENING: THE SETUP

Open your mystery novel with a dramatic scene in which something out of the ordinary happens. It might be a murder or just some **out-of-whack event** with an element of mystery to it.

Your novel might open with the murder itself. Or it might begin with your protagonist discovering that someone has been murdered. Or it might start with an event that happened years before the main story begins.

Your book has to start in an exciting or intriguing way by posing an **unanswered question** that provides a **narrative hook** that pulls the reader forward. You don't have to have a body drop in the first chapter. And you usually can't solve the problem of a flat, uninspired opening by inserting a prologue that flashes forward to the murder, followed by a chapter one that takes place earlier.

Here are some examples of award-winning bestsellers in which the opening scene sets up the book and pulls the reader forward without a murder:

> **Out-of-whack-event:** A baby is found abandoned on the steps of a church. (*In the Bleak Midwinter*, Julia Spencer-Fleming)
> **Unanswered question:** Who left the baby on the church steps, and what happened to the baby's mother?

Out-of-whack-event: A criminal defense attorney meets her new client—a woman accused of killing her cop boyfriend. The woman extends a hand and says, "Pleased to meet you, I'm your twin." (*Mistaken Identity*, Lisa Scottoline)

Unanswered question: Is this woman the defense attorney's twin, and is she a murderer?

Out-of-whack-event: PI Bill Smith receives a late-night telephone call from the NYPD, who is holding his fifteen-year-old nephew Gary. (*Winter and Night*, S.J. Rozan)

Unanswered question: Why would Gary ask for Smith? Smith hasn't seen his nephew for years and is estranged from Gary's parents.

A warning: Don't allow your opening scene to steal your book's thunder. It's tempting to write something that foreshadows the big secret, but keep in mind that in doing so you might weaken the reveal at the end.

So pick your opening gambit, and examine it with a critical eye. Be sure it sets up your novel, propels the reader forward, but doesn't rob your story of potential surprise by revealing too much too soon.

NOW YOU TRY: FIND YOUR OPENING SCENE 9.2

Review your crime scenario and your sleuth's quest. Think about where you want your story to start, and find a dramatic opening scene. Is it the crime itself? The start of the investigation? Or is it some other dramatic prelude to your story?

Write a one-paragraph description of your opening scene. Be sure your scene meets the criteria shown below.

CRITERIA FOR OPENING SCENE	DESCRIPTION OF OPENING SCENE
1. Dramatic	
2. Poses an unanswered question that propels the reader forward	
3. Sets up your story	
4. Doesn't give away too much too soon	

⬇ Download a printable version of this worksheet at www.writersdigest.com/writing-and-selling-your-mystery-novel-revised.

PLOT TWISTS

The plot twist is the most basic ingredient in a mystery. The unanswered question posed at the end of your opening scene is your novel's first plot twist. A twist might raise the stakes, exonerate one suspect or implicate another, or completely change the reader's understanding of the crime or the nature of one of the main characters. A major plot twist changes the direction—or the urgency of the investigation.

Plot twists should be surprising and credible at the same time. *If the reader sees a plot twist coming, it's not a twist.*

As you develop your plot, keep asking: *What does the reader expect to happen next? What could happen instead?* Brainstorm possibilities, and go in an unexpected but plausible direction.

Here are just a few of the many ways to twist your plot:

- A witness is discredited.
- A witness recants his story.
- A witness disappears.
- The victim isn't dead after all.
- New evidence is discovered implicating a new suspect.
- New evidence is discovered implicating the sleuth.
- The true implications of evidence that was previously misinterpreted are revealed.
- Evidence is discredited.
- Evidence disappears.
- A secret in a victim's past is revealed.
- A secret in a suspect's past is revealed.
- A threatening message is received.
- Another victim dies.
- A witness dies.
- The prime suspect dies.
- The sleuth is attacked.
- The sleuth is arrested.

At the end of each act, plan a dramatic climax that provides an ending to the story so far and a major plot twist that propels the reader forward to the next act.

THE FINAL CLIMAX AND CODA

Most mystery novels have a final climactic action scene fraught with mortal danger, during which the protagonist and the villain duke it out. That scene contains the payoff for the entire novel. It's one of the most important scenes in your book—second only to the dramatic opening.

After the climax, there's often a coda, a more contemplative scene in which all is explained. You can write three hundred pages of a great book, but if the final twenty don't fulfill the promise, it's a washout.

The ending should be **plausible**, **surprising**, and, most important, **satisfying**. In many mysteries, the protagonist triumphs, the villain is defeated, and justice is served. Don't feel bound by convention if a more unusual ending suits your story, but whatever you do, be sure that in the end it is crystal clear whodunit, why, and how. Readers should never be left scratching their heads.

PAGES, SCENES, CHAPTERS, AND ACTS

Scenes are the building blocks of a mystery novel. A scene contains the dramatic action of an event that occurs within a single time frame, in a single place, narrated throughout by one of the characters. When the time or place or narrator changes, this calls for a new scene. Every scene in a mystery novel should have a *payoff*—something that happens or changes to propel the story forward.

There's no ideal scene length. Several scenes may be grouped into a **chapter**, or a chapter may be one long scene, or a really long scene can be broken up across several chapters.

The **acts** in your novel are dramatic structures; they end with major turning points. While the text usually looks like the end of any chapter, it should *feel* to the reader as if a major part of your story has ended—tension has risen to a crescendo and a major plot twist has been introduced. The beginning of the next chapter is the beginning of the next act, and it feels as if the momentum is starting to build all over again: The tension has ratcheted down, and the characters take time to digest the implications of the latest plot twist.

The dramatic opening and Act I generally comprise the first quarter of the novel. Act II makes up roughly half of your total pages. Act III is the final quarter. Here's an example of how a three-hundred-page novel might lay out:

	# PAGES	# SCENES	# CHAPTERS
ACT I	75	11	9
ACT II	150	24	16
ACT III	75	13	10
TOTAL	300	48	35

To get the hang of how a mystery works, analyze the plot of a standard, one-hour crime show. These tend to be structured like mystery novels. They begin with a dramatic opening, and the commercial breaks impose a four-part structure. Usually there's a plot twist before each commercial. Often they end after the final dramatic scene, dispensing with a coda.

Watch a show and analyze the structure of the plot by filling out this scorecard:

	DESCRIPTION	MOST LIKELY SUSPECT AT THE COMMERCIAL BREAK
Opening scene: short scene at the very beginning, before the first commercial		
Plot twist before the next commercial break		
Plot twist before the next commercial break		
Plot twist before the next commercial break		
Final climax: final plot twist and resolution		

⬇ Download a printable version of this worksheet at www.writersdigest.com/writing-and-selling-your-mystery-novel-revised.

SUBPLOTS

Mysteries have secondary plots interwoven with the main one. Subplots can make the novel more complex and interesting and the characters more three-dimensional. They can also provide the reader with a breather or some comic relief from the ongoing, increasing tension of the main plot.

Subplots can be heavy or lightweight, tragic or comic, but they should always be integral to the novel, not slapped on. They should tie directly to the main plot, echo its themes, complicate the crime investigation, or provide the main character an opportunity to address inner demons.

Here are some different kinds of subplots:

- **A ROMANCE:** The main character becomes romantically involved. Now we have a character the protagonist cares about, someone who can be put in jeopardy, which ratchets up the stakes.
- **TRIALS AND TRIBULATIONS OF THE MAIN CHARACTER'S FRIENDS AND FAMILY:** Colorful relatives or friends can provide comic relief or complicate the protagonist's quest in interesting ways.
- **HEALTH ISSUES:** A character attempts to lose weight or get pregnant, deal with a disability, or fight a life-threatening disease.
- **CHALLENGES OF THE PROTAGONIST'S DAY JOB:** There are many ways to use the drama of the character's day job to complicate the story; for example, the character has an ongoing rivalry with a co-worker, deals with a demanding boss, tangles with bureaucracy, or gets fired.
- **INVESTIGATION OF ANOTHER, APPARENTLY UNRELATED CRIME:** A major plot twist occurs when this second crime ties into the main one.
- **UNRESOLVED EVENT IN A CHARACTER'S PAST:** The narrative seesaws back and forth between the present action and some unresolved past event. The ending of the book is doubly satisfying when the crime is solved *and* a past wrong is righted.

How many subplots does your story need? There should be at least one, and some novels can handle as many as five or six. While you should resolve the main plot at the end of the novel, a subplot can be left hanging—which is especially useful if you're writing a series. For instance, you can bring a romantic subplot to the brink of intimacy and then leave the reader panting to read the next book.

TO OUTLINE OR NOT TO OUTLINE

Is a detailed **scene outline** essential or a waste of time? Some writers can't start writing without one. Others say outlines are stifling and dry up their creative juices, preventing their characters from "taking over."

I've written books from detailed outlines and books from nothing but a whiff of an idea, and while the writing process is very different, I can't discern a difference in terms of final quality or overall writing time. When I do write an outline, it's a spare, dry working document, pure and simple.

Here's an example of the outline of the first scenes in my novel *There Was an Old Woman*.

SCENE	NARRATOR	SETTING/PLOT POINTS IN *THERE WAS AN OLD WOMAN*	TIME LINE
1	Mina	At home reading obits. Ambulance arrives for Mrs. Ferrante next door. Mrs. Ferrante asks her to "call Ginger" and "don't let him in until I'm gone."	DAY 1: Friday
2	Evie	At Empire State Building, retrieving B52 Bomber engine from elevator shaft. Gets call from sister, Ginger, which she doesn't answer.	
3	Evie	At historical society, bringing back engine. Gets message from Ginger: Mom's in the hospital.	
4	Evie	In Evie's office. Takes Ginger's call; they argue. "It's your turn"; agrees to go home and deal with Mom.	
5	Evie	Goes to Mom's. Stops at convenience store and reconnects with Finn. Sees house: it's a hoarder's nest, and her mother never was a hoarder.	DAY 2: Saturday
6	Evie	At home, sifting through the mess: cat food cans (her mother has no cats), empty liquor bottles (Mom's an alcoholic); broken bedroom window.	

Put in as much or as little detail as you need. Consider including these elements:

- sequential scene numbers (you can chunk scenes into chapters later)
- the viewpoint character (if you have more than one narrator)
- the setting
- the characters in the scene
- events and major plot points
- the date or day of the week and the time of day

An outline like this is useful when you start writing. It keeps your place, helps you see the big picture, keeps track of time elapsed, and provides scaffolding on which to hang your story. It's also easy to revise—you can move whole clumps of scenes from one place to another with a quick cut and paste.

Don't feel tethered to your outline. Consider it a starting point. Treat it as a working document, and revise it as you write to reflect your current draft.

While outlining the entire book in advance may seem daunting, mapping out the turning points is a good planning exercise. Briefly describe what's going to happen at a few key moments in your book.

KEY TURNING POINTS	WHAT'S GOING TO HAPPEN
Opening	
End of Act I	
Middle of Act II	
End of Act II	
Climax of Act III	

⬇️ Download a printable version of this worksheet at www.writersdigest.com/writing-and-selling-your-mystery-novel-revised.

WRITING A BEFORE-THE-FACT SYNOPSIS

In addition to (or instead of) an outline, you may want to write a **before-the-fact synopsis** of your book. As its name suggests, this synopsis is written *before* you start writing. It introduces the characters and the backdrop, and tells the story dramatically from start to finish. Here's the beginning of a before-the-fact synopsis I wrote for *There Was an Old Woman*.

> *There Was an Old Woman* [working title] tells the story of two women, one young and one old, who connect across generations in spite of the fact that, or perhaps because, they are not related.

Eighty-nine-year-old Wilhelmina "Mina" Yetner lives alone in the bungalow house where she grew up, in Taft Park in the Bronx, accompanied by her cat and surrounded by relics of her family's past. Her father built her house in the 1910s to replace even tinier summer cottages, reserving the prime river view of the Manhattan skyline and the Empire State Building for his own house. Mina's first job was as a secretary in the Empire State Building, and she was working there in 1945 when a B-52 bomber crashed into it. She's the last living survivor of the fire that ensued.

Thirty-year-old Evie Ferrante grew up next door to Mina. She's the daughter of Mina's neighbor and a curator at a New York historical society. She lives in Brooklyn and is mounting her first solo-curated exhibition on historic NYC fires, including the Empire State Building fire after the plane crashed into it.

The book opens as Mina's neighbor, Sandra Ferrante (Evie's mother), a longtime alcoholic, is carried out of her house. She begs Mina to "call Ginger" (her daughter) and tell her, "Don't let him in until I'm gone."

This synopsis goes on for fifteen pages, summarizing the events of a three-hundred-page novel. A synopsis like this can be shown to an editor or agent. In fact, some publishers require authors to submit a synopsis as the first deliverable of a book contract.

Writing this kind of synopsis makes you think through all the plot twists and turns and articulate how one part of the story connects to the next. Once I've written a thorough synopsis, I find I'm less likely to write myself into a corner.

MAPPING CHARACTER TIME LINES

Every character in your book had a life before your book opens. Some of their past experiences were shared, and some were not. Some past experiences matter to the plot you're writing. Some provide insight into why those characters do what they do in your novel.

A **multiple character time line** can help you keep track of your characters' most important past experiences, those that are critical to your story. Here's the time line I put together when I was writing *There Was an Old Woman*.

The shaded rows indicate Mina's and Evie's shared experiences that are pivotal to my plot, leading up to the book's opening.

	CHARACTER: MINA YETNER	CHARACTER: EVIE FERRANTE
Age on Page 1	89	30
1926	BORN	
1944	First job at Empire State Building @18	

1945	Survives Empire State Building fire @19	
1977		BORN
1982	Widowed @57	
1992	House fire next door; helps get Evie and her sister Ginger out @67	Her house burns @15
2008		Starts working at historical society
2012	Sister dies	Plans first solo-curated exhibit
2013/Page 1	Sees Evie's mother taken from house next door; calls Ginger who calls Evie @89	Gets Ginger's call that Mom is in the hospital; goes to mother's house and reconnects with Mina @30

✎ NOW YOU TRY: MAP A MULTIPLE-CHARACTER TIME LINE 9.5

Choose two major characters in your book, and list events from their pasts in chronological order; shade the rows for events they experienced together.

	CHARACTER:	CHARACTER:
Age on Page 1		
Year:		
Year:		
Year:		
Year:		
Year:		

Year:		
Year:		
Year:		
Year/Page 1:		

 Download a printable version of this worksheet at www.writersdigest.com/writing-and-selling-your-mystery-novel-revised.

ON YOUR OWN: STAKING OUT YOUR PLOT

Outline your story. Remember that you don't have to outline every single scene in your novel before you start writing; you can do some detailed planning at the outset, write some scenes or chapters, then return to planning, and so on. This approach can be less overwhelming than outlining the entire plot before moving on.

1. Create an outline that includes the following:
    • the opening scene (the out-of-whack event)
    • the rest of the scenes in Act I (Remember: every scene should have a payoff that moves the story forward.)
    • the final scene in Act I, which contains a dramatic climax and plot twist
    • a brief summary of what happens in Act II, plus a description of the climax and major plot twist
    • a brief summary of what happens in Act III, plus a description of the climax and major plot twist
    • the solution: whodunit and why
2. After you've written the scenes in one act, outline the scenes in the next act. While you're at it, revise the outline to reflect what you actually wrote.
3. Repeat step two until you've finished the book.

Write a before-the-fact synopsis. Start small, and then add on.

1. Write a one-paragraph synopsis that contains a dramatic summary of your novel. Include at least a summary of the dramatic opening, the crime, the investigation, and the solution.
2. Expand the synopsis to one page, adding a summary of each act and the major plot twists.
3. Expand it again, adding subplots.
4. Keep expanding until everything in your head is down on paper.

→ COMPLETE THE PLOT SECTION OF THE BLUEPRINT AT THE END OF PART I.

CHAPTER 10

PICKING A TITLE

"I start with a title. I use that as a springboard, then plunge into those dark, forbidding waters. The title keeps me focused throughout."

—Evan McBain (a.k.a. Evan Hunter)

■ ■ ■

Picking a title for your novel is more of an art than a science. Of course, you don't *need* a title to start writing, but just like typing *THE END* at the end of a completed draft, there's something therapeutic about typing a title at the beginning—if only to show yourself that you're officially off and writing.

Most writers consider the title they pick at this stage to be a *working title*, subject to change. Sometimes the book you start writing gets transformed by the time you get to the end, and you need a different title. Later, your publisher or agent may suggest a title change for what they perceive as marketing exigencies. Raymond Chandler wanted to call one of his novels *The Second Murder*; his publisher changed the title to *Farewell, My Lovely*, a change we can all agree was for the better.

WHAT'S IN A TITLE?

Like the cover art of your novel, the title should intrigue potential readers. You want a title that will pique the interest of your intended audience. It should tease with a hint of what lies between the covers.

Series writers often give their titles a common element. Sue Grafton captured the alphabet with hers, beginning with *"A" Is for Alibi*. John D. MacDonald splashed his Travis McGee novel titles with color, starting with *The Deep Blue Good-by*.

Here are the titles of the twenty mystery and crime fiction bestsellers listed on www.barnesandnoble.com in May 2016:

1. *15th Affair* by James Patterson
2. *The Last Mile* by David Baldacci
3. *Extreme Prey* by John Sandford
4. *Boar Island* by Nevada Barr
5. *The Girl on the Train* by Paula Hawkins
6. *Redemption Road* by John Hart
7. *The Pursuit* by Janet Evanovich and Lee Goldberg
8. *End of Watch* by Stephen King
9. *Knit to Be Tied* by Maggie Sefton
10. *The Crossing* by Michael Connelly
11. *The Butterfly Sister* by Amy Gail Hansen
12. *Mean Streak* by Sandra Brown
13. *Books of a Feather* by Kate Carlisle
14. *Family Jewels* by Stuart Woods
15. *Tall Tail* by Rita Mae Brown
16. *Ordinary Grace* by William Kent Krueger
17. *14th Deadly Sin* by James Patterson
18. *Murder in Morningside Heights* by Victoria Thompson
19. *Find Her* by Lisa Gardner
20. *The Highwayman* by Craig Johnson

Notice how many short titles there are.

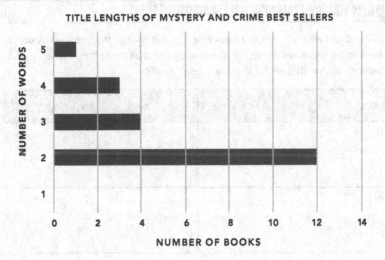

TITLE LENGTHS OF MYSTERY AND CRIME BEST SELLERS

A number of books on this list have recognizable series titles. James Patterson's *15th Affair* and *14th Deadly Sin* are in his Women's Murder Club series; *Extreme Prey* is a book in John Sandford's Prey series. Maggie Sefton's *Knit to Be Tied* has a punny title like the other cozy novels in her Knitting Mystery series.

Some titles provide a glimpse of setting (*Boar Island* and *Murder in Morningside Heights*). Others mine the theme of the book with an image or a phrase that has a double meaning (*The Crossing* and *Family Jewels*). "End of watch" is a police term used by officers in their reports to signify the end of their shift; fittingly, it's the final of three books focusing on a police detective. Finally, alliteration makes a title easier to remember (*Redemption Road* and *Tall Tail*).

It's also clear from a quick glance at the list that the author's name is far more important than the book's title. It's sad but true: Best-selling authors' names sell books. If no one knows your name, that's even more reason to have a great title.

Whatever title you pick, it should accomplish the following:

- accurately pitch your book
- intrigue potential readers
- be easy to remember

Titles can't be copyrighted, so there's no law against naming your book *Gone Girl* or *The Da Vinci Code*—but I wouldn't pick a title that's so instantly recognizable. On the other hand, if your favorite title has already been used for a book no one remembers, feel free to use it.

NOW YOU TRY: EXAMINING YOUR FAVORITE TITLES   10.1

Think about what you like in a book title. List five of your favorites—they don't have to be mysteries. What is it about each title that made it memorable, and what does that title evoke about the book itself?

FAVORITE TITLES	WHAT MAKES IT MEMORABLE AND WHAT IT EVOKES
1.	
2.	

3.	
4.	
5.	

⬇ Download a printable version of this worksheet at www.writersdigest.com/ writing-and-selling-your-mystery-novel-revised.

✏ ON YOUR OWN: PICKING A TITLE

1. Brainstorm title ideas. Review your blueprint, and pay special attention to the premise, the backdrop and setting, the major plot points, and the main character. Free-associate; make a list of the words and images that come to mind. Circle five or ten you like best, and turn them into titles.
2. Look up each of the five titles in an online bookstore to see how often it's been used.
3. Search for your potential titles online, and check each word in an online slang dictionary; that way, if you use a word like *shag* in your title, at least you'll know up front that it has more than one meaning.
4. Pick a title.

➡ WRITE YOUR TITLE IN THE FINAL FIELD OF THE BLUEPRINT, AND THEN TYPE IT ON THE FIRST PAGE OF YOUR MANUSCRIPT. YOU'RE READY TO START WRITING.

A BLUEPRINT FOR PLANNING A MYSTERY NOVEL

PREMISE: SUPPOSE ... AND WHAT IF ...

_____

_____

PROTAGONIST: THE MYSTERY SLEUTH

Name:

Reason for getting mixed up in investigating crimes:

_____

_____

Physical appearance:

_____

_____

Present status and ambitions:

_____

_____

Background:

Talents and skills:

Personality:

Tastes and preferences:

THE CRIME(S)			
	CRIME 1	CRIME 2	CRIME 3
Crime scenario: Victim, modus operandi, scene of the crime			
What appears to have happened			
What really happened			
Why this crime matters to this sleuth			

THE VILLAIN

Name:

Thumbnail sketch:

Apparent motive:

How this character justifies the crime(s):

VICTIMS

Victim's name:

Thumbnail sketch:

What put this victim in harm's way:	Secrets:

Victim's name:

Thumbnail sketch:

What put this victim in harm's way:	Secrets:

Suspect's name:	Relationship to victim:

Thumbnail sketch:

Apparent motive:	Secrets and lies:

Suspect's name:	Relationship to victim:

Thumbnail sketch:

Apparent motive:	Secrets and lies:

Suspect's name:	Relationship to victim:

Thumbnail sketch:

Apparent motive:	Secrets and lies:

SUPPORTING CAST		
Name	Relationship to sleuth (boss, brother, etc.)	Role in the story (adversary, sidekick, etc.)

CHARACTER WEB
Write the name; check the blocks that apply.

Character name	Helps the protagonist	Hinders the protagonist

SETTING

Time: year, season, concurrent events	
Location: geographic locale, exteriors, interiors	

Context: institutions and activities that provide the backdrop	

THE PLOT: MAIN TURNING POINTS

Dramatic Opening	Description
Out-of-Whack Event	Description:
End of Act I Plot Twist	Description:
Middle of Act II Plot Twist	Description:
End of Act II Plot Twist	Description:
End of Act III Climax	Description:
Subplots	Description:

⬇ Download a printable version of these worksheets at www.writersdigest.com/
writing-and-selling-your-mystery-novel-revised.

PART II

WRITING

"For me and most of the
other writers I know, writing
is not rapturous. In fact, the
only way I can get anything
written at all is to write really,
really shitty first drafts."

—Anne Lamott, *Bird by Bird:
Some Instructions on Writing and Life*

You've spent tons of energy and done a bang-up job researching and planning. Now you're ready to start writing the first draft.

At its most elementary, you'll be writing scenes that combine description, movement, dialogue, and internal dialogue to create these basic mystery novel components:

- **INVESTIGATION:** actions such as questioning suspects, examining the crime scene, going on stakeouts, doing searches, and so on
- **SUSPENSE:** rising tension and potential danger as the investigation continues; anticipation builds with the feeling that something is *going* to happen
- **DRAMATIC ACTION:** physical drama such as a car chase, a gunfight, or an assault
- **REFLECTION:** thoughts of what just happened and the review of clues and red herrings, then a moment of realization as a lightbulb goes off in the character's (and the reader's) head, and the story is propelled forward

To see how these elements work together, read the three-scene synopsis that follows.

Investigation | Concerned when lawyer Drew Fellon fails to show up in court, his buddy Jason Armitage goes to Fellon's apartment to look for him.

Jason finds Fellon's Porsche in the parking lot outside his apartment; the engine is cool.

Suspense | Jason goes to Fellon's apartment. The door is ajar. Cautiously he enters. He checks out the kitchen and the living room. Everything seems normal, but …

He notices an acrid smell. He enters the bedroom and finds Fellon lying on the bed, holding a pistol, with a bullet wound to the head. Jason picks

Dramatic Action | up the phone to call the police when he hears a toilet flush. The bathroom door opens, and a man wearing a ski mask charges out.

They struggle. Jason grabs for the gun, but before he can shoot the man, he's bashed in the head and it's lights out.

Reflection | Jason wakes up in an ambulance. At first he can't recall what happened. Then it comes back to him: He remembers going to his friend's apartment and finding him dead in what was meant to look like a suicide. Jason is angry and upset; he knows his friend was depressed, but he'd never shoot himself. Jason tries to visualize the intruder he saw coming out of the bathroom, and he wonders why the man only hit him in the head and didn't kill him. Then he realizes that his own clothes are covered in blood, his fingerprints are all over the gun that killed his friend, and the police officer leaning over him is reading him his Miranda rights.

Generally speaking, a mystery novel unfolds in waves of investigation, suspense, action, and reflection.

More investigation occurs earlier in the novel; toward the end there's more suspense and action. A well-paced novel takes time to develop characters and create a sense of place up front, all the while moving the story forward.

GETTING IT DOWN

Writing a first draft is like knitting a very long scarf. Your blueprint, outline, and synopsis provide a pattern to follow. Start at the beginning. Write scene one, and then write scene two. Keep at it, carrying along and interweaving the threads of subplots while you build the main story, varying the pattern and improvising as inspiration strikes. Sooner or later, you've inched your way to the end.

If it suits you, keep track of your progress and set a daily goal. I do because I'm anal and like to measure my progress. And also because I usually have a deadline, either self-imposed or set by my publisher. My goal is generally to write 500 new words a day, and I like to keep track of how far ahead or behind I am at reaching my ultimate goal.

Here's a portion of the chart I use to track my first-draft progress. The chart extends to 80,000 words over twenty-three weeks. I usually fall behind, but charting my day-to-day output gives me a realistic idea of when I'll actually reach the finish line.

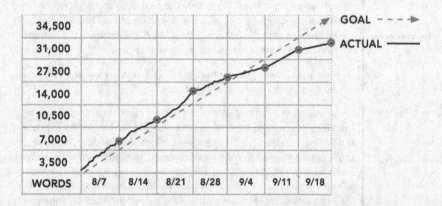

For me, writing the first draft is excruciating. I can plan to beat the band, research for hours on end, revise 'til the cows come home, but writing that first draft—every sentence, every page, feels like I'm pushing wood through a meat grinder. I read my e-mails or play solitaire to avoid writing. I'll even do laundry or balance my checkbook rather than write. Mystery author Kate Flora suggests hanging a sign *inside* your office door that says KEEP OUT. I tried it, but it didn't work.

I have found that it helps if I give myself permission to drop stitches. Writing a bad first draft is not only acceptable; it's expected. So silence your inner critic and nail down that first draft. If it's rife with highfalutin metaphors, arcane vocabulary, and long descriptive passages, you can cut and simplify later. If your writing is skeletal, more movie script than novel, don't worry about that either. You'll layer on nuance, character, and description when you revise.

Some writers start writing the first scene and go full-steam ahead, writing scene after scene, straight through to the end. But for the rest of us, writing is three steps forward, two steps back.

Every morning when I sit down to work, the first thing I do is reread and revise the scene I wrote the day before. Sometimes I revise an even larger chunk before writing new material. This is good—but only to a point. Have you heard that old saying, "Great is the enemy of good"? Well, "great" is also the enemy of "finished." And you've got to finish the first draft so you can get on to the revisions that will make it shine.

MANUSCRIPT LENGTH

There are no hard-and-fast rules, but generally speaking, a publisher expects a manuscript for a mystery novel to be somewhere between 70,000 and 100,000 words. Using 12-point Times New Roman font, double-spacing, and inch-wide margins, that's about 250 to 400 pages.

If your manuscript is more than 450 pages, an editor will be more reluctant to consider it. A 150-page manuscript, even when it's an entertaining cozy mystery, probably won't make it out of the slush pile either.

CHAPTER 11

WRITING A DRAMATIC OPENING

"I find that most people know what a story is until they sit down to write one."

—Flannery O'Connor

■ ■ ■

No pressure, but the opening of your book is the gatekeeper in determining whether your novel will sell. If your opening is weak, it won't matter if chapter two is a masterpiece. Editors and agents and booksellers and librarians and readers will stop reading before they get there.

If you completed your blueprint, you've already scoped out a dramatic scene to open your novel. You know who's in the scene and what's going to happen to propel the novel forward.

Your opening scene can be long or short. It can be action packed, or moody and rich in description, or skeletal and spare. It may contain a vivid sense of setting or a strong shot of character. Regardless of what's in that scene, the reader should have some idea of what the novel is going to be about after reading it, or at least have a good sense of the theme. Most of all, when they finish, readers should be *eager to keep reading.*

ANALYZING A DRAMATIC OPENING

So what makes for a good dramatic opening? In the absence of any useful rules, the best I can offer is an example. Consider this excerpt from the opening scene of Julia Spencer-Fleming's award-winning debut novel, *In the Bleak Midwinter*.

THINK ABOUT:	OPENING SCENE FROM *IN THE BLEAK MIDWINTER* BY JULIA SPENCER-FLEMING

• How does the opening sentence set up the scene?
 	
• What's the out-of-whack event, and how does it pull the reader forward?
 	
• In what tense is this told, and from which character's point of view?
 	
• What do we know about the setting?
 	
• What's the weather and time of day?
 	
• What do we learn about Russ Van Alstyne?
 	
• Why does this event matter to this protagonist?
 	
• What does this opening scene suggest that the book is going to be about?
 	
• Does this opening develop plot or character?
	It was one hell of a night to throw away a baby. The cold pinched at Russ Van Alstyne's nose and made him jam his hands deep into his coat pockets, grateful that the Washington County Hospital had a police parking spot just a few yards from the ER doors. A flare of red startled him, and he watched as an ambulance backed out of its bay silently, lights flashing.
	    "Kurt! Hey! Anything for me?"
	    The driver waved at Russ. "You heard about the baby?"
	    "That's why I'm here."
	    Russ waved, then pushed open the antiquated double doors to the emergency department.
	...
	"Hey! Chief!" A blurry form in brown approached him. Russ tucked his glasses over his ears and Mark Durkee, one of his three night shift officers, snapped into focus. As usual, the younger man was spit-and-polished within an inch of his life, making Russ acutely aware of his own non-standard-issue appearance: wrinkled wool pants shoved into salt-stained hunting boots, his oversized tartan muffler clashing with his regulation brown parka.
	    "Hey, Mark," Russ answered. "Talk to me."
	    The officer waved his chief down the drab green hallway toward the emergency room. The place smelled of disinfectant and bodies, with a whiff of cow manure left over by the last farmer who had come in straight from the barn.
	...
	"How's the baby look?"
	    "Fine, as far as they can tell. He was wrapped up real well, and the doc says he probably wasn't out in the cold more'n a half hour or so." Russ' sore stomach eased up. He'd seen a lot over the years, but nothing shook him as much as an abused child. He'd had one baby-stuffed-in-a-garbage-bag case when he'd been an MP in Germany, and he didn't care to ever see one again.

Plot and character take equal weight in this excerpt. It's as much about introducing police chief Russ Van Alstyne (one of the series' two protagonists) as it is about setting up the story of an abandoned baby. Every sentence, every detail is a deliberate choice, and by the end, the reader knows that the novel will answer two questions: Who abandoned that baby, and why?

> It was one hell of a night to throw away a baby.

Right away, the opening establishes the out-of-whack event: a baby has been abandoned. This intriguing opening is a line of internal dialogue that puts the reader firmly in Russ's head. The point of view is the third-person limited, and we experience this scene as if the camera is looking through Van Alstyne's eyes. His thoughts filter the images we see. It's written in the past tense, but the feeling is one of immediacy.

> The cold pinched at Russ Van Alstyne's nose and made him jam his hands deep into his coat pockets, grateful that the Washington County Hospital had a police parking spot just a few yards from the ER doors.

You've probably heard the author's adage "Show; don't tell." Throughout this brief passage, Spencer-Fleming shows us what Van Alstyne is like. She shows that he is chief of police: The ambulance driver addresses him as "Chief," and he parks his car in a police parking spot. She also shows how cold it is with the phrase "the cold pinched his nose" and with the way Van Alstyne jams his hands into his pockets. The bitter cold isn't mentioned just for ambience; it brings home to the reader how dangerous it was for that baby to be left on the church steps.

> The place smelled of disinfectant and bodies, with a whiff of cow manure left over by the last farmer who had come in straight from the barn.

In a few descriptive phrases, we get a visceral sense of place. We know this is a hospital, and we know it's located somewhere rural.

We get a detailed description of what Van Alstyne is wearing (*wrinkled wool pants shoved into salt-stained hunting boots*) as he mentally compares himself to a younger officer (*spit-and-polished within an inch of his life.*) Van Alstyne is a guy with more than a few miles on him who doesn't fuss with his appearance.

"How's the baby look?" Van Alstyne asks. He cares. And already we're wondering: Who left this baby on the church steps, and what happened to the baby's mother?

> "He was wrapped up really well, and the doc says he probably wasn't out in the cold more'n a half hour or so."

Clues!, thinks the astute reader. Someone wrapped that baby up well. Maybe that someone was even watching to be sure the baby was found in time.

Here's what Spencer-Fleming doesn't give the reader: a whole lot of backstory. Backstory is background information about how a character arrived at this particular place and time. When a load of backstory has been dumped into the opening chapter, it's a sure sign that the novel was written by a novice. At this point we get only a whiff of Van Alstyne's past and a hint of why an abandoned baby matters to him:

> He'd had one baby-stuffed-in-a-garbage-bag case when he'd been an MP in Germany, and he didn't care to ever see one again.

That's all the reader needs to know at this point.

 NOW YOU TRY: ANALYZE A DRAMATIC OPENING

Reread the opening scenes of some of your favorite mystery novels. Pay careful attention to how the authors handle these five elements:

1. the opening paragraph
2. the final paragraph
3. how characters are introduced
4. the setting and how it's established
5. the unanswered question that sets up the novel

SKETCHING OUT A DRAMATIC OPENING

As an exercise in chapter eight, you wrote a description of your opening scene. If you have a clear picture in your mind of exactly what happens in the scene, you may feel you can jump right in and write the dramatic opening of your novel. But if you find that blank page daunting, sketch out the scene before you try to write it.

Here's an example of what the sketch for a scene looks like, using the opening of *In the Bleak Midwinter* as an example.

Small town, Adirondacks, winter;   ⬅ Where
hospital parking lot and ER

Present, bitter-cold winter night   ⬅ When

Russ Van Alstyne (police chief, narrator);   ⬅ Characters in the scene
Kurt (ambulance driver); Officer Mark Durkee

Van Alstyne is in parking lot of Washington County Hospital;   ⬅ What happens
it's cold; an ambulance is leaving

Van Alstyne goes into ER; talks to Durkee; is relieved to
find out baby is fine, was well wrapped up; remembers the
discarded baby he found as MP in Germany

Who abandoned the baby, and why   ⬅ Question that propels
the reader forward

✎ NOW YOU TRY: SKETCH OUT A DRAMATIC OPENING   11.1

Review your description of your novel's dramatic opening. Then visualize the
scene in your mind. Sketch it out below.

WHERE:

WHEN:

CHARACTERS IN THE SCENE:

WHAT HAPPENS:

QUESTION THAT PROPELS THE READER FORWARD:

⬇ Download a printable version of this worksheet at www.writersdigest.com/
writing-and-selling-your-mystery-novel-revised.

WRITING THE DRAMATIC OPENING

One way to effectively launch the opening scene is to jump right into the action. Here are some opening lines that catapult the reader into the story:

> When the first bullet hit my chest, I thought of my daughter. (*No Second Chance*, Harlan Coben)

> She'd been brutally stabbed and slashed more times than Carella chose to imagine. (*Widows*, Ed McBain)

> Gordon Michaels stood in the fountain with all his clothes on. (*Banker*, Dick Francis)

> The house in Silverlake was dark, its windows as empty as a dead man's eyes. (*The Concrete Blonde*, Michael Connelly)

> I was fifteen years old when I first met Sherlock Holmes, fifteen years old with my nose in a book as I walked the Sussex Downs, and nearly stepped on him. (*The Beekeeper's Apprentice*, Laurie R. King)

> Augie Odenkirk had a 1997 Datsun that still ran well in spite of high mileage, but the gas was expensive, especially for a man with no job, and City Center was on the far side of town, so he decided to take the last bus of the night. (*Mr. Mercedes*, Stephen King)

> Annie Holleran hears him before she sees him. (*Let Me Die in His Footsteps*, Lori Roy)

Your opening line is important, but don't obsess about it. Just write an opening line that drops the reader into the scene, and keep going. You can perfect it later.

WRITING THE DRAMATIC OPENING

The first scene of your book presents some unique problems. Your primary job is to get your story moving. At the same time, you need to introduce your characters, the setting, and the situation. It's a tall order, and it's easy to bore the reader with too much information or to confuse him by laying too little groundwork.

Keep your eye trained on the story you're setting up—something intriguing has to happen. Lay in just enough character and setting description to orient the reader. You have the rest of the book to fill in the blanks.

Write the opening scene using the elements you sketched out. You can make revisions later, applying lessons from later chapters in this book, such as setting the scene, introducing characters, writing dialogue and internal dialogue, and creating action.

ENDING THE DRAMATIC OPENING WITH FORWARD MOMENTUM

End your dramatic opening scene with an unanswered question that is implied or stated. Your goal is to make it impossible for the reader to put down your novel.

Here's how Harlan Coben ends the opening scene of *No Second Chance*:

> So I like to think that as the two bullets pierced my body, as I collapsed onto the linoleum of my kitchen floor with a half-eaten granola bar clutched in my hand, as I lay immobile in a spreading puddle of my own blood, and yes, even as my heart stopped beating, that I still tried to do something to protect my daughter.

The reader wants to know: Did he die? Was his daughter okay? And what was he trying to protect his daughter from?

Review the sketch of your opening scene. Decide how you should end it to achieve maximum forward momentum. Steer clear of a "Had I but known" ending or a generic "Boy, was I surprised and terrified by what happened next" statement that could be tacked on to the end of any novel's opening.

 ON YOUR OWN: WRITE A DRAMATIC OPENING

1. Write the opening scene for your novel.
2. Review your scene, and examine your choices:
   - Does the first sentence set up the scene?
   - What's the out-of-whack event?
   - Does the scene pose an unanswered question?
   - In what tense is this scene told, and which character is the narrator? Are you happy with these choices?
   - Have you dumped a load of unnecessary backstory into the opening?
3. Revise, and move on.

CHAPTER 12

INTRODUCING THE PROTAGONIST

"Years ago I was in Botswana, staying with friends in a small town called Mochudi. A woman in the town wished to give my friends a chicken to celebrate Botswana National Day. I watched as this woman—traditionally built, like Mma Ramotswe—chased the chicken round the yard and eventually caught it. She made a clucking noise as she ran. The chicken looked miserable. She looked very cheerful. At that moment I thought that I might write a book about a cheerful woman of traditional build."

—Alexander McCall Smith

■■■

BRINGING THE CHARACTER ONSTAGE

In mystery fiction, as in life, first impressions matter. Make the most of your sleuth's first appearance on the page with the following elements.

Description

Raymond Chandler introduces Philip Marlowe with **description** and sets the bar high in *The Big Sleep*, published in 1939:

It was about eleven o'clock in the morning, mid October, with the sun not shining and a look of hard wet rain in the clearness of the foothills. I was wearing my powder-blue suit, with dark blue shirt, tie and display handkerchief, black brogues, black wool socks with dark blue clocks on them. I was neat, clean, shaved and sober, and I didn't care who knew it. I was everything the well-dressed private detective ought to be. I was calling on four million dollars.

Aside from being beautifully written, this introduction is packed with information about Marlowe. As a first-person narrator, Marlowe talks directly to the reader. He tells us he's a private dick and a clotheshorse in his powder-blue suit, fancy hankie, and socks with clocks—Bogie's portrayal of the character notwithstanding. You can almost smell the aftershave. We know he likes his liquor hard—otherwise why mention being sober? Then he offers the in-your-face line "… and I didn't care who knew it."

He adds, "I was everything the well-dressed private detective ought to be." Here's a guy with a chip on his shoulder, an outsider, a self-deprecating smart-ass. "I was calling on four million dollars." And finally we have a hint of what he's up to.

Dialogue

Another way to introduce a character is with **dialogue**. Here's Robert B. Parker using dialogue to introduce his main character, Spenser, in *Bad Business*:

"Do you do divorce work?" the woman said.

"I do," I said.

"Are you any good?"

"I am," I said.

"I don't want likelihood," she said. "Or guesswork. I need evidence that will stand up in court."

"That's not up to me," I said. "That's up to the evidence."

She sat quietly in my client chair and thought about that.

"You're telling me you won't manufacture it," she said.

"Yes," I said.

"You won't have to," she said. "The sonovabitch can't keep his dick in his pants for a full day."

"Must make dining out a little awkward," I said.

She ignored me. I was used to it. Mostly I amused myself.

No description. No setting. With a deadpan style, Parker jumps directly into a verbal sparring match between Spenser and a woman who wants to hire him to snoop on her soon-to-be ex. From the dialogue alone, we get a strong taste of Spenser's wry sense of humor, we know he's a detective, and we easily infer that he can take or leave this particular assignment.

Action

A third way to introduce a protagonist is to show him in **action**. That's how Michael Connelly introduces police detective Harry Bosch a few pages into his award-winning debut novel, *The Black Echo*:

> Harry Bosch could hear the helicopter up there, somewhere, above the darkness, circling up in the light. Why didn't it land? Why didn't it bring help? Harry was moving through a smoky, dark tunnel and his batteries were dying. The beam of the flashlight grew weaker every yard he covered. He needed help. He needed to move faster. He needed to reach the end of the tunnel before the light was gone and he was alone in the black. He heard the chopper make one more pass. Why didn't it land? Where was the help he needed? When the drone of the blades fluttered away again, he felt the terror build and he moved faster, crawling on scraped and bloody knees, one hand holding the dim light up, the other pawing the ground to keep his balance. He did not look back for the enemy he knew was behind him in the black mist. Unseen, but there. And closing in.
>
> When the phone rang in the kitchen, Bosch immediately woke.

This is an action sequence that turns out to be a dream. It shows us that Harry Bosch fought in the military, and we get hints of his darkest fears and of a tragedy from his past.

Description, dialogue, action—any of these can be used effectively, alone or in combination, to introduce your protagonist. Your goal is to create a sense of immediacy, to show the reader the character's physical presence and personality. The character should pop off the page. Then, while the reader is paying attention to the fireworks, you can slip in basic information and a hint of what formative event drives him.

GIVING THE READER THE BASICS

There's much debate among writers concerning how much the reader needs to be told right away about a main character. Lawrence Block never describes Bernie Rhodenbarr, his series protagonist, and readers don't complain. Sarah Caudwell wrote a series of suspense novels featuring Professor Hilary Tamar of Oxford and never told the reader if Professor Tamar was a man or a woman.

Nevertheless, within the first few pages of a character's introduction, most mystery authors let the reader know these basic bits of information:

- name
- gender
- approximate age
- job
- physical appearance

It's important to give the reader a hint, at least, of your character's physical presence right away. In the absence of a description, readers will quickly form their own competing images.

The challenge is to slip in the facts without giving the reader a boring curriculum vitae to read. If you're writing a character who acts as a narrator, speaking directly to the reader, telling the basics is no problem at all. Sue Grafton handily gets away with this information dump in "*G*" *Is for Gumshoe*:

> For the record, my name is Kinsey Millhone. I'm a private investigator, licensed by the State of California, (now) thirty-three years old, 118 pounds of female in a five-foot-six frame. My hair is dark, thick and straight. I'd been accustomed to wearing it short, but I'd been letting it grow out just to see what it would look like. My usual practice is to crop my own mop every six weeks or so with a pair of nail scissors. This I do because I'm too cheap to pay twenty-eight bucks in a beauty salon. I have hazel eyes, a nose that's been busted twice, but still manages to function pretty well I think. If I were asked to rate my looks on a scale of one to ten, I wouldn't. I have to say, however, that I seldom wear makeup, so whatever I look like first thing in the morning at least remains consistent as the day wears on.

Like a character in a movie who suddenly turns and addresses the audience, Kinsey speaks directly to the reader. In one dense paragraph, we get all the basics about her, plus a shot of her feisty, nonconformist personality.

Here's another example from *The Magician's Tale* by William Bayer (a.k.a. David Hunt). Though the passage is also written in the first person, the character, photographer Kay Farrow, describes herself as part of the storytelling rather than speaking directly to the reader.

> The sun is about to set. I check myself in the mirror—glowing eyes, dark brows, small triangular face, medium-length hair parted on the side. I brush down some wisps so they fall across my forehead, then dress to go out—black T-shirt, jeans, black leather jacket, sneakers, Contax camera around my neck.

WRITING & SELLING YOUR MYSTERY NOVEL

I wear black to blend in. My hope is that by dressing dark and with my face half concealed by my hair, I can slink along the streets, barely seen, covertly stealing images.

I pause at my living room window. Dusk is magic time, the sky still faintly lit. Streetlamps are on and lights glow from windows, making the city look mysterious and serene. The view's so spectacular it's hard to tear myself away: North Beach, Telegraph Hill, the Bay Bridge sharply defined, all still, silent, glowing behind the glass.

Hunt has this character look into a mirror and tell us about her own appearance. Plenty of books on writing tell you this is a clichéd technique, but it turns up all the time in successful novels, and the passage above is an example of how it can be done well.

From the telling details Hunt reveals, the reader infers a great deal. This character is young (*black T-shirt, jeans* ...), a resident of San Francisco (*North Beach* ...), a photographer (*Contax camera around my neck*). The character feels somewhat androgynous, but the mention of *medium-length hair* suggests she's a woman. Beyond that, we know she's highly visual, curious, and secretive. A page later, she's prowling an unsavory neighborhood, and a street kid calls out to her: "You blind, girl? What's with the shades, Bug?" Her response tells us that she suffers from complete color-blindness. Soon she meets a man who addresses her as "Kay," which tells us her name. Within the first four pages, Hunt covers all the basics, introducing his protagonist and blending the information seamlessly into an ongoing narrative.

Linda Barnes takes another approach to introduce Carlotta Carlyle in *The Big Dig*:

> He was studying my face like he'd never seen green eyes, a pointy chin, or flaming hair before. Made me wonder whether I looked drawn or pale. I widened my smile, hoping the extra wattage would substitute for a blusher.

Notice that Barnes has another character look at Carlotta Carlyle, and Carlotta tells us what she thinks he sees.

You may want to convey a lot of information about your main character to your reader. Restrain yourself. There's no rush. Make the introduction memorable but not overwhelming. Carefully select details. Reveal your character's backstory as you go along, and in support of ongoing drama.

NOW YOU TRY: GIVE THE READER THE BASICS

1. Refer to your blueprint. Make a list of twenty things about your protagonist's past, personality, or appearance that you want the reader to know right away.
2. Cross out the fifteen that can wait until later in the novel.
3. Write (or rewrite) the first scene your protagonist appears in, conveying the remaining five basic things about your character without writing an information dump.

 ## ON YOUR OWN: INTRODUCE THE PROTAGONIST

1. Look at the openings of a half dozen of your favorite mysteries. Analyze how the author introduces the protagonist:
   • Does the author use description? Dialogue? Action? A combination?
   • How (and when) does the author convey the character's name, gender, job, age, and physical appearance?
   • What character traits does the author initially reveal, and how?
   • How much of the character's background does the reader learn at the beginning?
2. Try different approaches to introducing your protagonist: first-person narration, description, dialogue, action. See which one works best.

CHAPTER 13

INTRODUCING MAJOR AND MINOR CHARACTERS

"Don't say the old lady screamed. Bring her on and let her scream."

—attributed to Mark Twain

■■■

Not all characters are created equal, but each one appears on the page and makes a first impression. How big an impression should be in direct proportion to the size of the role that character plays in the novel:

- **MAJOR CHARACTERS** get to have opinions and take action; they're necessary to the integrity of the story. Take one out and the plot collapses. Major characters in a mystery include the protagonist, the villain, the suspects, the sidekick, and the supporting cast.
- **MINOR CHARACTERS** play small but necessary roles. They may appear only once or twice. For instance, the barmaid who serves up that double-Scotch and listens to your sleuth complain about the case, or the victim's bereaved mother whom your protagonist questions to get the names of the victim's close friends.

- **WALK-ONS** are usually nameless characters who deliver, at most, a few lines of dialogue; their presence lends a dash of realism to a scene, then they are seen no more.

MAKING INTRODUCTIONS: CONJURING THE DETAILS

When a character first appears in your novel, take a few paragraphs, at most, to create an impression. Here's the kind of impression you want to avoid making:

> An attractive young brunette sat at the desk. She had on glasses, and she wore a dark top. She looked up and saw me.

What's wrong with this introduction? It's pallid and generic. *Attractive* is one of those waffle words that don't carry a specific meaning. *Dark top?* Was it a scruffy T-shirt? A ruffled blouse?

Consider this revision:

> A skinny adolescent girl sat at the desk. She had dark eyes and pale skin, and her short dark hair was streaked with red. She had on wire-rimmed glasses and wore black jeans and a black T-shirt. A leather lace was tied around her wrist, and there were silver rings on all her fingers.

Is this any better? At least there are more details. Too many, in fact, and they are pure surface features—eye color, skin color, glasses, clothing, jewelry. We get the sense that this girl might be a rebel and into Goth. But verbs like *sat* and *had on* and *wore* are weak and fail to communicate anything about the character's presence. We know she's probably an edgy teenager, but she's more shop-window mannequin than real human being

How about this description?

> Olivia was slumped at a desk facing me, staring intently at a computer screen. She looked nothing like the lively six-year-old or the mousy preadolescent I remembered. A long neck and bony elbows stuck out of her loose black T-shirt. But the hair was what you noticed—black spikes with poster-paint red streaks running through them.
>
> She took off her round, wire-rimmed glasses, picked up a bottle of eye drops from alongside her keyboard, tipped her head back, and squeezed some drops into each eye. She had a leather lace tied around her wrist and silver rings on all her fingers, including the thumb.

Now the character makes more of an impression with details like that long neck and bony elbows sticking out of a loose black T-shirt, the "poster-paint red streaks" in her hair, and the thumb ring. These are more than a bunch of descriptions that communicate appearance; they are details that show who Olivia is. Still more information is conveyed by what she does—she puts drops in her eyes.

Where do you reach to find the details you need? How do you get past clichés? I know some writers conjure intriguing characters from dust. I can't. Sometimes it feels as if all I've got in my head are caricatures from Charles Dickens's novels and *The Love Boat*.

Fortunately, the world is full of real people who can inspire fictional characters. For example, the character I described above is based on a girl who sat across from me on a subway. Here are my notes from that train ride:

> Young woman. 18? Skinny Goth look. Spiky short hair, black T-shirt, short skirt, braided leather straps on her wrist. Hunched over, eyes closed. Headsets. Silver rings on every finger, including thumb. Green Doc Martens.

All kinds of real-life people make good jumping-off points for characters. Yourself, for example. The protagonist in one of my novels (I won't say which one) feels intensely autobiographical to me. She's got my hair, stature, and inability to suffer fools.

I don't recommend creating a character who walks and talks like your best friend, but certainly you can create a character who is a composite of relatives, friends, or acquaintances.

Public figures or actors make good starting points for fictional characters, as do strangers you see all around you. Watch people. Take advantage of the time you spend waiting in a doctor's office or airport terminal, or riding a bus.

Can you create a nosy next-door neighbor based on your boss? A nefarious killer based on your ex? A two-bit crook based on the bully who tortured you in high school? Sure. But make sure that by the time you're finished writing the character, the real person is unrecognizable. You don't want to get sued.

 ## Q&A: BASING CHARACTERS ON REAL PEOPLE: THE LEGAL RISKS

Q. SUPPOSE A CHARACTER IN YOUR NOVEL IS BASED ON A REAL PERSON. CAN THAT PERSON SUE FOR LIBEL?
A. Maybe. The law defines libel as the publication of a false statement of fact that harms the reputation of a living individual. (The dead cannot be defamed

because, the law says, a person's reputation dies when a person dies.) So, yes, living individuals can be libeled in works of fiction. They can sue you.

Q. WHAT DOES SOMEONE NEED TO WIN THE CASE?

A. To win, the person must show (a) that the portrayal is recognizable and (b) that his reputation has been damaged as a result. If the person is a public official or public figure, then in addition he must prove that the portrayal is false and was published with "actual malice." The Supreme Court defines actual malice as knowledge of a statement's falsity or reckless disregard for a statement's truth or falsity.

Q. SO WHAT'S THE BOTTOM LINE?

A. Protect yourself, and disguise the character. Change the name, gender, ethnicity, age, physical description, geographic location, job function or title, and alter the details of the events to make an individual unrecognizable.

Q. DOES DISGUISING A CHARACTER PROVIDE SUFFICIENT PROTECTION?

A. Usually. But be careful that the features you use to disguise the character are not themselves defamatory. If you disguise your former teacher as a physically repulsive woman who tries to seduce her students, the disguise itself may be defamatory.

INTRODUCING MAJOR CHARACTERS

When a major character appears, take the opportunity to make proper introductions. In these memorable paragraphs, Raymond Chandler introduces the villain of his short story, "Spanish Blood":

> Big John Masters was large, fat, oily. He had sleek blue jowls and very thick fingers on which the knuckles were dimples. His brown hair was combed straight back from his forehead and he wore a wine-colored suit with patch pockets, a wine-colored tie, a tan silk shirt. There was a lot of red and gold band around the thick brown cigar between his lips.
>
> He wrinkled his nose, peeped at his hole card again, and tried not to grin. He said: "Hit me again, Dave—and don't hit me with the City Hall."

This is the essence of showing, not telling. Here are some of the basics to get across to the reader whenever you introduce a major character:

Full Name and Gender

> Big John Masters was large, fat, oily. He …

Right away, the reader finds out the character's name and that he's a man. The name itself (*Big John Masters*) suggests a large, imposing figure. If your narrator doesn't know the character's name, then have him refer to the character some other way. For example, he might refer to a character as *Liam's boss* or call him *Tweeds* if he's wearing tweeds, or refer to him as *Baby Face* if he reminds the narrator of a cherub. Start using the character's name only after the narrator learns it.

Physical Appearance

> He had sleek blue jowls and very thick fingers on which the knuckles were dimples.

Hair, clothing, and finally the cigar—not a single piece of the description is throwaway. Sketch out your character's physical features and/or clothing with a few telling details. His cologne, a broken nose, and a bulge under the arm of his suit jacket, which suggests he's carrying a gun, may be enough. Don't go on and on with paragraphs of description.

Personality

> He wrinkled his nose, peeped at his hole card again, and tried not to grin. He said: "Hit me again, Dave—and don't hit me with the City Hall."

Convey the impression your character makes—his attitude, effect, and demeanor. In this example, Chandler uses a *one-two punch* character intro. After a description, the character does something—in this case, he looks at his cards, tries not to grin, and delivers a line of dialogue.

This combination of description with action and dialogue effectively communicates attitude and personality. How your character stands, moves, talks, breathes, and chews his food can convey a sense of someone who's flat and depressed, larger-than-life and menacing, all business and professional, or jovial and easygoing.

Relationship to the Narrator

The reader should know immediately whether this character is a stranger, an acquaintance, a colleague, or a longtime friend of the narrator's. In this case, the narrator is a fellow poker player. Though Chandler never says it outright, the reader also gleans that Big John Masters is corrupt.

 NOW YOU TRY: ANALYZE THE INTRODUCTION OF A MAJOR CHARACTER

Analyze this passage in which Linda Barnes introduces detective Eddie Conklin, a former cop who offers Carlotta Carlyle a job investigating in *The Big Dig*. Use the questions on the left to guide you.

HOW DOES THE AUTHOR CONVEY:	EXCERPT FROM *THE BIG DIG* BY LINDA BARNES—
• physical appearance? • profession? • personality? • his relationship to Carlotta and their history? **IS THIS AN UNBIASED VIEW OF EDDIE?**	I used to work with Happy Eddie Conklin when I was a cop. … Eddie, now head of Foundation Security's Boston office, was early, wearing a gray suit that did its best to make him look ten pounds lighter, seated at a table barely big enough to handle two plates and a teapot. He rose, clasping my hand in both of his, yanking me into an embrace. "Business, I tell ya, fantastic. Boomin' don't come close to it. Lack of trust in this town, geez, it's amazin'. Due diligence alone, bodyguardin' alone—I could run my own freakin' police department, ya know? Ya like this place? Ya want something to start?" He relayed my order of hot and sour soup to the hovering waiter and demanded "egg rolls, spring rolls, whatever ya call 'em," as well. "Bring that sweet sauce, ya know? The duck kind." I poured steaming tea into small white cups. Eddie looked preposterous from his silk tie to his tasseled slip-ons. His gray hair was short, his jaw freshly shaven. He glanced around to discourage eavesdroppers at neighboring tables, lowered his voice half a notch. "So how's your boy Mooney?

Happy Eddie makes a strong first impression. Did you notice the use of contrast to show us how big he is? The guy is wearing a suit designed to make him look thinner, and he's sitting at an itty-bitty table with dainty teacups.

He's gruff and kind of goofy, the way he "yanks" Carlotta into his embrace and asks her if she likes the restaurant. The dialogue is written in dialect, ("*I tell ya …*" and "*…geez it's amazin*"), suggesting a Boston accent. The grammar shows us Eddie hasn't gone to Harvard ("*Boomin' don't come close to it.*")

Eddie could have been a typical hard-boiled private detective, but he's much more interesting. He's garrulous and anxious to please, more overstuffed teddy bear than stuffed shirt. Whenever you bring a character onstage, think about what the stereotype would be, and then surprise yourself by writing something different.

Is this an objective picture of Eddie? Of course it isn't. That's because we're seeing him through Carlotta's eyes. She's the narrator, and this description is all internal dialogue coming from Carlotta's head, so we get a strong sense of Carlotta's *attitude* toward Eddie. She's got a soft spot for the big lunk. She comes right out and says, "He looked preposterous ..." From the way he embraces her, we suspect they go way back.

When you write a description of a major character, keep the narrator's voice in your head, and describe the character showing your narrator's attitude to that character. Here are two passages that describe the character similarly, but the narrator's attitude is quite different.

Lola stepped into the room and started for the corner. She was gorgeous, as always, with her flaming red hair and dress that fit her like quicksilver. She seemed oblivious to all the men in the room who were watching her like a pack of hunting dogs who'd just caught a scent.	Lola slinked into the room and started for the corner table. That silver lamé dress looked as if it had been painted on. She tossed her silky red hair back, nonchalant, like she didn't notice the men's eyes following her.

With subtle differences (*Lola stepped* versus *Lola slinked*, for example), the first description conveys sympathy; the second description conveys contempt. By carefully picking the words you use to describe a character, you can show the reader both the character's presence and the narrator's attitude toward the character.

NOW YOU TRY: INTRODUCE A MAJOR CHARACTER   13.1

1. Write the first appearance of a major character using the one-two punch method. First describe the character; show with a few telling details. Then use dialogue and/or action to give the reader more insight into his attitude and personality.

INTRODUCE A MAJOR CHARACTER	DETAILS YOU MIGHT WANT TO INCLUDE
	• full name
	• gender
	• physical appearance
	• clothing
	• posture
	• hygiene
	• speech patterns or dialect
	• habits
	• voice
	• movement or gait

2. Now revise that first appearance, tweaking your word choices to convey as much as you can about the *narrator's attitude* toward this character.

REWRITE THE PASSAGE TO CONVEY THE NARRATOR'S ATTITUDE.

⬇ Download a printable version of this worksheet at www.writersdigest.com/ writing-and-selling-your-mystery-novel-revised.

INTRODUCING MINOR CHARACTERS

Minor characters should definitely make an impression when they come on the scene—just not a big splash. You don't want the reader to get too attached to them.

Here's how Jasper Fforde introduces Chief Boswell, the protagonist's boss, in *The Eyre Affair*:

> I worked under Area Chief Boswell, a small, puffy man who looked like a bag of flour with arms and legs. He lived and breathed the job; words were his life and his love—he never seemed happier than when he was on the trail of a counterfeit Coleridge or a fake Fielding.

For all its brevity, this description shows the reader what Boswell looks like, what he does, and that he loves his job. And talk about terrific visual images—you can't beat *a bag of flour with arms and legs*.

Here's another example from *Devices and Desires* by P.D. James. With a flash of vivid description, action, and dialogue, Manny Cummings makes his debut:

> The door was already closing when he heard running footsteps and a cheerful shout and Manny Cummings leapt in, just avoiding the bite of the closing steel. As always he seemed to whirl in a vortex of almost oppressive energy, too powerful to be contained by the lift's four walls. He was brandishing a brown envelope. "Glad I caught you, Adam. It is Norfolk you're escaping to, isn't it? If the Norfolk CID do lay their hands on the Whistler, take a look at him for me, will you, check he isn't our chap in Battersea."

Is Manny tall or short? Fat or thin? Balding or sporting a crew cut? Who knows, and who cares? It's what he does that counts: He leaps into the elevator, arriving like whirlwind, delivers three lines of dialogue with a hint of an Irish brogue, and gives the protagonist an all-important brown envelope that pushes the plot along.

Despite the lack of particulars, Manny makes a vivid impression. Then the reader is content to let him fade away.

A minor role is no place for a complex character. Don't imbue one with a lot of mystery that your reader will expect you to explain. A name, a few details, and a bit of action or dialogue are more effective than a long, drawn-out description.

Write a one-paragraph first appearance of a minor character.

INTRODUCE A MINOR CHARACTER	DETAILS YOU MIGHT WANT TO CONVEY
	• full name
	• gender
	• role (co-worker, neighbor, etc.)
	• approximate age
	• a few telling details
	• a bit of action or dialogue

⬇ Download a printable version of this worksheet at www.writersdigest.com/writing-and-selling-your-mystery-novel-revised.

INTRODUCING WALK-ONS

The world of your novel should be full of walk-on characters who provide texture and realism. Each one may also have some small role in facilitating the plot, but for the most part, walk-on characters are there to make scenes feel authentic. Your protagonist takes a stroll; the street needs pedestrians. She goes to the bank to withdraw money; the bank needs tellers and security guards. The same goes for hotel clerks, waitresses, salesmen, and all the rest.

Walk-ons should get no more than a sentence or two of introduction. They don't need names, and a touch of description is plenty. The details you choose can be a kind of shorthand commentary on the neighborhood or context. Maybe the playground skateboarder is dressed in baggy jeans and a Rasta hat. Or a PTA mother has a four-carat rock on her finger. Used in this way, walk-ons are as much elements of *setting* as they are characters.

A walk-on can also provide side commentary on the action. Here's an example of how *Bonecrack* by Dick Francis uses this walk-on character:

Beyond the yard, out on the gravel, there was parked a large white Mercedes with a uniformed chauffeur standing by the bonnet.

...

I walked up through the yard and out into the drive. The chauffeur folded his arms and his mouth like barricades against fraternization. I stopped a few paces away from him and looked toward the inside of the car.

The chauffeur doesn't have a name, but his stance telegraphs his sense of entitlement and disdain for the narrator.

Be careful not to mislead the reader. If you go on for sentences about what a walk-on looks like, you set the expectation that the character will have a prominent role in the book.

Occasionally, you'll write a walk-on who refuses to simmer down. When that happens, keep writing and see who this character is, what he does, and what interesting detours he inserts into your story. If all he creates is an unnecessary diversion, you'll have to stifle him or save him for a short story. But if he adds just the spice your story needs, then by all means, promote him to a bigger role and integrate him into the plot.

NOW YOU TRY: INTRODUCE A WALK-ON   13.3

Write the appearance of a walk-on character. All it takes is a sentence or two.

WRITE THE APPEARANCE OF A WALK-ON CHARACTER	DETAILS YOU MIGHT WANT TO CONVEY
	• role (waitress, pedestrian, etc.)
	• gender
	• a telling detail or two

⬇ Download a printable version of this worksheet at www.writersdigest.com/writing-and-selling-your-mystery-novel-revised.

HELPING THE READER KEEP YOUR CHARACTERS STRAIGHT

Have you ever started reading a book and felt as if your brain was about to explode because the author introduced a dozen characters in the first ten pages and you can't keep them straight? Help the reader by spreading out the character introductions. Don't try to write a cocktail party until your protagonist and a handful of your other main characters are well anchored in your readers' heads.

Another way to confuse readers is to refer to the same character by a bunch of different names. Suppose you introduce Officer James Dazzle. A sentence later you write "James went to the door." A paragraph later, it's "Dazzle's jaw dropped." On the next page you write, "Jim scowled." Later: "The patrolman scratched his head." The hapless reader thinks these are five different characters. Do this with two characters in the same scene and what's supposed to be an intimate conversation will read like a crowd scene.

When a character is introduced for the first time, tell the reader the character's whole name. After that, call the character by the name the *narrator* would use to refer to him. For instance, if the narrator is James Dazzle's brother, he'd probably refer to him as "Jim." If the narrator is James's boss, he might refer to him as "Dazzle." If the narrator is an attorney prepping him to testify in court, he might call him "Officer Dazzle." Remember: It's the *narrator's relationship to the character* that determines how you refer to that character in the narrative.

 ON YOUR OWN: INTRODUCING MAJOR AND MINOR CHARACTERS

1. Take along a little notebook or index cards when you're out, especially when you know you're going to be waiting. Observe people. Capture telling details you might use in writing characters. Jot down snippets of conversation.
2. Create a file—manila or electronic—where you save your observations.
3. Scan a favorite mystery novel for character introductions. Look at how the author does it:
   • Is this an introduction of a walk-on, a minor, or a major character? How can you tell?
   • What telling details does the author pick?
   • How does the author convey the impression this character makes on others?
   • How does the author convey this character's relationship to other characters?

4. Pause before you write each character's first appearance. Get a firm visual image of the character, and then think about what you want to convey to the reader and how you can *show* rather than tell. For any major character, try writing a one-two punch intro: description followed by action and/or dialogue.
5. Give each character in your book a full name, and decide how you will consistently refer to that character throughout the narrative. Decide how others in the book will address that character.

CHAPTER 14

DRAMATIZING SCENES AND WRITING CHAPTERS

"Usually, when people get to the end of a chapter, they close the book and go to sleep. I deliberately write a book so when the reader gets to the end of the chapter, he or she must turn one more page. When people tell me I've kept them up all night, I feel like I've succeeded."

—Sidney Sheldon

■ ■ ■

On the first day of a class I once took on writing fiction, the instructor said, "The most important single piece of advice I have for anyone trying to write a novel is this: Write scenes." Months later, when I really *got* what he was talking about, I wrote those words on a Post-It and stuck it to my computer.

Write scenes. In other words, don't *tell* the story. *Show it.* Bring it to life. Make it unfold cinematically. This is excellent advice, given how today's readers have been weaned on movies and television.

SCENE: A DEFINITION

Scenes are the atomic particles of a novel. Scenes can be short (less than a page) or long (spanning thirty or more pages).

A **scene** is a unit of storytelling that:

- takes place in *one specific contiguous setting.*
- takes place in *a more or less continuous time period.*
- is *narrated throughout from one character's viewpoint.*

If the location changes or the time shifts or a new narrator takes over, it's time to insert a break and start a new scene. Most authors group scenes into chapters of approximately equal length, separating scenes within chapters by a visual break like a double-carriage return.

DRAMATIZING A SCENE

A few sentences of scene description in an outline can turn into pages of drama.

Here's an example of the start of a dramatic scene based on the scene description presented earlier. As you read, think about what makes it dramatic.

SCENE DESCRIPTION	BEGINNING OF A DRAMATIC SCENE
Day 1, 20 minutes later. Jason Armitage goes to Drew Fellon's apartment. The door is ajar. Cautiously, he enters. He checks out the kitchen, the living room. Everything seems normal. He notices an acrid smell. He enters the bedroom and finds Drew lying on the bed, holding a pistol, a bullet wound to the head.	Jason stepped out of the elevator. Traffic had been light, and he'd gotten there in less than twenty minutes. He didn't remember the gold-flocked wallpaper or the brass wall sconces that lined the hall, but then it had been a year at least since he'd last been to Drew's apartment. His old friend had been married back then to the woman he now referred to as Bonnie Simple. The door had been recently painted too, a creamy white, now scuffed and gouged along the bottom. Jason reached up to knock when he noticed the door was ajar. He tried to ignore the queasy feeling in the pit of his stomach. Nothing to worry about. His friend probably overslept and left in such a rush that he forgot to lock up. Jason pushed the door open a crack. Maybe. But where was Drew's dog? Usually the damned Doberman started barking the minute the elevator doors opened. Yapping and snarling. Had the beast escaped? Jason cast an uneasy glance up and down the hallway, hoping that the sound he heard was the elevator descending and not Fang's teeth-bared snarl. A jolt went down Jason's spine when the phone in the apartment rang. He inhaled and pressed his shoulder against the wall. Rrrring. No claws scrabbling on the wood floor. Rrrring. No footsteps. Rrrring. A click, and there was Drew's voice. "Sorry I can't come to the phone …"

Notice the setting is contiguous, moving from the hall into the apartment. The time frame is continuous. And the entire passage is narrated from a single viewpoint: Jason's.

Here are some tips for turning scene description into dramatic fiction:

Begin the Scene as Late as Possible

> Jason stepped out of the elevator.

Notice that the scene doesn't begin with Jason driving to Drew's apartment, parking the car, or getting into the building. Begin a scene as late as possible, when the drama begins. Avoid any coming and going that doesn't serve your story. (Caveat: If this scene had been at the beginning of the book, I might have shown Jason leaving the office and the drive over as a way to introduce him to the reader.)

Orient the Reader

> ... he'd gotten there in less than twenty minutes.

Near the beginning of the scene, tell the reader where we are and how much time has elapsed since the previous scene ended. Make it brief. This isn't dramatic, but it keeps the reader from being confused and therefore distracted from the drama you're creating.

Keep the Reader in One Character's Head

> He tried to ignore the queasy feeling in the pit of his stomach. Nothing to worry about.

Write the scene as if you are inside a character's head, using internal dialogue (the character's thoughts). In a mystery, that character is often the sleuth. Here, the reader walks down the hall with Jason, sees what Jason sees, is privy to Jason's thoughts, and, along with Jason, grows increasingly uneasy.

Show Some Telling Details

Pick ordinary details like the *gold-flocked wallpaper*, and extraordinary details like the bottom of the door that looked *scuffed and gouged along the bottom*. In a mystery, some of these details turn out to be clues.

Exploit the Senses

> *Rrrring.*

Give the reader the sounds, smells, and other sensations that the point-of-view character experiences.

Keep It Relevant

In an earlier draft of this scene, I included a whole description of the exterior of the building, parking the car, a conversation with the doorman, a paragraph-long description of Drew's ex-wife, and some sentences about fall weather in New England. I deleted all of that because the novel didn't need it. Avoid pointless dialogue, aimless introspection, unnecessary travel, weather, setting, food, or even sex if it doesn't *serve your story*.

Give Yourself Permission to Write Beyond the Scene You Planned

Where did that ringing phone and the dog come from? Neither was in my outline. All I can tell you is that when I wrote the scene, I put myself in Jason's head and the missing dog showed up and the phone rang. Unexpected plot points like Fang appear uninvited as you write, and it's glorious when they do. It's up to you to deal with these uninvited guests. Maybe the dog will show up dead in the bedroom with the deceased lawyer … or maybe not. Readers of mystery fiction are not as partial to dead dogs as they are to dead lawyers.

End a Scene as Early as Possible with a Hook

Don't allow a scene to trail off at the end. End as early as possible, and wind up with a hook that makes the reader want to turn the page.

NOW YOU TRY: CONTINUE WRITING THE SCENE   14.1

Continue the scene. You decide if the caller hangs up or leaves a message. You furnish the apartment. Is it a jumble of legal briefs and law books covering coffee table and desk, or is it neat as a pin, all chrome and glass on white carpeting? Pick details that convey to the reader, in a few brushstrokes, something about the attorney who lives there. Put us inside Jason's head as he moves from room to room. What does he think when he notices the acrid smell? What does he see when he gets into the bedroom? Where's the Doberman? Convey how Jason feels by *showing the reader his reaction*, not by telling.

A jolt went down Jason's spine when the phone in the apartment rang. He inhaled and drew back, pressing his shoulder against the wall. *Rrrring*. No claws scrabbling on the wood floor. *Rrrring*. No footsteps. *Rrrring*. A click, and there was Drew's voice. "Sorry I can't come to the phone …

Download a printable version of this worksheet at www.writersdigest.com/writing-and-selling-your-mystery-novel-revised.

THE PAYOFF

In a mystery, every scene should contain a **payoff**—something that happens, or some change that occurs, that propels the main plot or one of the subplots forward. In my version of the scene above, the payoff is Jason finding his friend dead.

The payoff might be immediate. Maybe the sleuth learns something that brings investigators a step closer to discovering the truth (**clue**) or learns something that sends the investigators down a blind alley (**red herring**). Maybe something dramatic happens that ratchets up the tension—for instance, the sleuth receives a message warning her to back off, or else. Or something happens that raises the stakes, like a character gets kidnapped. Or a roadblock is thrown at the sleuth—he might get pulled off the street and put on desk duty by the superintendent in charge of the investigation.

A scene might have a delayed payoff. For example, later in the novel Jason might meet another friend of Drew's who is wearing steel-toed work boots that are scuffed with white paint. He remembers that the bottom of Drew's door was gouged and scuffed, and he suspects that this so-called friend kicked in Drew's door.

If a scene has no payoff, if all it does is introduce a situation or character or setting, then it doesn't belong in your mystery novel.

SUBTLE ORIENTEERING

Give your readers visual cues so they'll know where a scene ends and a new one begins. Many authors insert a double space or put a place marker, such as several asterisks, on a separate line to indicate a scene break.

The next scene could be five minutes or five days later, in Drew's apartment or on a desolate mountaintop twenty miles away. The new scene may have the same characters or different ones, and it can be narrated by the same or a different narrator.

Some writers think they're building suspense by making the reader wait to discover where the new scene takes place, when it happens, and who's talking. It doesn't. It only builds confusion. A reader who is confused about the where, when, and who of a scene is likely to scan ahead seeking answers.

Whenever you start a new scene, you must quickly clarify:

- **WHEN** it takes place and how much time has transpired since the last scene ended
- **WHERE** it takes place
- **WHO** is in the scene

Here's an example at the start of a scene in Laura Lippman's *The Sugar House*:

> Within a day, dental records obtained from a Silver Spring orthodontist made it official. The Dead Girl Formerly Known as Jane Doe was Gwen Schiller. Martin Tull was impressed, and generous enough not to hide it.
>
> "I can't believe how much you did with so little," he kept saying to Tess. They were sitting in a sub shop near police headquarters.

Without feeling at all like a news bulletin, Lippman lets the reader know where we are (the sub shop), when it is (a day later), and who is in the scene (Tess and Martin Tull).

GROUPING SCENES INTO CHAPTERS

Some authors let their scenes stand alone as chapters, even if they're very short. James Patterson's Women's Murder Club series, for example, has single-scene chapters that can be as short as a single page. Other authors group short scenes together in chapters of approximately equal length. They can decide whether to end a chapter at the end of a scene or in the middle of one, depending on the dramatic effect they want to create.

- *Ending the chapter at the end of a scene* gives the reader a sense of completion as a series of events has come to its conclusion. A settled ending gives the reader a break, time to take a breath before continuing.
- *Ending a chapter in the middle of a scene* at a particularly suspenseful moment has the opposite effect. The reader feels breathless as forward motion is suspended in midair. A cliff-hanger ending makes it hard for a reader to put the book down.

Kathy Reichs is a master of the cliff-hanger chapter ending. Here are a few chapter endings and next-chapter beginnings from her novel, *Monday Mourning*:

> **Chapter end:** The line went dead.
> **Next chapter beginning:** I jiggled the button, trying to get the switchboard operator's attention.
>
> **Chapter end:** Black space gaped between the open door and jamb.
> **Next chapter beginning:** Through the gap, I could make out disordered shadows and an odd luminescence, like moonlight on water.
>
> **Chapter end:** My heart dropped like a rock.

Next chapter beginning: LaManche's voice grew distant. The room receded around me.

Both settled and cliff-hanger chapter endings belong in your novel. Plan for settled endings early in an act, and use more cliff-hanger endings as your book barrels along toward an act-ending climax.

A WORD ABOUT PACING

As you write, keep an eye on **pacing**—the speed and intensity of your story. Bunch all your suspense and action sequences together and you risk numbing the reader; pile on too many paragraphs of plot exposition and lush, descriptive setting and the reader is apt to start paging ahead, looking for something to happen.

Generally speaking, the intensity of your story should build, with more leisurely storytelling at the beginning and more tense suspense and slam-bang action toward the end.

 ON YOUR OWN: WRITING SCENES

1. Pick a favorite mystery by an author whose work you aspire to emulate.
   - Notice how the story is divided into scenes and whether the scenes are grouped into chapters.
   - Skim through the story, reading only scene endings and next-scene beginnings. Notice how the author orients the reader at the start of a scene. Notice which chapters seem to have settled endings and which end with cliff-hangers.
   - Pick a scene at random, and read it carefully. Notice how the author brings the drama to life, how she modulates the pace, and the effect she achieves by starting and ending scenes where she does. Find the scene's payoff.
2. Continue writing scenes. Use this checklist to guide your work:

   ____ Orients the reader at the outset to who, where, and when

   ____ Starts as late as possible and ends as early as possible

   ____ Has a single character narrating throughout the scene

   ____ Dramatically conveys what the point-of-view character sees, hears, smells, touches, thinks, and feels

   ____ Has a payoff: a reason for being in the novel

   ____ Ends with a punch

CHAPTER 15

NARRATIVE VOICE AND VIEWPOINT

"I think point of view is a bugaboo for many beginning writers because so many terrifying things have been said about it. It is entirely a matter of feeling comfortable in the writing, the question of through whose eyes you should tell the story."

—Patricia Highsmith, *Plotting and Writing Suspense Fiction*

■ ■ ■

Writing is all about making choices, and one of the first choices you make when you sit down to write is *who narrates*. Which characters will get to tell their version of what happened? Will you be in one character's head throughout, or will you let several characters speak to the reader?

When you read a Sherlock Holmes story, you get Watson's version of events. Stephanie Plum puts her pungent spin on what goes down in Janet Evanovich's Stephanie Plum series. One thing that made Gillian Flynn's *Gone Girl* such a blockbuster is that readers doesn't know which of its two narrators, Amy or Nick, to believe. Then it turns out both of them are lying.

PICKING NARRATORS

Usually in a mystery, the sleuth tells some or all of the story. He functions much like a camera, and the scenes he narrates are filtered through his personal lens. The reader has access to his senses, emotions, and thoughts.

Some mystery novels have one narrator throughout. Others have two. Others have many. More than convenience should drive the decision to give a character viewpoint. There should be something important in that character's firsthand experience of the events in the novel or in the past that will add complexity and power to the overall tale.

In Tess Gerritsen's series featuring detective Jane Rizzoli and medical examiner Maura Isles, both characters get to narrate. Sometimes Gerritsen has to pick which one will one narrate a scene they're both in. I asked her how she decides, and her answer surprised me. She said she chooses the character who is feeling the most off balance.

When you allow a character to narrate, you are inviting the reader inside that character's head. In a mystery novel this can be a tricky proposition if that character knows a secret that you want to withhold from the reader.

Changing the Narrator Changes the Story

Who narrates a scene is a critical decision. The reader sees only what that character sees, is privy to his interpretation of the events, which are biased by his personality and past.

Here are two versions of the same action, written from the point of view of two different characters. Read each version, and think about how the change in point of view affects the story. Notice that only the dialogue (bolded) remains the same.

SHARON'S POINT OF VIEW	BOB'S POINT OF VIEW
"Sharon?" The voice echoed in the courtyard.	When I got there, Sharon was walking across the courtyard. Looked as if she was heading for her car. A minute later and I'd have missed her.
I turned, and immediately wished I'd just kept going. **"What do you want now, Bob?"**	
My voice sounded strident. If only he'd back off, ease up on the full court press. I just wanted to get away, be by myself for a while.	I hid the flowers behind my back. I'd surprise her.
"Hold up a sec."	**"Sharon?"** I yelled. My voice echoed in the courtyard.
I stood there, barely able to keep myself from bolting for my car. His boot heels stomped across the concrete, crunching bits of broken glass.	She paused and turned back. **"What do you want now, Bob?"**
The flowers he held out were roses, shopworn, their heads already starting to droop. Pathetic, really. I suppressed a groan.	I felt my shoulders sag. Why had I bothered? *You're so pathetic—you just can't take no for an answer,* I heard my ex-wife's hectoring voice in my head. But I couldn't turn back now.
	"Hold up a sec."
	I closed the space between us. Her eyes were hard, and there were lines of tension in her forehead. When I held out the flowers, her expression changed to pity.
	Should have known. Why the hell had I bothered?

In both versions, the same action takes place: Bob calls out; Sharon stops; he gives her flowers. The dialogue is identical. The differences are in the *narrator's internal dialogue*—and what a difference that makes.

✎ NOW YOU TRY: REVISE THE NARRATOR   15.1

Revise the scene between Sharon and Bob. Use only this dialogue:

> **BOB:** "Sharon?"
>
> **SHARON:** "What do you want now, Bob?"
>
> **BOB:** "Hold up a sec."

COMMUNICATE THIS WITH INTERNAL DIALOGUE—

From Bob's point of view: Bob is a private investigator, deliberately acting like a goofball so he can get close to Sharon without revealing his true identity.

From Sharon's point of view: Sharon is madly in love with Bob, but afraid to show her true feelings because he sees her as a friend.

⬇ Download a printable version of this worksheet at www.writersdigest.com/writing-and-selling-your-mystery-novel-revised.

MAKING EACH NARRATOR'S VOICE MEMORABLE

If you were writing a memoir, the narrator's voice would be your own. You'd tell the story of the events in your life from your perspective, sharing your thoughts and feelings along the way. Your language and word choice, jokes, cultural references, and metaphors would reflect who you are.

The challenge of writing fiction is to tell a story in a voice that's *not* your own. You conjure the personality behind it and show who he is by how he tells the tale.

What does a strong voice look like? Meet Christopher John Francis Boone, a fifteen-year-old boy in Mark Haddon's *The Curious Incident of the Dog in the Night-Time*:

> It was 7 minutes after midnight. The dog was lying on the grass in the middle of the lawn in front of Mrs. Shears' house. Its eyes were closed. It looked as if it was running on its side, the way dogs run when they think they are chasing a cat in a dream. But the dog was not running or asleep. The dog was dead. There was a garden fork sticking out of the dog. The points of the fork must have gone all the way through the dog and into the ground because the fork had not fallen over. I decided that the dog was probably killed with the fork because I could not see any other wounds in the dog and I do not think you would stick a garden fork into a dog after it had died for some other reason, like cancer for example, or a road accident. But I could not be certain about this.

What happens in this brief passage? Not much, right? It's narrated in the first person with Christopher trying to figure out what happened to his neighbor's dog. But through what he observes, and how he tells us about it, we learn a great deal about him. He is logical, precise (he tells us it's *7 minutes after midnight*). Even though finding a dead dog might be traumatic to most boys, he is unemotional and observant, noticing the concrete facts of the situation, not its horror. This is amplified by his short, precise, and complete sentences; he never uses contractions. He almost sounds like a robot.

Consider next this excerpt in which Stella Hardesty confronts a friend's abusive husband in *A Bad Day for Sorry*:

> Stella lowered her gun to her side and let the Raven hang there casually. She could go from full dangle to aimed and ready to shoot in about a tenth of a second. That was a trick she'd worked on most of last winter when business was slow at the shop—sitting on her stool behind the cash register and practicing her draw, tucking the gun into the drawer when the bell at the door signaled a customer's arrival.

She's also taught herself to spin the thing on her finger just like Gary Cooper in *High Noon*, but that trick was strictly for her own enjoyment. She didn't mind having a little flair, but she wasn't an idiot: guns, after all, were serious business.

Again, not much happens. Stella is just standing there, her gun at her side. She's narrating in third person. Her voice is tough and direct, and her sentences are laced with colorful phrases and a regional twang.

An analysis of the differences between Christopher Boone and Stella Hardesty reveals some pointers on how to create your own strong narrator:

- **DIRECTNESS:** Christopher speaks in the first person, directly to the reader. Stella is rendered in third person, though it feels just as direct.
- **WORD CHOICE, SENTENCE STRUCTURE:** Christopher speaks in short, subject-verb-object sentences filled with specific details and simple language. Stella's speech is much more colorful, her sentences varied in structure and laced with humor.
- **EMOTION:** Christopher's words feel like a blank façade; Stella's are packed with dry humor and innuendo. We get the sense that Stella has a great deal of insight into her own emotions and actions, whereas Christopher does not.
- **TONE:** Christopher's passage, even though it's devoid of emotion, reveals to the reader how vulnerable he is because he doesn't understand the nuance of the situation. Stella seems like someone who's had all the protectin' she needs in this lifetime, thanks very much.

To create a strong narrative voice, incorporate all these elements into your prose: directness, sentence structure, word choice, and tone. Channel your character's personality. Revise until you've developed a narrative voice that satisfies you. Try to keep that voice in your head and on the page whenever that character narrates, all the way to the end of the book.

DETERMINING POINT OF VIEW (POV)

Decide at the outset in what point of view (POV) you're going to write, and how many of your characters will narrate. This sounds pretty simple, and sometimes it's clear to the writer which POV and narrative strategy is going to work best for a given manuscript. Other times the writer struggles, starting in first person and discovering part way through that it's too limiting, or he starts the novel in third person, with multiple narrators, but then feels the story loses its focus and needs the emotional intensity of a single first-person narrator.

Of course you can begin writing in first person, for example, and then decide that third person works better. But you'll have to rewrite everything you've written up to that point. I know because I've done it. To avoid a major rewrite halfway through, experiment early with different point-of-view choices. See which feels right for the story you want to tell.

Here are the point-of-view choices:

- **FIRST PERSON:** One character holds the camera; the narrative is written using the pronouns *I* and *me*.
- **THIRD-PERSON LIMITED:** One character holds the camera; the narrative is written using the pronouns *he/she* and *him/her*.
- **MULTIPLE THIRD PERSON:** One character *at a time* holds the camera; the narrative is written using the pronouns *he/she* and *him/her*.
- **OMNISCIENT:** The camera can be anywhere; the narrative is written using the pronouns *he/she*, *him/her*, and *they/them*.

Let's take a closer look at the strengths and weaknesses of each of these choices.

First-Person POV

Many mysteries are written entirely from the point of view of a sleuth who is a first-person narrator. Series authors often choose first person because it helps create a bond between the reader and the protagonist, which is essential in a successful series.

Robert B. Parker wrote *Hugger Mugger,* a Spenser series novel, in first person. Read this example to see how an expert wields first-person viewpoint:

> I was at my desk, in my office, with my feet up on the windowsill, and a yellow pad in my lap, thinking about baseball. It's what I always think about when I'm not thinking about sex. Susan says that supreme happiness for me would probably involve having sex while watching a ball game. Since she knows this, I've never understood why, when we're at Fenway Park, she remains so prudish.

With a first-person sleuth narrator, Parker gives the reader an intense and personal inside view of his character. First-person narrative also reinforces the illusion that the sleuth and the reader are solving the puzzle together, finding clues, getting lured into blind alleys, surviving physical peril, until they finally discover the truth.

Series authors with first-person sleuth narrators include some of the biggies: Sue Grafton, Jonathan Kellerman, Lawrence Block, Kathy Reichs, Linda Fairstein, and James Patterson.

A single first-person narrator is the simplest to manage for new writers. It's easier to get a single point of view under control, and you only have to create one strong narrator's voice.

But here's the rub: When a first-person narrator gets locked in a dark, dank basement for days, your story gets held captive with him. If your first-person narrator isn't present when something dramatic (like the murder) happens, you can't dramatize it. Your character has to find out indirectly by visiting the scene of the crime, hearing it described by another character, reading the autopsy report or newspaper article, or interviewing surviving witnesses. Events perceived after the fact or secondhand don't pack nearly the wallop as those experienced firsthand and dramatized as they unfold.

Third-Person Limited POV

You can convey an equally strong sense of the main character by writing in third-person limited. The story is still narrated by one character, but writing in third-person limited enables you to insert more distance between the character and the reader, providing a **narrator's filter** for the point-of-view character's experience.

Consider this example from P.D. James's *Devices and Desires*:

> By four o'clock in the morning, when Alice Mair woke with a small despairing cry from her nightmare, the wind was rising. She stretched out her hand to click on the bedside light, checked her watch, then lay back, panic subsiding, her eyes staring at the ceiling, while the terrible immediacy of the dream began to fade, recognized for what it was, an old spectre returning after all these years, conjured up by the events of the night and by the reiteration of the word "Murder," which since the Whistler had begun his work seemed to murmur sonorously on the very air.

Did you notice how James inserts distance between the reader and the point-of-view character? It's written as if we're looking down on Alice, interpreting her actions, reading her thoughts.

If you want to insert this kind of distance between your point-of-view character and the narrative, write in third person instead of in first person. You'll be able to draw back the camera from time to time and show the reader a bigger picture than what your point-of-view character can see.

Keep in mind, though, that narrative written in the third-person limited is more difficult to control than narrative written in first person. It's easy to slip out of one character's head and into another's or slide into omniscience. And you're still limited in what you can show the reader since a single character tells the story.

Multiple Third-Person POV

Thriller writers often opt for multiple points of view. They write in third person, with the camera close over the shoulder of *one character at a time*. Different scenes can be narrated by different characters.

With multiple points of view, you have more flexibility in telling your story. Shifting the point of view enables you to create considerable dramatic tension and suspense. For example, suppose you have two main characters, partner sleuths. When one of them gets trapped in a cave, you can let the other character take over, narrating his struggle to find her. Shift back to the trapped partner, and show her feeling colder and wetter as water rises. Shift back to the other partner, searching frantically, trying to find the cave entrance.

Using multiple points of view can feel liberating. You can dramatize virtually anything—just shift to the point of view of a character who's there. You can even write scenes from the villain's point of view.

Best-selling authors who excel at using multiple points of view include Lisa Scottoline, Val McDermid, Tony Hillerman, and Dennis Lehane. These authors are also big talents with a lot of writing experience under their belts.

Don't underestimate the skill it takes to create a single strong, distinct narrator's voice, never mind more than one. Too often, inexperienced writers attempt to write in multiple points of view, resulting in a book that feels disjointed, without a coherent story line or an emotional core.

Third-Person Omniscient POV

With an omniscient viewpoint, the narrator is a disembodied presence, a storyteller who sees all and knows all. The omniscient narrator can hover above the action, offer ongoing commentary that goes beyond the perspective of the individual characters, provide emotional insight, and even disclose information that none of the characters knows.

Omniscient viewpoint was often used in nineteenth-century novels like *Pride and Prejudice.* It's a technique modern writers use more often in fantasy and science fiction. Examples include Philip Pullman's *The Golden Compass,* Frank Herbert's *Dune,* and the Harry Potter books.

The omniscient-third-person point of view offers the narrator the advantage of going anywhere and seeing anything. If the sleuth gets trapped in a cave, the narrator can describe the deserted scene a few feet outside the cave's wall where birds are singing and the sun is shining.

However, an omniscient narrator who picks and chooses what information to share can make the reader feel distanced and manipulated, turning the mystery into more of a tease than a puzzle. In addition, using the omniscient third person can weaken the bond between the reader and the sleuth.

Many authors shun the omniscient voice, concerned that it seems stilted and old-fashioned. Still, it has its place. Plenty of authors use it occasionally to pull the camera back and show the reader a bird's-eye view of the goings on.

Here's an example of a modern master using the omniscient point of view from P.D. James's *Death Comes to Pemberly*.

> It was generally agreed by the female residents of Meryton that Mr. and Mrs. Bennet of Longbourn had been fortunate in the disposal in marriage of four of their five daughters. Meryton, a small market town in Hertfordshire, is not on the route of any tours of pleasure, having neither beauty of setting nor a distinguished history, while its only great house, Netherfield Park, although impressive, is not mentioned in books about the county's notable architecture. The town has an assembly room where dances are regularly held but no theatre, and the chief entertainment takes place in private houses where the boredom of dinner parties and whist tables, always with the same company, is relieved by gossip.

In an authorial voice, James introduces the readers to Meryton and establishes the context for this modern murder-mystery sequel to *Pride and Prejudice*.

A little omniscience goes a long way in a mystery novel, so use it sparingly.

Sliding Point of View (Head Hopping)—A No-No

Whether you tell your story in first or third person, or have a single point-of-view character or several, anchor the narration in each scene in a single character's head.

If Bob is the narrator, you can show his thoughts and feelings:

> Bob *was afraid* he was going to throw up.

If Linda is the narrator, the same content becomes:

> Bob *looked like* he was going to throw up.

Don't let the viewpoint slide from head to head. For instance, suppose you write a scene in which police arrive and investigate a shooting. You begin writing the scene from the point of view of the detective in charge. You can show the detective observing blood spatter, gunshot residue, and the position of the corpse. You can show the detective questioning the victim's boyfriend and interpreting his reactions. But to reveal what the boyfriend really thinks and feels would require a viewpoint shift.

Reading a scene where the point of view slides from one character's head to another can feel like riding in a car with loose steering. Here's an example. Cover up the discussion on the right, and try to find the spots where the viewpoint slides. Then read the discussion.

PASSAGE WITH POINT-OF-VIEW SLIDES	DISCUSSION
Cecilia tiptoed to the door. She peered out and listened. All quiet. At last, she could share what she'd learned.	*No problem here. We're in Cecilia's point of view. She's the narrator.*
She closed the door and addressed William with a solemn face, her voice ominous.	*Cecilia can't see her own face. The point of view slides to omniscient.*
William tried not to show his disdain. She was so full of herself.	*These are William's thoughts. The point of view slid again; William is now the narrator.*

To keep the point of view from sliding, keep asking yourself: Who is telling the story? Then, as you write, anchor yourself in that character's head. Write the scene as that character experiences it, revealing his thoughts and feelings, his *observations* of other characters, and his *interpretation* of what other characters might be thinking and feeling.

You can have a different narrator tell the story in the next scene, but try not to head hop within a single scene.

NOW YOU TRY: SLIPPING AND SLIDING POINT OF VIEW 15.2

Read the passage below and find the point-of-view shifts.

PASSAGE	POINT-OF-VIEW SHIFTS
When Corrigan looked up, he saw Mary gazing at him like a lost puppy. He looked away, got up, and made for the door. As she watched him leave, her look hardened. "So you think you don't owe me anything?" she said, her voice raspy and dull. He whipped around, his eyes blazing. "I don't owe you a damned thing." He had no business treating her like that. Mary stumbled to her feet, her fists clenched.	

Revise the entire passage so Corrigan is the only narrator.

⬇ Download a printable version of this worksheet at www.writersdigest.com/
writing-and-selling-your-mystery-novel-revised.

✏ ON YOUR OWN: NARRATIVE VOICE AND POINT OF VIEW

1. Scan through some of your favorite mysteries; examine the point-of-view
   choices the authors make:
   • First person or third?
   • Single or multiple narrators?

2. Open one of your favorite mysteries to scenes at the beginning, middle, and end of the book. In each scene, analyze how the author creates a distinct, compelling narrative voice. Look at each of the following:
   • directness
   • sentence structure
   • word choice
   • tone
3. Examine the scenes you've written so far, and ask yourself:
   • Are you satisfied with your choice of first- or third-person narrative?
   • Are you satisfied with the character(s) you picked to tell the story?
   • Have you kept control of the point of view, or have you allowed it to slip and slide?
4. Continue writing. Keep in mind that in every scene, you should be telling the story in a single character's (and not your authorial) voice.

CHAPTER 16

WRITING DIALOGUE

"Dialogue should be allowed to stand alone, pure and simple. Except when it shouldn't."

—Lawrence Block, *Telling Lies for Fun & Profit*

■■■

Most authors have an Achilles' heel, some aspect of their writing that they need to improve. Mine is dialogue. I have to work to make each character's dialogue feel authentic, individual, and natural.

This may be related to the fact that I can never remember anyone's exact words in real life. After a party, for example, ask me what was on the walls of the host's home, what people were wearing, what food was served, and I can give you chapter and verse. But ask me what anyone said, and I can only paraphrase.

Paraphrasing isn't dialogue. If you paraphrase what your characters say, every conversation in your novel will sound like you, or even worse, like no one. In other words, you'll be stuck with weak dialogue.

WRITING CONVINCING DIALOGUE

Elmore Leonard wrote the proverbial book on dialogue. Just about everything you need to know is illustrated in this brief two-part excerpt from his novel *LaBrava*:

> Cundo Rey said to Nobles, "Let me ask you something, okay? You ever see a snake eat a bat? Here is a wing sticking out of the snake's mouth, the wing, it's

still moving, this little movement, like is trying to fly. The snake, he don't care. You know why? Because the other end of the bat is down in the snake turning to juice, man. Sure, the snake, he don't even have to move, just lay there and keep swallowing as long as it takes. He don't even have to chew," Cundo Rey said, watching Richard Nobles eating his Big Mac and poking fries in his mouth a few at a time, dipped in ketchup. "Mmmmmm, nice juicy bat."

...

[Nobles] said, mouth full of hamburger, "I ate a snake. I've ate a few different kinds. You flour 'em, deep fry 'em in some Crisco so the meat crackles, they're pretty good. But I never ate a bat. Time you skin it, what would you have?"

There—if the Cuban was trying to make him sick he was wasting his time.

Leonard uses content and tone, grammar and word choice, dialect, simple attributions, and more to craft his perfectly tuned dialogue. Use these same techniques to give your characters authentic, unique voices:

- **CONTENT AND TONE.** *You ever see a snake eat a bat?* What your character talks about and how he phrases it—that's the fundamental choice you make when you write dialogue. Here, there's something sinister, weird, and confrontational about Cundo Rey's monologue about how snakes eat bats. His words contain a not-so-veiled threat, and we get the sense of a ruthless, cold individual who gets his jollies watching another creature tortured.
- **GRAMMAR AND WORD CHOICE.** *The snake, he don't care.* Use grammar to show the character's personality and background. Here, the grammatical error suggests a character who is tough and uneducated, possibly not a native English speaker. You might choose other words to convey a speaker who is casual and hip (*That snake, he could care less*), or painstakingly formal and correct (*From the snake's perspective, it matters not.*)
- **HINT AT DIALECT.** *You flour 'em, deep fry 'em …* Characters mispronounce words and speak with accents. Do you have to render what's said phonetically in order to make the character sound real? You can, but more than a touch of phonetically rendered dialect can be distracting and difficult to decipher. Not only that, dialect can turn character into caricature. Write the occasional phonetic version of a phrase to give the reader the flavor of how a character sounds, but do so sparingly. Trust the reader to mentally apply what you suggest to the remaining dialogue.

- **USE SIMPLE ATTRIBUTIONS OR NONE AT ALL.** *Cundo Rey said ...* New writers think they need to vary their verb choice to express how someone spoke; they use attributions like *chimed, chirped, responded, hissed, retorted, bellowed,* and *queried.* Equally egregious is when an author writes something like, *"Thanks," he grinned,* as if grinning has anything to do with speaking. (It's fine to write, *"Thanks," he said, grinning,* or *"Thanks." He grinned.*) You can occasionally use *whispered* or *shouted* if the character actually does so. But *said* and *asked* are perfectly sufficient 98 percent of the time and are more or less invisible to the reader. Often you can omit an attribution entirely if the context makes it clear to the reader who's talking.
- **LIMIT ADVERBS.** You rarely find an adverb with *said* in Leonard's prose, nor should one show up in yours. Using adverbs alongside dialogue is a clunky way to *tell* the reader something that's better *shown* through dialogue and the character's accompanying behavior.
- **COMBINE DIALOGUE AND ACTION.** *... watching Richard Nobles eating his Big Mac and poking fries in his mouth a few at a time, dipped in ketchup. "Mmmmmm. Nice juicy bat."* How do you convey the tenor of dialogue to the reader? Pack emotion into the speaker's words as well as the physical gestures and body language that accompany them. Combine dialogue with the right action and the result is more than the sum of the parts—as the example shows with the combination of eating French fries with the dialogue, "Mmmmmm. Nice juicy bat."
- **BRING THE CHARACTERS' RELATIONSHIP TO LIFE.** *"I ate a snake. ..."* The thrust and parry of dialogue shows the relationship between the characters. When Nobles responds, the reader sees that these two guys are evenly matched for bravado.
- **SPRINKLE LIGHTLY WITH INTERNAL DIALOGUE.** *There—if the Cuban was trying to make him sick he was wasting his time.* During an exchange of dialogue, use internal dialogue to show your reader what's going on in the point-of-view character's head and to add dimension to the interaction. Notice that internal dialogue need not sound or look like dialogue. Here, Nobles's thoughts are more grammatically correct, with less swagger, and without the staccato sentences of his spoken dialogue. Notice also that internal dialogue doesn't require quotes, italics, or even the attribu-

tion *he thought* to cue the reader that these words are thoughts. Leonard maintains tense and point of view (here, it's past tense and first person) and just writes the thought.

MAKING DIALOGUE FEEL AUTHENTIC

Good dialogue is not realistic conversation. People digress, pause, use the wrong words, repeat themselves, fail to clearly express themselves, or go on and on, boring everyone around them while they work their way to whatever point they're trying to make. So how do you write dialogue that sounds authentic without making it *too* real?

Take a cue from how real people talk. They speak in sentence fragments. They drop nouns and verbs. They use jargon, vernacular, and sometimes profanity. If you edit out the meanderings, repetitions, digressions, and irrelevancies, you'll have something that approaches good fictional dialogue. Remember: Dialogue shouldn't call attention to itself. If it's too clever, get rid of it.

Here's an example. In this dialogue from S.J. Rozan's *Absent Friends*, notice how Zannoni drops words; uses sentence fragments, profanity, and police jargon; and comes off sounding like the tough, jaded, retired homicide detective he's supposed to be.

> "I was a detective at the 124 then," he said. "Later got transferred to the Bronx. Christ what a schlep. Those days, right after the Knapp Commission—you heard of that?—they didn't have this community policing thing like now. They wanted you to live outside your precinct. Keep down graft. Pile of crap. Cops running all around the goddamn city, damn waste of time. I retired eight years ago."
>
> Zannoni took a gulp of tea. A fresh breeze blew in from the Narrows, got trapped in the cul-de-sac balcony. It lifted a page from Laura's notebook; it brought with it the scent of sea.
>
> "Officers responded to a shots-fired, found Malloy," Zannoni said.

To check whether your dialogue is working, read it aloud to yourself. Wooden dialogue is more obvious when you hear it than when you read it.

NOW YOU TRY: ANALYZE DIALOGUE

Janet Evanovich writes funny, smart dialogue, and she gives each of her characters a unique voice. Analyze this excerpt of dialogue among three characters in Evanovich's *Four to Score*:

THINK ABOUT THE FOLLOWING:	EXCERPT FROM *FOUR TO SCORE*
How is each character's dialogue made distinct and authentic? Consider: • content • grammar • word choice • dialect • sentence structure • profanity and vernacular • internal dialogue and action combined with dialogue	"I still don't like this," Kuntz said. "Maxine is crazy. Who knows what she'll do. I'm gonna feel like a sitting duck out there." Lula was standing behind me on Kuntz's porch. "Probably just another dumb-ass note taped to the bottom of the bench. Think you should stop your whining," she said to Kuntz, "on account of it makes you look like a wiener. And with a name like Kuntz you gotta be careful what you look like." Eddie cut his eyes to Lula. "Who's this?" "I'm her partner," Lula said. "Just like Starsky and Hutch, Cagney and Lacey, the Lone Ranger and What's-his-name." Truth is, we were more like Laurel and Hardy, but I didn't want to share that information with Kuntz. "We'll be in place ahead of time," I said. "Don't worry if you don't see us. We'll be there. All you have to do is show up and go sit on the bench and wait."

INJECTING DIALOGUE WITH CONFLICT

Dialogue that sparks with conflict is inherently more interesting than dialogue that merely conveys information. Compare these brief dialogue interchanges:

"You're back. Where were you?" Verna asked.

"The library and then the market," Michael said. "I got stuck in traffic on the way back."

"You're back. Where were you?" Verna asked.

"The library and then the market," Michael said. "I got stuck in traffic on the way back."

"Really? I was just at the market, too. Didn't hit traffic coming or going."

"You're back. Where were you?" Verna asked.

"None of your business," Michael said. "And stop asking me."

"You're back. Where were you?" Verna asked.

"Where were you?" Michael said.

"You're back. Where were you?" Verna asked.

"That man called again," Michael said.

All but the first of these interchanges have an element of conflict that creates tension and interest. Sometimes conflict can be *overt* (*"None of your business"*), and sometimes it's present even though the characters are talking past each other (*"That man called again"*). As you write dialogue, look for opportunities to add an edge to the interchanges by layering in conflict. But as with everything else, beware of the downside: A character who's constantly nasty and quarrelsome gets old fast.

SHOWING EMOTIONS

Presencing is a term that a wonderful writing teacher, Arthur Edelstein, used when urging his students to write characters that feel physically present on the page. For example, when a character is listening, is she leaning forward, grasping the speaker's arm? Shredding a tissue? Checking herself out in a mirror and smoothing her hair? Staring off into the middle distance? Those physical cues suggest the character's unstated emotions and thoughts. You don't have to say she was interested, upset, or bored and self-obsessed.

This is why authors give characters props. What a character does with a drink while she's talking, for example, can alter how the reader perceives the dialogue delivered.

Here are two examples with identical dialogue:

"Did you know him long?" I asked.

She stirred her drink and stared into it. "Too long, and not long enough."

"Did you know him long?" I asked.

She knocked back her drink and slammed the empty glass down on the table. "Too long, and not long enough."

Just about anything in a scene—a drink, a cigarette, gum, a necktie, a belt, shirt buttons, and so on—can be used, in combination with dialogue, to show different mental states. You don't even need props. A character can wring his hands, crack his knuckles, pick at a pimple, or take a quick intake of breath. Choose the action that effectively nuances the dialogue the character delivers and you don't have to explain.

NOW YOU TRY: SHOW EMOTIONS

Mixing and matching from the suggestions below, revise the following basic dialogue using different props and showing different emotions.

DIALOGUE	ACTION/PROP	EMOTION
"Did you know him long?"	chewing gum	anger
"Too long, and not long enough."	twirling a strand of hair	resignation
	fiddling with a ring	disgust
	adding sugar to coffee	sadness
	crossing legs and shifting position	ambivalence
	doodling on a scrap of paper	grief
		boredom

 NOW YOU TRY: WRITE DIALOGUE

1. Write a simple dialogue exchange between two characters consisting of ten or twelve lines. Don't include any actions—just dialogue.
2. Make a list of what you want to reveal about each character's emotions during this exchange. (It could be boredom, anger, fear, sexual attraction, stubbornness, or so on.)
3. Add body language, gestures, and props to show the characters' inner states.
4. To further illuminate, add some internal dialogue for the point-of-view character.

SUMMARIZING INSTEAD

Not everything your characters would logically say in a given situation needs to be spelled out in dialogue. Sometimes it's better to summarize and fast-forward through the necessary but unexciting bits than risk bogging down your story.

For instance, "He introduced himself, and we shook hands" is a fine alternative to a lot of hello-and-how-are-you-ing—unless you're using the characters' greeting to show the relationship between them. If your character has to tell his partner about a visit to Nina's house, and that visit was dramatized a chapter earlier, then "I told him about my visit to Nina's house" is all you need. But if he's going to lie or obfuscate or omit something that happened during the visit, by all means dramatize (rather than summarize) that dialogue.

Use dialogue only when it moves your story forward or illuminates your characters and their relationships with each other. Never make a character deliver a speech with the sole purpose of providing the reader with information. It will feel flat and forced, and many readers will skip over it.

ON YOUR OWN: WRITING DIALOGUE

1. Pull out a few of your favorite novels. Skim for sections of dialogue. Read those sections aloud to see how the author uses dialogue to create drama, push the story forward, or develop the relationships between characters.
2. List the characters who deliver the bulk of the dialogue in your book. To give each one a distinctive voice, make notes for yourself describing how you want each one to sound. For example, direct or evasive, self-assured or uncertain, powerful or weak, worldly or naïve, educated or uneducated, old or young. Add ethnicity, regional identity, and socioeconomic status.
3. Using the list you just developed, revise some dialogue you've written to make your characters sound more unique and compelling.
4. Be on the lookout for dialogue in your novel that would be better summarized. Conversely, look for summarized dialogue that would be better dramatized. Revise accordingly.
5. Read aloud passages of dialogue you've written to make sure they sound natural and effective.

CHAPTER 17

CREATING A SENSE OF PLACE

"In many cases, when a reader puts a story aside because 'it got boring,' the boredom arose because the writer grew enchanted with his powers of description and lost sight of his priority, which is to keep the ball rolling."

—Stephen King

■■■

Mystery readers are looking for great plots and interesting characters. If you include too much detailed description of places and things, the reader is likely to skip ahead, looking for action.

Still, a strong sense of place can catapult your novel from just okay to great. Readers relish revisiting the settings as well as the characters in some of today's best-selling mystery fiction. Examples include Carl Hiaasen's Miami, Craig Johnson's Wyoming, and Donna Leon's Venice.

SETTING SCENES

A vivid glimpse of setting can be used to open a scene and provide a backdrop for the characters. Imagine being there: the smell of Los Angeles after a brush fire, the sulfurous humidity of a Louisiana swamp, or the colorful crush of people at a Mexican open market. Use all of your senses to make settings come alive. Pick details that define the place and time.

Read this opening of Thomas Wheeler's *The Arcanum*, and notice the techniques he uses to create a vivid setting:

London—1919

A September storm battered a sleeping London. Barrage after barrage of gusting sheets drummed on the rooftops and loosened clapboards. Raindrops like silver dollars pelted the empty roads and forced families of pigeons into huddled clumps atop the gaslights.

Then it stopped.

The trees of Kensington Gardens swayed, and the city held its breath. It waited a few dripping moments, then relaxed.

Just as suddenly, a Model-T Ford swerved past Marble Arch in Hyde Park and buzzed around Speakers' Corner, peals of laughter following in its wake.

Inside the car, Daniel Bisbee held the steering wheel with one hand and patted Lizzie's plump thigh with the other.

Cinematically, it's as if a camera pans first from a distance and an omniscient narrator describes the setting. We feel the power of the rain, and then quiet descends upon London streets as the downpour stops. The camera zooms in for a close-up of the Model-T, and the laughter of its occupants breaks the silence.

Here are some of the elements that make this passage opening so effective:

- **PLACE AND TIME:** *London—1919*
  A simple notation of place and year at the beginning anchors the characters in place and time.

- **CONTRAST:** *The storm battered a sleeping London.*
  The juxtaposition of the storm battering and London sleeping creates a mood for the scene.

- **SENSORY IMPRESSIONS:** *Barrage after barrage of gusting sheets drummed on the rooftops and loosened clapboards.*
  This passage exploits the auditory and visual senses.

- **COMPARISON:** *Raindrops like silver dollars …*
  The use—but not overuse—of simile paints a vivid picture.

- **DETAILS, NOT GENERALIZATIONS:** *… forced families of pigeons into huddled clumps atop the gaslights.*
  This single image is much more effective than "It was a dark and stormy night."

- **DRAMA:** *The trees of Kensington Gardens swayed, and the city held its breath. It waited a few dripping moments, then relaxed.*

  Here the rain becomes almost like a character; rain stopping becomes a dramatic moment.

Notice what are *not* there: adjectives and adverbs. We're taught in school that these parts of speech carry descriptive power. But do they?

Examine the passage again. Make a list of the adjectives and adverbs in the passage. I find only six: *September, gusting, silver, empty, huddled, dripping, suddenly,* and *plump.* A small amount for a highly descriptive passage.

Where does the descriptive power come from? Read the passage again, and see if you can figure it out.

I think it's in the verbs: *battered, drummed, pelted, swayed, swerved,* and *buzzed.* Moreover, notice that nearly half of the adjectives in this passage are verbs in disguise (*gusting, huddled, dripping*).

When you set a scene, use sensory impressions, details, comparisons, and contrasts. Make your scene descriptions dramatic, and choose verbs for maximum impact.

 NOW YOU TRY: ANALYZE A DRAMATIC DESCRIPTION OF SETTING

Analyze the passage from Tony Hellerman's *Listening Woman.*

THINK ABOUT THE FOLLOWING:	EXCERPT FROM *LISTENING WOMAN*
• How does the "camera" move? • What are the contrasts? • What sensory impressions does Hillerman create; what senses does he exploit? • What details does Hillerman choose to make the scene come alive? • How does Hillerman create drama without any human action or dialogue? • Find the adjectives and adverbs. Now find the verbs. Which carry the descriptive power?	The southwest wind picked up turbulence around the San Francisco peaks, howled across the emptiness of the Moenkopi plateau, and made a thousand strange sounds in the windows of the old Hopi villages of Shongopovi and Second Mesa. Two hundred vacant miles to the north and east, it sandblasted the stone sculptures of Monument Valley Navajo Tribal Park and whistled eastward across the maze of canyons on the Utah-Arizona border. Over the arid immensity of the Nokaito Bench it filled the blank blue sky with a rushing sound. At the hogan of Hosteen Tso, at 3:17 p.m., it gusted and eddied, and formed a dust devil, which crossed the wagon track and raced with a swirling roar across Margaret Cigaret's old Dodge pickup truck and past the Tso brush arbor. The three people under the arbor huddled against the driven dust.

USING SETTING IN A MYSTERY NOVEL

Mystery writers never write setting for setting's sake. It's there *in support* of story and character.

There are a number of ways that setting functions to support story and character.

- **TO ORIENT THE READER AND SITUATE THE CHARACTERS.** The most basic use of setting is to answer the question *Where are we now?* This can be done quickly at the beginning of a scene, as in this chapter opening from Chuck Hogan's *Prince of Thieves*:

  > Malden Center smelled like a village set on the shore of an ocean of hot coffee. With the coffee bean warehouse so close, sitting in Dunkin' Donuts was a little redundant, like chewing nicotine gum in a tobacco field. But that's what they were doing, Frank G. in a soft black sweatshirt, nursing a decaf, and Doug M. looking rumpled in a gray shirt with blue basketball-length sleeves, rolling a bottle of Mountain Dew between his hands.

  Hogan tells us where we are (*Malden Center*), that it's set *on the shore*, and that it *smelled* pungently of coffee. Then he drops his two characters (one *nursing a decaf* and the other *rolling a bottle of Mountain Dew*) into the setting. The characters are anchored and drama can begin.

- **TO SHOW TIME PASSING.** In a scene in which a character drives to work or waits on a park bench for a skittish informant to show up, the author might use setting to show the passage of time. Here's an example from Raymond Chandler's *The High Window*:

  > I pulled the phone over and looked at the number on the slip and called it. They said my package could be sent right over. I said I would wait for it.
  >
  > It was getting dark outside now. The rushing sound of the traffic had died a little and the air from the open window, not yet cool from the night, had that tired end-of-the-day smell of dust, automobile exhaust, sun-light rising from hot walls and sidewalks, the remote smell of food in a thousand restaurants, and perhaps, drifting down from the residential hills above Hollywood—if you had a nose like a hunting dog—a touch of that peculiar tomcat smell that eucalyptus trees give off in warm weather.
  >
  > I sat there smoking. Ten minutes later the door was knocked on …

Chandler uses a paragraph of pure atmospherics to kill ten minutes between the time that Marlow calls for package delivery and when the package arrives. Talk about exploiting the senses. I grew up in Southern California, and I know exactly that eucalyptus smell he's talking about.

- **TO DRIVE A SUSPENSE SCENE.** Setting can be used to build tension in a suspense scene. In this example from William G. Tapply's *Bitch Creek*, protagonist Stoney Calhoun stakes out the villain:

> The sun wasn't scheduled to rise for another hour, but already the black sky had begun to fade into a pewtery purple. Calhoun leaned forward so he could see through the bushes. He caught a shadowy movement on the far side of the parking area, then made out a dark shape easing along the edge of the opening, just inside the woods.

The reader is enjoying that pewter sky when *shadowy movement* and a *dark shape* trigger tension. Is it only a deer, or something more sinister like a skulking gunman?

- **TO GIVE THE READER A BREATHER.** A paragraph or two of setting after a scene of high drama and action can be used to give your characters and the reader a chance to catch their breaths.

INCORPORATING SETTING DETAILS

Setting can be applied in broad brushstrokes, as in the examples above. In addition, dabs of setting can be judiciously added throughout a novel to heighten the sense of time and place.

Here are just a few examples:

- **HOW PEDESTRIANS CROSS THE STREETS:** Do they wait for the green light or dart across against the red light when there's a break in traffic?
- **CLOTHING:** 1950s women wore shirtwaist dresses; in the 1970s they wore micro-minis.
- **HOUSEHOLD EFFECTS:** The furniture, household appliances, and accessories reflect time and place, poverty or wealth. An egg chair belongs in a 1960s suburban family room, just as a "Hoosier" cabinet belongs in a 1940s kitchen in the Midwest.
- **VEGETATION:** Does your character scramble down a hillside dense with bougainvillea or pockmarked with saguaro cacti?

- **DIALECT:** When a character addresses two or more people, is it "You," "Y'all," or "Youze guys"?

Read this brief excerpt from Lee Child's *Killing Floor*. Think about how details convey the setting:

> I was arrested in Eno's diner. At twelve o'clock. I was eating eggs and drinking coffee. A late breakfast, not lunch. I was wet and tired after a long walk in heavy rain. All the way from the highway to the edge of town.
>
> The diner was small, but bright and clean. Brand-new, built to resemble a converted railroad car. Narrow, with a long lunch counter on one side and a kitchen bumped out back. Booths lining the opposite wall. A doorway where the center booth would be.
>
> I was in a booth, at a window, reading somebody's abandoned newspaper about the campaign for a President I didn't vote for last time and wasn't going to vote for this time. Outside, the rain had stopped but the glass was still pebbled with bright drops. I saw the police cruisers pull into the gravel lot. They were moving fast and crunched to a stop. Light bars flashing and popping. Red and blue light in the raindrops on my window. Doors burst open, policemen jumped out. Two from each car, weapons ready. Two revolvers, two shotguns. This was heavy stuff. One revolver and one shotgun ran to the back. One of each rushed the door.

Notice how the prosaic details of this diner (we've all been to one like it), along with the way Reacher calmly has his breakfast, contrast with the violence of the police storming in. Is he worried? From the dispassionate way he observes the lights refracted off the raindrops in the window, the reader thinks not. The passage continues with Reacher finishing his eggs, leaving a tip, folding the newspaper, and draining his coffee before he reacts to their presence.

✏️ **NOW YOU TRY: WRITE A DINER OF YOUR OWN**   17.1

Write a paragraph or two in which your character is sitting in a diner reading a menu in rural Vermont, Malibu, Tijuana, your home town, or the town where you've set your novel. Pick details that give that setting its own unique flavor.

WRITE A DINER OF YOUR OWN.

⬇ Download a printable version of this worksheet at www.writersdigest.com/
writing-and-selling-your-mystery-novel-revised.

 ON YOUR OWN: WRITING SETTING

1. Go to a place that resembles a setting in your book. Bring a notebook, and
   jot down what you see and hear; tune in to all the other sensory impressions, and note the quirky details that define this particular place. Then
   write the scene. Remember: You want to evoke a place, not render it in
   painstaking detail.
2. Revise passages you've written that describe a setting. Try to do the following:
   • Replace generalizations ("a beautiful day," "a nice breeze," "a hand-
     some man") with specifics, details that show rather than tell.
   • Use a range of sensory images.
   • Use contrasts.
3. Go back and add dabs of setting to scenes you've written.

CHAPTER 18

WRITING INVESTIGATION

Clues, Red Herrings, and Misdirection

"Another clue! And this time a swell one!"

—Joe to Frank in *The Tower Treasure*, the first Hardy Boys mystery
by Franklin W. Dixon

■■■

Investigation is the meat and potatoes of a mystery novel. The sleuth talks to people, does research, snoops around, and makes observations. Facts emerge. Maybe an eyewitness gives an account of what he saw. A wife has unexplained bruises on her face. The brother of a victim avoids eye contact with his questioner. A will leaves a millionaire's estate to an obscure charity. A bloody knife is found in a laundry bin. A love letter is discovered tucked into last week's newspaper.

Some of this evidence will turn out to be **clues** that eventually identify the villain. Others are **red herrings**—evidence that **misdirects** the reader and leads to false conclusions. On top of that, some of the information your sleuth gathers will turn out to be nothing more than the irrelevant minutiae of everyday life, inserted into scenes to give a sense of realism and to camouflage the clues.

INVESTIGATING: OBSERVING AND INTERROGATING

A sleuth's investigation centers on two main activities: observing and asking questions. If your sleuth is a professional detective or a police officer, then investigating might include examining the crime scene, questioning witnesses, staking out suspects, pulling rap sheets, checking DMV records, and going undercover.

If your sleuth is a medical examiner, we're talking autopsies and X-rays, analysis of stomach contents and DNA. If your character is an amateur sleuth, he's going to sneak around, ask a lot of questions, and cozy up to the police.

How your sleuth investigates should reflect his skills and personality. Here is an example from one of Peter Robinson's DCI Banks mystery novels, *Friend of the Devil*. DCI Banks observes the crime scene:

> "Looks like we have manual strangulation to me, unless there are hidden causes," Burns said, stooping and carefully lifting a strand of blond hair, gesturing toward the dark bruising under her chin and ear.
>
> From what Banks could see, she was young, no older than his own daughter Tracy. She was wearing a green top and a white miniskirt with a broad pink plastic belt covered in silver glitter. The skirt had been hitched up even higher than it was already to expose her upper thighs. The body looked posed.

Banks is a pro. He's unemotional and analytical in his observations, even though the victim is the same age as his daughter. His years of experience have shown him what dead bodies look like, so he knows when one seems "posed."

Whether your sleuth schmoozes over tea with the victim's neighbor, makes telephone calls to witnesses, formally interrogates a suspect, or huddles with colleagues to discuss blood spatter, your sleuth asks questions and gets answers. Talk, talk, talk. It can get pretty boring if all you're doing is conveying information. So create a dynamic between the characters during the Q&A to hold the reader's interest. Interrogation becomes interesting when the relationship between the characters has an electrical charge, some inner dynamic, as in this passage in which DCI Banks interrogates a suspect later in *Friend of the Devil*:

> "Never mind the bollocks, Mr. Austin," said Banks. "You told DC Jackman that you weren't having an affair with Hayley Daniels. Information has come to light that indicates you were lying. What do you have to say about that?"
>
> "What information? I resent your implication."
>
> "Is it true or not that you were having an affair with Hayley Daniels?"
>
> Austin looked at Winsome, then back at Banks. Finally he compressed his lips, bellowed up his cheeks and let the air out slowly. "All right," he said. "Hayley and I had been seeing one another for two months. We started about a month or so after my wife left. Which means, strictly speaking, that whatever Hayley and I had, it wasn't an affair."
>
> "Semantics," said Banks. "Teacher shagging student. What do you call it?"
>
> "It wasn't that," said Austin. "You make it sound so sordid. We were in love."

"Excuse me while I reach for a bucket."

"Inspector! The woman I love has been murdered. The least you can do is show some respect."

"How old are you, Malcolm?"

"Fifty-one."

"And Hayley Daniels was nineteen."

With his word choice (*bollocks*, *shagging*) and attitude (*"Excuse me while I reach for a bucket."*), Banks shows his working-class roots and his disdain for Malcolm Austin. He's not at all impressed with this man's pedigree as a teacher, and he doesn't suffer fools. His disgust with this man who seduced a young woman is more than professional; it's personal—the victim reminds Banks of his own daughter.

Notice how Robinson uses **body language as subtext**, conveying to the reader a character's emotions without spelling it out, letting the reader do the work of interpreting:

> *Austin looked at Winsome, then back at Banks. Finally he compressed his lips, bellowed up his cheeks and let the air out slowly.*

That physical description, inserted in the middle of spare back-and-forth dialogue, highlights a **tipping point**—a transition between Austin's insistence that he wasn't having an affair with the victim and his confession that he was. Instead of rushing past this key moment, Robinson opens it up , slowing the reader down and drawing attention to the shift by inserting a physical description between the lines of dialogue.

Look for tipping points in your novel where the emotional balance shifts or a revelation comes to light. Open those tipping points by slowing down the narrative, but don't bang your reader over the head with them or spoon-feed conclusions. Often you can let the reader interpret what it means.

✏ NOW YOU TRY: NUANCE Q&A

Here are two examples in which body language conveys inner dynamics and shows the relationship between characters. The bolded dialogue in both passages is identical. Read and analyze. Which Cassandra is more likely telling the truth, and how does the body language suggest that?

Q&A 1	Q&A 2
I reached out and touched Cassandra's arm. **"Are you going to tell me what happened?"**	I pulled over a chair and pushed Cassandra down into it. **"Are you going to tell me what happened?"**
She looked away. **"Well—"**	**"Well—"** She shrugged me off and fluffed her hair.
"What did you see?"	
She looked around, frantic for a moment, cornered, then swallowed and sat back in her chair.	**"What did you see?"**
	She gave me a sideways look, the flicker of a smile. **"I saw a car."** She stared down at her fingernails, picked at the peeling candy-apple red polish. **"Red. Coming fast. I got the hell out of the way."**
"I saw a car," she said. **"Red. Coming fast. I got the hell out of the way."**	

In *Q&A 1*, I intended to make the reader think that Cassandra is telling the truth. By having her seem frantic and then resigned, and swallowing before she says what she saw, I tried to convey fear and reluctance and to suggest that she may be telling the truth. Cassandra in *Q&A 2* shrugs, doesn't seem to care, gives a flicker of a smile, and then picks at her red nail polish before she says the car was red—maybe it occurs to her at that moment that she should say the car is red. These details are designed to suggest that she's lying.

✏ NOW YOU TRY: ADDING BODY LANGUAGE
18.1

Combine physical gestures, internal dialogue, and body language with the dialogue below to develop one of these scenarios. Alter the word choice and add more dialogue to convey the dynamics of the scenario you pick.

BASIC DIALOGUE	SCENARIOS
"Are you going to tell me what happened?" "Well—" "What did you see?" "I saw a car. Red. Coming fast. I got the hell out of the way."	• A PI questions a seven-year-old boy who's afraid that if he admits what he saw, he'll be punished. (He was supposed to be in school.) • A reporter questions the bereaved mother of the murder victim. • A police officer questions a local thug who, until now, has denied he witnessed anything.

Write the Q&A, adding physical gestures and body language to convey one of the scenarios.

⬇ Download a printable version of this worksheet at www.writersdigest.com/writing-and-selling-your-mystery-novel-revised.

Blending Clues and Red Herrings

A clue can be just about anything:

- an object the sleuth discovers (a bloody glove)
- the way a character behaves (he keeps his hands in his pockets)
- a revealing gesture (a woman straightens her boss's collar)
- what someone says ("Julia Dalrymple deserved to die.")
- what someone wears (a locket stolen from the victim)
- an item that doesn't fit with the way the person presents himself or his history (a suspect's fingerprint is lifted from a room the suspect says she was never in)

Here are some techniques that enable you to play fair and, at the same time, keep the reader guessing:

- **EMPHASIZE THE UNIMPORTANT; DEEMPHASIZE THE CLUE.** The reader should see the clue but not recognize its significance. For example, the sleuth investigates the value and provenance of a stolen painting and pays little attention to the identity of the woman who sat for the portrait.
- **ESTABLISH A CLUE BEFORE THE READER CAN GRASP ITS SIGNIFICANCE.** Introduce the key information before the reader understands the context it fits into. For example, the sleuth strolls by a character spraying her rose bushes before discovering that a neighbor was poisoned by a common herbicide.
- **HAVE YOUR SLEUTH MISINTERPRET THE MEANING OF A CLUE.** Your sleuth misinterprets evidence that takes the investigation to a dead end. For example, the victim is found in a room with the window open. The sleuth thinks that's how the killer escaped and goes looking for a witness who saw someone climbing out of the house. In fact, the window was opened to let out telltale fumes.
- **HAVE THE CLUE TURN OUT TO BE SOMETHING THAT SHOULD BE THERE BUT *ISN'T*.** The sleuth painstakingly elucidates what happened, failing to notice what should have happened but didn't. The most famous example is from the Sherlock Holmes story "Silver Blaze." Holmes deduces there could not have been an intruder because the dog didn't bark.
- **SCATTER PIECES OF THE CLUE IN DIFFERENT PLACES AND MIX UP THE LOGICAL ORDER.** Challenge your reader by revealing only part of a clue at a time. For instance, the sleuth might find a canary cage with a broken door in the basement, along with other detritus; later the sleuth has a "Wait a minute!" realization when he discovers the dead canary with its neck wrung.

- **HIDE THE CLUE IN PLAIN SIGHT.** Tuck the clue among so many other possible clues that it doesn't stand out. For example, the murder weapon, a nylon stocking, might be neatly laundered and folded in the victim's lingerie drawer. Or the sleuth focuses on the water bottle, unopened mail, pine needles, and gas station receipt on the floor of the victim's car and fails to recognize the significance of a telephone number written in the margin of the map.
- **DRAW ATTENTION ELSEWHERE.** Have multiple plausible alternatives vying for the reader's attention. For example, the sleuth knows patients are being poisoned. He focuses on a doctor who gives injections and fails to notice the medic who administers oxygen.
- **CREATE A TIME PROBLEM.** Manipulate time to your own advantage. For example, suppose the prime suspect has an alibi for the time of the murder. Later the sleuth discovers that the time of the alibi or the time of death is wrong.
- **PLACE THE REAL CLUE RIGHT BEFORE A FALSE ONE.** People tend to remember what was presented to them last. For example, your sleuth notices that the stove doesn't light properly and immediately after that discovers an empty prescription bottle, marked with the label "Poison," stuffed in the trash. Readers (and your sleuth) are more likely to remember the hidden bottle than the malfunctioning stove that preceded it.
- **CAMOUFLAGE A CLUE WITH ACTION.** If you show the reader a clue, insert some extraneous action at the same time to distract attention. For example, your sleuth gets mugged while reading a flyer posted on a lamppost; the mugging turns out to be irrelevant, but the flyer contains an important clue.

✎ NOW YOU TRY: MIX UP CLUES AND RED HERRINGS 18.2

Write a few paragraphs in which your sleuth does one of the following:

- inspects a murder scene
- searches a victim's bedroom
- examines a suspect's car

Have your sleuth find at least one real clue that implicates the villain, but camouflage it among false clues and extraneous details of everyday life.

⬇ Download a printable version of this worksheet at www.writersdigest.com/
writing-and-selling-your-mystery-novel-revised.

PLAYING FAIR

In a mystery novel, it's considered bad form to flat-out withhold information
that the narrator knows. It can be infuriating when an author withholds, even
temporarily, some important piece of information that the point-of-view character knows.

Here's an example:

> Sharon's cell phone rang.
>
> "Sorry," she told Bob. "This could be important."
>
> She flipped the phone open and pressed it to her ear. "Hello?"
>
> Sharon recognized the caller's voice, the last person she'd expect to call her
> after all that had happened. "What's up?" she said, trying not to sound surprised.
>
> "You need to know this—" the caller began.

As Sharon listened, she found herself pressing against the car door, trying to insert a few extra inches between herself and Bob. Bob was eyeing her closely, and his unconcerned look suddenly seemed no more than a thin veneer.

The chapter ends, and the reader doesn't discover for twenty pages the identity of the caller or what troubling information that person imparted. Never mind that we've been hanging out in Sharon's head for the last hundred pages and she's been blabbing everything she sees, hears, feels, and thinks. Now, all of a sudden, she plays coy with this critical tidbit.

The reader and the sleuth should realize the identity of the culprit at about the same time. Authors succumb to the temptation of withholding information the narrator knows to create suspense. When they do, they cheat the story and exasperate readers. I know, I know, mystery authors get away with this shtick all the time, but it's a cheap trick. Here's my advice: Don't succumb.

This is why guilty narrators are problematic in a mystery. They know too much. But plenty of mystery writers have managed to pull off a villainous narrator, keeping the character's identity hidden without enraging their readers. For example, Peter Clement's *The Inquisitor* is written from the point of view of a particularly chilling villain who gets his jollies bringing terminal patients near death:

> "Can you hear me?" I whispered, holding back on the plunger of my syringe.
>
> "Yes." Her eyes remained shut.
>
> I leaned over and brought my mouth to her ear. "Any more pain?"
>
> "No. It's gone."
>
> "Do you see anything?"
>
> "Only blackness." Her whispers rasped against the back of her throat.
>
> "Look harder! Now tell me what's there." I swallowed to keep from gagging.
> Her breath stank.
>
> "You're not my doctor."
>
> "No, I'm replacing him tonight."

Notice that by writing this passage in first person, Clement not only conceals the villain's identity but also the villain's gender. This subterfuge leaves the author free to cast suspicion on both male and female characters.

But it's cheating to spend chapter after chapter in a character's head, only to reveal in a final climactic scene that she's been hiding one small detail: She did it. You might get away with it if the character is an *unreliable narrator* who can't remember (she has amnesia), doesn't realize (she's delusional, naïve, simpleminded, or bamboozled), or can't admit even to herself that she's guilty.

CONFUSION: AN INTEREST KILLER

Your goal is to misdirect but never to confuse. Lead the reader down a series of perfectly logical primrose paths—your reader must always feel grounded, even if the story is veering onto a false path. Set too many different possible scenarios spinning at once, or overwhelm your reader with a cacophony of clues, red herrings, and background noise, and your baffled reader will get frustrated and set the book aside—permanently.

As you write, keep track of the different scenarios and of the clues that implicate and exonerate each suspect. Also, be sure to track who knows what and when they know it—particularly if you're writing from multiple viewpoints. If you're confused, your reader is sure to be.

COINCIDENCE: A CREDIBILITY KILLER

All of us are tempted, from time to time, to insert a coincidence into a storyline. Wouldn't it be cool, you say to yourself, to have a character run into the twin sister she never knew she had in a hall of mirrors at a county fair? Dramatic, yes. Credible, no.

Never mind that Agatha Christie wrote a story that turns on a similar coincidence: A man runs into his unknown twin brother coming out of a drugstore; the evil twin then commits a murder and implicates his brother. Never mind that you once read a newspaper article about separated twins who ran into each other in a supermarket. Life is full of bizarre coincidences. You can't put a coincidence like that in a mystery novel today and expect your work to be taken seriously.

Coincidence is most likely to creep in when you maneuver your character into position for the sake of your plot. Maybe your character needs to find out when and where a crime is going to occur, so you have him coincidentally find that information in a letter someone drops on the sidewalk. Or maybe your character needs to find a buried clue, so you give her the inexplicable urge to plant petunias and dig in just the right spot. Or maybe your character needs to know the scheme two characters are hatching, so he happens to pick up the phone extension and overhears them planning.

It's much more satisfying if you come up with logical ways to maneuver your character into position to find the clues and red herrings your plot requires. Repeat after me: *Thou shalt not resort to coincidence, intuition, clairvoyance, or divine intervention.* In a mystery, logic rules, and credibility is paramount.

If you do put coincidence in your story, at least have your point-of-view character comment on the absurdity of the coincidence. While it's not the most elegant solution, at least it will keep the reader from dismissing you as a hack.

 ON YOUR OWN: WRITING INVESTIGATION

1. Check out a how-to book about magic. Mystery authors do well to take a few pages from magicians, who have perfected the art of misdirection. My favorite is the classic by Henning Nelms, *Magic and Showmanship*. Take to heart his distinction between diversion (good showmanship) and distraction (poor showmanship).

2. Write a scene in your novel in which your sleuth questions one of the other characters. Show the dynamic between the characters.

3. Keep track of your clues, noting the key pieces of information you reveal throughout the investigation:
   • the clue
   • what it reveals
   • who knows it and when
   • whom it implicates

CHAPTER 19

WRITING SUSPENSE

"A character who unknowingly carries a bomb around as if it were an ordinary package is bound to work up great suspense in the audience."

—Alfred Hitchcock

■ ■ ■

Suspense happens when a scene becomes charged with anticipation. It's the possibility of what *might* happen that keeps readers on the edge of their chairs.

Think of the classic suspense scene in the Alfred Hitchcock movie *Suspicion*. The Joan Fontaine character believes that her charming husband, played by Cary Grant, is an embezzler and a murderer who is going to kill her. There's a long shot as Grant mounts the stairs, and then the camera focuses on the nightly glass of milk he carries up to her. Everyone in the audience is wondering: *Is it poison?* To heighten the threat and foreboding, Hitchcock placed a lightbulb in the glass so the milk gives off an eerie glow.

To create suspense, your job is to do the literary equivalent of what Hitchcock did by putting that lightbulb in the milk: Build dramatic tension by making the ordinary seem menacing. Two writing tools for achieving this are **sensory detail** and **the slowing down of time**.

TURNING UP SENSORY DETAIL

By focusing on the right sensory detail, you can heighten the sense of potential menace in everyday objects.

Read this example from my suspense novel *Never Tell a Lie*. In it, Ivy Rose, who is hugely pregnant with her first child, realizes someone has been in her house.

> Ivy toweled off the dog in the mudroom, locked the door, and hung the spare key back on its hook. She was halfway through the dark kitchen when she stopped. Turned back.
>
> Something was off.
>
> She flipped on the switch, and the overhead fixture flooded the room with light. Her purse was not on the kitchen counter, where she was sure she'd left it. Her keys were gone, too.
>
> Instead, on the counter sat one of her grandmother's red glass dessert plates. On it lay the newspaper clipping of Ivy and David's engagement announcement.
>
> A siren went off in Ivy's head. Someone was in the house. She had to get out of here. But she couldn't take her eyes off the clipping. Yellow and curled, it looked like the copy she'd found in Melinda's bedroom at her mother's house.
>
> But how could it be? Hadn't Jody gathered up all that material from Ivy's hospital bed and burned it?
>
> Ivy stepped closer. Where her own face had been cut out, another face now filled the hole. She turned the clipping over and ripped away the photograph that had been taped onto the back.
>
> It took her a moment to process what she was seeing—the face was in a frame from one of the photo-booth strips she'd found in Melinda's old bedroom.
>
> A low growl sent a chill rippling across Ivy's back. Phoebe stood in the doorway to the mudroom, teeth bared and snarling, staring past Ivy toward the dining room.

In that short passage, the tenor gradually shifts from normal to fully charged with tension. Taking apart the pieces, here's what happens and the details that are used to create the suspense:

WHAT HAPPENS	DETAILS TO INCREASE TENSION
Ivy realizes someone is in the house.	• Ivy's purse isn't where she left it, and her keys are missing.
	• A newspaper clipping Ivy thought was destroyed is on display on the counter.
	• Ivy's face in the newspaper clipping has been cut out, and Melinda's face has been taped into the hole.
	• The dog growls and snarls, alert.

Ivy reacts in stages:

1. She realizes that something is off.
2. A siren goes off in her head.
3. In internal dialogue, she asks herself, how could it be?
4. A chill ripples across her back.

By making your character hyper-aware and ratcheting the dramatic tension in stages, you create a feeling of impending danger. Suspense is sustained by the absence of anything terrible happening and the continued focus on unnerving details.

When you write suspense, remember that your goal is to heighten anticipation. Here are some useful devices for doing so:

- **ATMOSPHERICS:** Building storm clouds, a flash of lightning, or distant thunder suggest something bad is about to happen, even if they are a bit clichéd.
- **SHADOWS THAT COVER OBJECTS, OR A BRIGHT LIGHT THAT REVEALS SOMETHING THAT WAS HIDDEN:** Create the suggestion of hidden menace with closed curtains, a tarp covering something, a folding screen set up in the corner of a room, a closed (or just barely ajar) door, a shadow, and so on. Or flood the setting with light to suddenly reveal something that was previously obscured.
- **INTERNAL SENSATIONS:** Show that your character feels the anticipation, too. She might pull up her coat collar, pat her pocket to be sure she's got her mace, or feel her scalp prickle.
- **SOMETHING THAT'S NOT QUITE RIGHT:** A telephone off the hook, a broken window, a single high-heeled shoe discarded on a front walk, water left running in a kitchen sink—these not-quite-right details create suspense.

TURNING DOWN THE VELOCITY

Slowing down time increases suspense. I deliberately drew out the moment when Ivy realizes her face has been torn from the old engagement announcement and Melinda's pasted in.

Here are some tools for slowing things down:

- **COMPLEX SENTENCES.** To create a feeling of apprehension about what might happen next, use longer, more complex sentences rather than a rat-a-tat subject-verb-object structure.
- **INTERNAL DIALOGUE.** Let the reader hear your character's thoughts.
- **CAMERA CLOSE-UP.** You want the reader as close as possible, experiencing firsthand the tension the narrator is feeling.
- **QUIET AND DARKNESS.** Stillness, shadows, and dark suggest hidden menace.
- **EXPOSED TIPPING POINT.** Isolate and expand the moment when things go from being okay to not okay. In this example, the words "Something was off," which stand alone as a paragraph by themselves, serve that function.

MODULATING SUSPENSE

Building suspense takes time. No matter how much menace your descriptions carry, the reader will lose interest if you pile on sensory detail after sensory detail. Break the tension by inserting a pause in the tension.

There are many ways to insert a pause into suspense. A telephone rings. One of the characters cracks a joke; in real life, we use humor to get through tense times. Or something that seemed menacing is revealed to be ordinary: A scary shape turns out to be the shadow of a moonlit tree; scuffling outside a window is just a squirrel; the person placing a hand on your protagonist's shoulder at a tense moment turns out to be his best buddy.

Or suspense can continue to rise as *something bad happens*. Here's how *Never Tell a Lie* continues:

> Ivy turned. A figure emerged from the shadows. The woman who'd been at their yard sale stood there, staring at Ivy. Was this Melinda? Ruth?
>
> Raw terror clawed its way up Ivy's throat. "Get out of my house."
>
> The woman stepped into the bright kitchen. She was not pregnant.
>
> "Keep away from me!"
>
> The woman took a step closer.
>
> "Why are you doing this?"
>
> The woman's gaze dropped to Ivy's belly. "Because that's my baby."
>
> Ivy backed up fast, banging against the kitchen counter. She grabbed one of the knives from the block and held it out in front of her, the tip wavering, the blade catching the light.
>
> "Stay away!" Ivy screamed.

FORESHADOWING VERSUS TELEGRAPHING

Creating a suspense sequence that ends harmlessly is a good way to **foreshadow** something more sinister that happens later in your novel. For example, in chapter three, your protagonist goes into a dark, dank basement and emerges, joking about spiders and things that go bump in the night. In chapter twenty-three, she goes down into that same basement, and this time she finds the villain waiting for her. Just be careful you're foreshadowing and not **telegraphing**. Giving away too much too soon is guaranteed to ruin the suspense.

The line between foreshadowing and telegraphing is a subtle one. Let's say your female sleuth meets a man who turns out to be a serial rapist/murderer who preys on young businesswomen whom he picks up in bars at fancy restaurants.

What would be foreshadowing, and what would be telegraphing? Consider this list of possibilities. Where would you draw the line?

1. The man is charming; his nails are manicured, and he smells of expensive aftershave. She finds herself feeling a bit uneasy around him, but she can't put her finger on why.
2. The man's eyes linger on her chest when they're introduced.
3. When the man shakes her hand, he places his other hand on the small of her back.
4. When she gets ready to leave, he offers to walk her to her car, saying there have been some muggings in the neighborhood.
5. She finds his direct, penetrating blue eyes unnerving.
6. She notices a scratch on his face; he notices her noticing and says his cat scratched him.
7. She's repelled by the man. He reminds her of the college football player who tried to rape her years earlier.
8. The man opens his briefcase; she notices a copy of *Hustler* magazine tucked inside.
9. The man opens his briefcase; she notices a roll of duct tape and handcuffs inside.
10. The man's name is Vlad Raptor.

For me, it's around number seven when foreshadowing starts to tip over into telegraphing.

When you insert a hint of what's to come, look at it critically and decide whether it's something the reader will glide right by but remember later with an *Aha!* That's foreshadowing. If, instead, it's like a blinking neon sign that tells the reader what's coming, you've telegraphed.

ENDING SUSPENSE WITH A PAYOFF

You can write a suspense sequence early in your novel that ends with nothing more than a harmless tabby padding off into the night. But as you near one of your novel's end-of-act climaxes, the suspense sequence should pay off. In other words, the bad thing should happen.

The payoff can be an unsettling discovery of evidence of a crime: a dead body, bloodstained clothing, a weapons cache, or a dug-up basement floor.

Or the payoff might be the revelation of a secret. Finding love letters or a personal diary might reveal a hidden relationship between two characters. Finding drug paraphernalia in a car might suggest that a suburban housewife has a secret life.

Or the payoff can be a plot twist. The bad guy confesses. The sleuth gets attacked, locked in a basement, or lost in a cave. Someone else is murdered. Or the police show up and arrest the sleuth.

Here's an excerpt from an end-of-act suspense sequence in Michael Connelly's *9 Dragons*. It's set in the dark, creepy, empty hull of a ship; Harry Bosch is looking for evidence that his missing daughter was kept there:

> There was no trash here. A battery-powered light hung from a wire attached to a hook on the ceiling. There was an upturned shipping crate stacked with unopened cereal boxes, packs of noodles and gallon jugs of water. Bosch looked for any indication that his daughter had been kept in the room, but there was no sign of her.
>
> Bosch heard the hinges on the hatch beneath him screech loudly. He turned just as the hatch banged shut. He saw the seal on the upper right corner turn into locked position and immediately saw that the internal handles had been removed. He was being locked in. He pulled the second gun and aimed both weapons at the hatch, waiting for the next lock to turn.
>
> It was lower right. The moment the bolt started to turn Bosch aimed and fired both guns repeatedly into the door, the bullets piercing metal weakened by years of rust. He heard someone call out as if surprised or hurt. He then heard a banging sound out in the hallway as a body hit the floor.
>
> Bosch moved to the hatch and tried to turn the bolt on the upper right lock with his hand. It was too small for his fingers to find purchase. In desperation, he stepped back a pace and then threw his shoulder into the door, hoping to snap the lock assembly. But it didn't budge and he knew by the feel of the impact on his shoulder that the door would not give way.
>
> He was locked in.

The payoff comes when his search is interrupted by the hatch banging shut. He springs into action, shooting at the door and then trying to force it open. Connelly brings the action to a standstill with that short sentence that sits so effectively on a line by itself: "He was locked in."

Analyze this passage from Hank Phillippi Ryan's *The Wrong Girl*:

> Jane couldn't move. Couldn't risk it. From her place against the wall—light switch stabbing her in the back through her jacket—her line of sight was a narrow sliver.
>
> She couldn't see the office door across the carpeted hall. She'd have to listen for the click of the latch. Listen for footsteps.
>
> When whoever it was got close enough to her, she'd have them in view. Briefly. Long enough to know the score. If it was Jake and all was well she'd stay hidden, and he'd never know she was there. Nor would anyone else.
>
> In that case, she'd leave, come back later. Make an appointment. All by the book.
>
> Her eyes hurt from having to look sideways. Her neck was complaining. But she couldn't risk a move.
>
> Footsteps. A door closing.
>
> They were coming.

WHAT HAPPENS	SENSORY DETAILS THAT CREATE SUSPENSE

⬇ Download a printable version of this worksheet at www.writersdigest.com/writing-and-selling-your-mystery-novel-revised.

Using the simple scene description below, make a list of sensory details you might use to create suspense. Try to use details that incorporate all the senses. Decide what the payoff will be. Then write the scene.

WHAT HAPPENS	SENSORY DETAILS TO CREATE SUSPENSE	PAYOFF
Janie M. locks the door to her office building and walks across the parking lot to her car. As she gets nearer, she realizes her car window is partly open (didn't she remember to close it?) and she catches a glimpse of a dark shape in the back seat.		

WRITE THE SCENE.

⬇ Download a printable version of this worksheet at www.writersdigest.com/writing-and-selling-your-mystery-novel-revised.

ON YOUR OWN: WRITING SUSPENSE

1. Pick a novel you've read that is filled with suspense. If you can't think of one, pick anything by Jeffery Deaver or Mary Higgins Clark. Skim the last third until you find a scene with rising suspense. Examine how the author creates dramatic tension and the sense of anticipation. Does the author provide moments of respite, and how? What's the payoff?

2. Write (or rewrite) a suspense sequence from your outline, focusing on sensory detail and slowing down time to create rising tension.

3. Continue writing. Use this suspense checklist to guide your work:

____ Use sensory detail to make everyday objects seem menacing.

____ Consider using the weather, obscured objects, or your character's internal sensations.

____ Don't rush. Use description, internal dialogue, and complex sentences to slow the pace.

____ Pull the camera in close.

____ End suspense with a payoff.

____ Foreshadow; don't telegraph.

CHAPTER 20

WRITING ACTION

"I once started a detective story to make money—but I couldn't get the murder to take place! At the end of three chapters I was still describing characters and the milieu, so I thought, this is not going to work. No corpse!"

—Mary McCarthy

■ ■ ■

Every mystery novel includes action sequences. An action sequence can be a getaway, a chase, or a desperate rush to catch a plane. It can be a confrontation: an attack, a fistfight, a gun battle, or a murder. Your character could get tied up and thrown in a car trunk or stumble through a forest in the dead of night while being tracked by attack dogs. To make it work, you have to write convincing physical action.

In the hands of a master, writing action seems simple. Take this passage from Lee Child's *The Enemy*, in which Jack Reacher beats a hasty retreat:

> I stood up and raced the last ten feet and hauled Marshall around to the passenger side and opened the door and crammed him into the front. Then I climbed right in over him and dumped myself into the driver's seat. Hit that big red button and fired it up. Shoved it into gear and stamped on the gas so hard the acceleration slammed the door shut. Then I turned the lights full on and put my foot to the floor and charged. Summer would have been proud of me. I drove straight for the line of tanks. Two hundred yards. One hundred yards. I picked my spot and aimed carefully and burst through the gap between two main battle tanks doing more than eighty miles an hour.

This paragraph leaves the reader breathless. Take a minute to reread, analyzing Child's word choice and sentence structure.

Here are some things that make it work:

- **"AND … AND … AND …":** A run-on sentence of short action statements connected by *ands* creates a sense of urgency and a repetitive drum-beat rhythm: *I stood up* **and** *raced the last ten feet* **and** *hauled Marshall around to the passenger side* **and** *opened the door* **and** *crammed him in the front.*
- **SENTENCE FRAGMENTS:** Sentence fragments starting with the verb (*Hit that red button…; Shoved it into gear…*) suggest quick actions.
- **POWERFUL ACTION VERBS:** The sentences aren't freighted with complex phrases, descriptions, adjectives, or adverbs; the verbs (*stood, raced, hauled, crammed, climbed, dumped, hit, shoved*) do all the heavy lifting.
- **ACTIONS AND REACTIONS:** Just like in the real world, when something violent happens, there's a reaction: *… stamped on the gas so hard the acceleration slammed the door shut.*
- **A MOMENT OF INTROSPECTION:** A bit of internal dialogue (*Summer would have been proud of me*) allows the reader to catch a breath in the middle.
- **THE COUNTDOWN:** *Two hundred yards. One hundred yards. I picked my spot and aimed carefully …* Internal dialogue like this puts the reader in the middle of the action, moving forward, closing in.

I asked Lee Child to explain his approach to writing this action sequence. Here's what he told me:

> There's a lot of visualization. I used to be a TV director, and all this stuff is choreographed in my head, like I'm watching a phantom screen.
>
> Also, I try to pre-explain anything that would slow the scene in question. Much earlier in the book, I established that Humvees are low and wide inside, so it seemed okay that Reacher could be shown climbing over Marshall and diving for his own seat. And earlier in that Reacher/Marshall scene, I had established the big red button instead of a regular key. That was quasi-researched inasmuch as I'm pretty sure I read it somewhere. I think it's accurate. But even if it's not, it sounds right, which is 99 percent of my research process.

How many revisions did it take Lee Child to craft an action sequence of this quality? I nearly cried when he gave me his answer: "With climax pieces like that one, I always use the first draft. No revision at all. I'm usually in a zone by then, and that makes the first pass the best."

What I wouldn't give to get a ticket to whatever "zone" he's talking about. For me, and for most writers I know, it takes quite a few rewrites to achieve action that's this spare and effective.

✏ NOW YOU TRY: ANALYZE ACTION   20.1

Read the following action sequence from Kate Flora's *Liberty or Death*. List the ways Flora uses the language and sentence structure to convey action. Notice, also, how she conveys heroine Thea Kozak's complete exhaustion, despite the action that's going on.

EXCERPT FROM *LIBERTY OR DEATH*	HOW LANGUAGE AND SENTENCE STRUCTURE CONVEY ACTION
I took some quick steps forward, raised my gun, supporting it in two hands as I'd been taught, and fired. I kept it pointed toward Belcher and kept on firing until the gun was empty. Fired at his back. Fired at his side, fired as he turned to face me. Fired as he took a step forward and brought his gun the rest of the way up. I fired until he fell onto the ground and lay still. If I'd had more ammunition, I would have gone right on firing. I sat down then, a surprised collapse, the sudden boneless fall of a baby just learning to walk. Still holding the gun, I brought my knees to my chest, and rested my head on them.	1. 2. 3. 4. 5.

⬇ Download a printable version of this worksheet at www.writersdigest.com/writing-and-selling-your-mystery-novel-revised.

VISUALIZING IN ADVANCE

The first step in writing an action sequence is to visualize what you want to happen. Some people can visualize the whole scene from start to finish. Usually I can see what's going to happen at the beginning and how it's going to end, but the middle is a blur. I have to write my way into the action in spurts.

Action sequences are about *action and reaction*, action and response. A useful approach is to map out an action before you write it: choreograph it in your head, and then list the main points:

- where the action takes place
- what happens
- what the characters do in relationship to one another, step by step

For example, here's how Flora's action sequence might be mapped out:

- **WHO:** Thea Kozak and Roy Belcher
- **WHERE:** In a field behind the house
- **WHAT HAPPENS:** Thea shoots Belcher

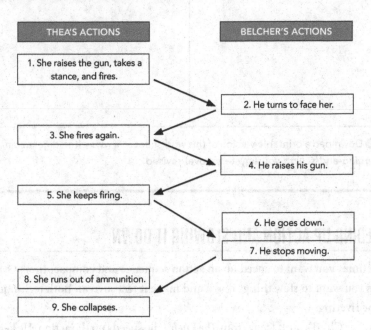

THEA'S ACTIONS	BELCHER'S ACTIONS
1. She raises the gun, takes a stance, and fires.	
	2. He turns to face her.
3. She fires again.	
	4. He raises his gun.
5. She keeps firing.	
	6. He goes down.
	7. He stops moving.
8. She runs out of ammunition.	
9. She collapses.	

Mapping out the action before dramatizing it in writing helps you visualize what your characters are going to do in the scene.

1. Find a two-character action sequence from a television show or movie.
2. Play one minute of this scene with the sound turned off, and replay it as many times as necessary to map out the sequence below.

WHO:

WHERE:

WHAT HAPPENS:

CHARACTER ONE'S ACTIONS	CHARACTER TWO'S ACTIONS

⬇ Download a printable version of this worksheet at www.writersdigest.com/writing-and-selling-your-mystery-novel-revised.

SPEEDING UP ACTION AND SLOWING IT DOWN

Sometimes you want to speed up an action sequence and compact time. Other times you want to slow things down and make it feel surreal. Both techniques can be riveting.

In Lee Child's tank scene from *The Enemy*, he speeds up the action. He keeps the camera zoomed in and presents the action at a rapid-fire pace. His goal is to get his character the hell out of Dodge and leave the reader panting for breath.

In Kate Flora's shoot-out, she slows down the action. Her character is exhausted, on the brink of collapse. By pulling the camera back and slowing down the sequence, she gives the sequence a dreamlike quality.

Here's a guide for modulating the pace of an action sequence:

TO SPEED UP THE ACTION	TO SLOW DOWN THE ACTION
Focus, and pull the camera in close.	Pull the camera back.
Limit extraneous detail.	Provide descriptive detail.
Keep sentences short and direct; drop the pronouns.	Use longer, more complex sentences.
	Convey some introspection.
Minimize internal dialogue.	

MAKING ACTION BELIEVABLE

A successful action sequence must be believable. Lapses in logic distract the reader from the drama you're trying to create.

If your action has guns in it, make sure you know what you're talking about. Are the characters using handguns, rifles, or shotguns? If they're using handguns, are they revolvers or a semiautomatic pistols? I don't know Glocks from Mausers, but if you're writing about them, you should. You need to know how to load, aim, and fire, what the recoil feels like, what happens to the spent shell casing (if there is one), whether the gun gets hot, and, most important, whether your character could handle that particular weapon.

Kate Flora told me how she learned about guns:

> One day I was sitting in a police station talking with an officer who was a good friend. When I mentioned that I had never shot a handgun, he looked at his watch, shook his head, and said, "We'll have to fix that."
>
> He then took me to a shooting range in the basement of the department and walked me through the process of shooting. He taught me about how to hold the gun and the proper stance for shooting and bracing for recoil, and then I squeezed the trigger (not pulled) and everything I'd ever seen on TV or read about guns was literally blown away.
>
> It was a big gun with a big jump and a flash of flame and a thunderous noise followed by a gust of smoke. The air filled with the smell of exploding gunpowder, the ejected shell flying back at me, and it left me stunned, shaken, and rubber-limbed. Shooting a gun is not a small thing.

If guns play a major role in your book and you don't know a friendly cop who will take you to a firing range, take a firearms class.

Writing a physical fight requires some know-how, too. If you're like me and you've survived this long by fleeing rather than fighting, you'll need to do some research. There are many books and handbooks on the subject. For instance, the U.S. Army has an official training manual on hand-to-hand combat that covers different moves such as choke holds, throws, kicks, and blocks. Watch a hand-to-hand combat video, or, better yet, take a self-defense class—many community police departments sponsor them.

Get the medical detail in your action sequence correct. Ask any doctor, and you'll quickly discover that a single blow to the head is almost never fatal. Rarely is death instantaneous from a stab or gunshot wound either. The pool of blood around a corpse's head shouldn't grow—dead men don't bleed.

A good source for this kind of information is *Forensics: A Guide for Writers* by D.P. Lyle, M.D. (Writer's Digest Books).

So do your homework, get the details right, but don't show off. One guaranteed way to deflate a gun battle is to dump everything you've learned about semiautomatic pistols into the middle of it.

KILLING ACTION WITH CLINICAL DETAIL

You can also kill an action sequence by describing the action with excruciating detail. Here's an example of what *not* to do:

> He took three steps forward and stood facing me, inches away. His breath smelled like he'd been chewing on old tires. I averted my face a quarter turn to the right and poked my left index finger into the middle of his chest. He stepped back six inches, tilted his head twenty degrees, and batted away my hand.

This is an exaggeration, but you get the idea. The only detail I like in this passage is the bit about bad breath and the verb *poked*. Red flags should go up in your mind if you start writing about quarters and halves, left and right, inches and degrees. Yes, these details describe action, but all that measurement and specificity bring it to its knees.

Here's an example from my novel *Never Tell a Lie*. Note how much leaner the description is, and yet the passage is still easy to visualize.

> Ivy dropped the receiver, grabbed the teakettle from the stove and brought it down as hard as she could on the woman's head. Then she raced into the mudroom. The spare key was there, hanging from the hook by the door.
> She felt movement behind her. *Hurry!*

She jammed the key in the lock, turned it. She had the door barely open when the woman's forearm clamped around her neck. Before Ivy could resist, she was shoved hard against the door, slamming it shut. The sound seemed to explode in her skull

Something stuck into Ivy's side—the knifepoint, she realized, pricking through the sweatshirt and into her skin. She tried to pull away. Winded and breathing heavily, the woman wrapped her arm more tightly around Ivy's neck and twisted the knife tip against Ivy's ribs.

Ivy's head throbbed, and patterns of yellow and black kaleidoscoped in front of her tightly shut eyes.

"Lock the door and give me the key," the woman said, her voice low.

Ivy hunched her back, struggling to make a safe hollow for the baby. She screamed as the knife cut into her skin. She tried to angle her body to keep the baby from being crushed inside her, trying to ease the pressure of the knifepoint.

In an action sequence, less is more. Provide just enough detail to show the reader what's going on, using simple sentences and powerful verbs. Establish crucial details in advance. Trust the reader to fill in what you judiciously leave out.

✏️ **NOW YOU TRY: REVISE TO ELIMINATE CLINICAL DETAIL**   20.3

Rewrite this action sequence, getting rid of the clinical detail.

ACTION INFESTED WITH CLINICAL DETAIL	YOUR LEAN AND VISCERAL REVISION
He took three steps forward and stood facing me, inches away. His breath smelled like he'd been chewing on old tires. I averted my face, a quarter turn to the right, and poked my left index finger into the middle of his chest. He stepped back six inches, tilted his head twenty degrees, and batted away my hand.	

⬇️ Download a printable version of this worksheet at www.writersdigest.com/writing-and-selling-your-mystery-novel-revised.

AVOIDING DETOURS DURING ACTION: ESTABLISHING IN ADVANCE

If you find yourself taking a pause in the middle of an action sequence to explain something to the reader, be aware that you are slowing the forward momentum. For instance, suppose your character is being chased along the edge of a cliff and you describe to the readers how high it is, how the waves crash on jagged rocks a hundred feet below. If you don't, you reason, how will they appreciate how dangerous this is? They won't. But ask yourself: Is this the best place to insert the description?

Don't dump explanation into an action sequence unless you want to modulate the forward momentum. Instead, *establish* this setting earlier. Have your character walk his dog there while he's thinking through the clues or searching for evidence. Describe the breathtaking view from this spot, or have his dog scrabble back from the edge. Then, later in the novel, when you get to the action sequence at that cliff's edge, you can let 'er rip.

 NOW YOU TRY: WRITE AN ACTION SEQUENCE

Dramatize the action sequence you mapped out earlier in this chapter. Then, follow these steps:

1. Underline all your verbs. Are they strong enough? Replace the ones you feel need strengthening.
2. Examine your sentence structure. Is it appropriate to the feeling you're trying to convey—simple and straightforward if you want the scene to move fast, or more complex if you want it to slow down?
3. Are you writing with the camera as close as you need it to be? Remember: Zooming the camera in heightens intensity and speeds up action; drawing back gives the scene a dreamlike feel and slows things down.
4. Is the writing clear and lean?
5. Is there anything in this scene that needs to be established earlier in the novel? Make a note in your outline to establish that information where you think it belongs.

ON YOUR OWN: MAKING ACTION

1. Pick a novel you've read that's filled with a lot of action. If you can't recall one, pick anything by Lee Child or Lisa Scottoline. Skim the last third for an action sequence. Read and analyze it. What's the overall effect of the scene, and how does the writer achieve it?

2. Plan to research certain topics for the action sequences in your book. For instance, if you know your plot involves guns or hand-to-hand combat, your plan might include taking a firearms or self-defense class.

3. Write action sequences, mapping them out in advance if you like. Use this checklist to guide your work:

____ Use powerful verbs.

____ Use active voice.

____ Use simple sentences.

____ Keep introspection to a minimum unless you're deliberately slowing down the action.

____ Keep description to a minimum unless you're deliberately slowing down the action.

____ Make sure actions have reactions.

____ Establish in advance anything that will bog down the scene.

CHAPTER 21

PUZZLING IT OUT

Writing Reflection

"In mysteries, the penny-drop comes when the sleuth hears, sees, tastes, smells, touches or otherwise experiences something that, when combined (usually mentally) with a fact or facts gleaned earlier, tells the detective that 'til now, everyone has been following false leads."

—Thomas B. Sawyer, head writer/producer of *Murder, She Wrote*

■ ■ ■

A mystery is about solving a puzzle. Puzzle solving requires *thinking*, so throughout your novel, and especially after suspense and action sequences, take time to pause, turn down the volume, and let your character (and the reader) think about what's happened so far and put together the clues.

It's all about getting to the **aha moment** when the sleuth realizes the significance of something which, up to that point, has seemed unimportant. For example, the aha moment might be the revelation of a secret that establishes a character's motive for murder. It might be the discovery of evidence that explains how a crime was committed. When the metaphorical bulb lights up inside the sleuth's head, facts and events snap into focus and the story is propelled forward.

You have two tools for dramatizing reflection:

- **DIALOGUE:** Characters discuss what happened and think aloud. Your sidekick and supporting cast become sounding boards for the sleuth.
- **INTERNAL DIALOGUE:** The reader is privy to a character's thoughts.

REFLECTING IN DIALOGUE

One of the main reasons Sherlock Holmes needs Watson is so he can discuss the case and astound Watson and the reader with his mental acumen. Here's an example of how it works.

This conversation between Holmes and Watson occurs near the end of "The Speckled Band":

> "Well, there is at least the curious coincidence of the dates. A ventilator is made, a cord is hung, and a lady who sleeps in the bed dies. Does that not strike you?"
>
> "I cannot as yet see any connection."
>
> "Did you observe anything very peculiar about that bed?"
>
> "No."
>
> "It was clamped to the floor. Did you ever see a bed fastened like that before?"
>
> "I cannot say that I have."
>
> "The lady could not move her bed. It must always be in the same relative position to the ventilator and to the rope—for so we may call it since it was clearly never meant for a bell-pull."
>
> "Holmes," I cried. "I seem to see dimly what you are hinting at. We are only just in time to prevent some subtle and horrible crime."

Though this passage feels a bit wooden by today's standards, every good mystery needs sequences of dialogue in which the characters puzzle things out and advance the story. Here's what this bit of dialogue accomplishes:

- **REVIEWS WHAT HAPPENED:** In case the reader missed anything in the preceding tumult, the characters highlight the clues (some may turn out to be red herrings): the coincidence of the dates, the nailed-down bed, and the rope that's not a bell-pull.
- **PRESENTS THE AHA MOMENT:** The sleuth realizes the significance of a clue. Holmes concludes that the bedroom was arranged in that very peculiar way to facilitate a murder.
- **SHOWS CHARACTERS' REACTIONS:** The characters sense the gravity of the implications. Even Watson gets it ("*We are only just in time to prevent some subtle and horrible crime.*")
- **RAISES QUESTIONS:** Unanswered questions propel the story forward. In this example, the reader wonders about that sinister rope hanging from the ceiling—how was it used to commit a crime? And what crimes lie ahead?

Create opportunities like this for your sleuth to discuss the case and draw conclusions after turning points in the story.

In this passage from Jonathan Kellerman's *Twisted*, analyze how Detective Petra Connor and intern Isaac Gomez puzzle out the pattern behind a series of killings.

THINK ABOUT THE FOLLOWING:	EXCERPT FROM *TWISTED*
What clues are explained? What conclusions are drawn during the aha moment? How does Isaac show his reaction to this train of thought? What unanswered questions propel the story forward?	"There's another discrepancy between Marta and the others. They were beaten to the ground and left there. She was killed on the street but placed in her car. You could look at that as her being treated with a bit more respect. Which would also fit with a killer who knew her well." He grimaced. "I should have thought of that." ... "That's why it's good to brainstorm," said Petra. They reached Santa Monica Boulevard. Traffic, noise, pedestrians, gay hustlers loitering on corners. Petra said, "Here's another distinction for Doebbler: She was the first. When Detective Ballou told me he thought Kurt Doebbler's reaction was off, and then after I met Kurt, it got me thinking: What if the bad guy never set out to commit a string of murders. What if he killed Marta for a personal reason and found out he liked it? Got himself a hobby. Which brings us back to Kurt." "A once-a-year hobby," said Isaac. "An anniversary," she said. "What if June 28 is significant to Kurt because he happened to kill Marta on that day? So he relives it." He stared at her. "That's brilliant."

REFLECTING IN INTERNAL DIALOGUE

Reflection can also be expressed through internal dialogue. For example, in this passage from Laura Lippman's *Wilde Lake*, state's attorney Luisa Brant thinks about why she was attacked:

The EMT guys decide to let her go home, although with muttered imprecations about concussions, and while Lu scoffs at them, she finds herself unaccountably nervous as bedtime nears. She drinks cognac, knowing it's a terrible idea—it will knock her out anyway. She simply cannot sleep. It's not that she experiences the attack when she closes her eyes. Instead she has the strangest sense of déjà vu. That whooshing noise. A man running. Rudy at the door of the courtroom, so close to the outdoors for which he longed. Yes, the attack on her was a diversion, an attempt to throw the court into chaos. So why didn't he then break for daylight, as the saying goes?

Because he's crazy. But not crazy in the way that counts.

Reflection in internal dialogue achieves the same goals as spoken dialogue:

- **REVIEWS WHAT HAPPENED:** Lu remembers the noise, the man running but not fleeing: *… she has the strangest sense of déjà vu.*
- **SHOWS THE CHARACTER'S REACTION:** *She drinks cognac… . She simply cannot sleep.* Lu doesn't have to say, "I was upset." The reader can see from how she behaves that she is. As your character reflects, allow the memories to trigger an emotional response you can show the reader.
- **RAISES QUESTIONS.** *… why didn't he then break for daylight, as the saying goes?* Lu moves point by point, frame by frame, raising questions that may send the story in a new direction.
- **PRESENTS THE AHA MOMENT.** Lu realizes how dangerous this man is (*Because he's crazy.*). The character puts together the clues and makes sense of what happened, and in this case it raises the stakes to a higher level.

USING CONFLICT TO ADD SPICE TO REFLECTION

Conflict adds another dimension to reflection. It can be played out in dialogue (argument, debate) or internal dialogue (disbelief, self-doubt).

Here's an example from Dennis Lehane's *Moonlight Mile*. Patrick Kenzie argues with himself as he tries to sort out what he thinks:

There was zero connection between her whistle-blowing and her getting shot by some dumb, fucked-up kid in a parking lot at three in the morning. No connection whatsoever.

But it's all connected.

This should not be about that, a voice said. *You're just pissed off. And when you're pissed off, you lash out.*

I leaned back in my seat, closed my eyes. I saw Beatrice McCready's face—pained and prematurely aged and possibly crazed.

Another voice said, *Don't do this.*

That voice sounds uncomfortably like my daughter's.

Leave it be.

I opened my eyes. The voices were right.

I saw Amanda from my morning dream, the envelopes she'd tossed in the bushes.

It's all connected.

No it's not.

Here are some examples of the different kinds of conflict you can inject into reflection:

- **THE ODD COUPLE:** Characters with opposite personalities have different takes on the same evidence. Think about how Mulder and Scully approach their investigations in the television series *The X-Files*. Or, for instance, how an older, jaded male homicide detective might pressure a less-experienced female medical examiner to highlight evidence that supports his theory about the murder, but she goes on to point out all the inconsistencies.
- **OPPOSING DESIRES OR PRESSURES:** One character wants to move ahead with the investigation while another character wants to hold back. For instance, a reporter is eager to investigate a recent death that police have labeled a suicide; her editor wants her to stick to covering town politics.
- **CREDIBILITY:** Characters argue over the existence of evidence. For instance, an innkeeper hears a scream outside in the middle of the night and sees shadowy shapes moving about in the field. The police officer, who finds no evidence of a crime and no one else who heard those sounds, wonders if the innkeeper is dotty.
- **SELF-DOUBT:** The character saw or felt something. He then questions his own senses and wonders if he's overreacting, embellishing, or making it up.
- **THE WAR WITHIN:** The character chokes on a decision he has to make to move forward. For example, a reporter has to decide whether revealing a source is ever justified, even to catch a killer.
- **WITHHOLDING INFORMATION:** One character tells another a partial recap of events but lies about or withholds the complete picture. For example, a character might tell her father about what's going on in a case but leave out the parts that would make her father worry about her safety; he's no pushover, so he calls her on it.

Your protagonist wakes up in pain and in a small confined space, up to his ankles in cold water. Write an introspective scene as he deduces that he's in a basement closet and the water is rising.

⬇ Download a printable version of this worksheet at www.writersdigest.com/ writing-and-selling-your-mystery-novel-revised.

NOW YOU TRY: PLAN AND WRITE REFLECTION

Pick a place in your outline where your characters need to stand back and reflect. Decide how you're going to write that passage:

- Will you use dialogue, internal dialogue, or both?
- How can you include conflict?
- What's the aha moment?
- What's your point-of-view character's emotion, and how are you going to show it to the reader?
- What unanswered question will propel the reader forward?

Now write that scene.

 ## ON YOUR OWN: WRITING REFLECTION

1. Skim for action and suspense sequences in a few of your favorite mystery novels. After each sequence, does the author take time to let the characters think? Can you find an aha moment in each reflection sequence?
2. Flag places in your outline where you think it would be appropriate to have your character sit back and reflect about what happened.
3. Continue writing. Whenever you write a reflection sequence, use this checklist to guide your work:

____ Use sensory images to bring the thoughts alive.

____ Show your character's emotional response.

____ Write the aha moment when your character realizes the significance of a clue or impending danger.

____ End with an open question that propels the reader forward.

____ Inject conflict (self-doubt, argument) wherever it makes sense.

CHAPTER 22

LAYERING IN BACKSTORY

"The first draft of my second novel, Common Murder, *began with five beautifully crafted chapters of backstory for my protagonist, Lindsay Gordon. When I sent it off to my agent, she said, 'Lose the first five chapters. They're lovely, but they don't tell the story. Everything you've told us here can be fed in as and when we need to know it.'"*

—Val McDermid

■ ■ ■

Suppose you're writing a novel that starts with a brutal rape and murder. In the opening scene, medical examiner Renata Ruiz examines the body. The reader doesn't know that Renata grew up poor on a farm in central California, put herself through college, modeled for *Playboy* magazine in college to make ends meet, and, most important, was the victim of a brutal rapist who also raped and murdered her best friend. You want to convey all these aspects of this **backstory** because, by the end of the novel, you want Renata to triumph on two levels—first, by putting this sexual pervert in jail, and second, by coming to terms with her own survivor's guilt.

Question: When do you reveal Renata's backstory?

Answer: A little at a time.

Too much backstory in the beginning can bog down your novel before you get it off the ground. Initially, your reader may need to know only that Renata is an experienced medical examiner with special expertise in sex crimes and that she doesn't tolerate anyone kidding around when the corpse of a woman victim is on the autopsy table. Once your story is airborne, slip in more details of Renata's past at opportune moments.

The really dramatic information that resonates with this investigation—that Renata was herself a rape victim and that her best friend was murdered by the rapist—is best revealed in layers as part of the unfolding drama. You might slip in, early on, that Renata was a crime victim. Later, you might reveal that she was raped, and, later still, that her best friend was raped and also murdered. At a major turning point in the novel, perhaps when Renata is about to confront the villain, you might write a vivid flashback that dramatizes the rape or her dead friend's funeral.

The stronger and more compelling your front story, the more backstory it can hold. Here are three rules of thumb to keep in mind:

1. Hold the backstory until your novel is launched.
2. Gradually layer in backstory wherever it resonates with your main story, letting the past drama reinforce the present drama.
3. Tell the backstory in a variety of ways.

There are a number of different strategies for telling that backstory.

BACKSTORY STRATEGY: NARRATOR TELLS ALL

The narrator can simply *tell* the reader about a character's past. In this example from Denise Mina's *Field of Blood*, narrator Paddy Meehan has just walked into the Press Bar. She's the only woman in a sea of men.

> Paddy didn't like men or want to keep their company, but she did want to have a place among them, to be a journalist instead of a gofer. She would have felt like an interloper in the bar if she hadn't been on *News* business, here to get the picture editor's tankard filled.

Voilà. Here's a snapshot of who she is and who she aspires to be. We're already privy to her insecurities and biases. Talking directly to the reader like this is an efficient, economical way to convey a character's background. In small doses, it's highly effective.

BACKSTORY STRATEGY: SLIPPING IT INTO DIALOGUE

An equally simple but somewhat more artful way of layering in backstory involves dialogue. In this example from *Mr. Churchill's Secretary*, author Susan Elia MacNeal has Maggie Hope deliver a monologue explaining why she's annoyed at being turned down for a job and why apologies don't cut it:

"You're sorry? *Sorry?*" she said, her voice rising in pitch.

…

"Perfect. You're sorry. But it doesn't change anything." Her pronunciation became
more distinct. "It doesn't *change* that when I interviewed for the private secretary
job, I was *more* than qualified. It doesn't *change* that Dicky Snodgrass was a
condescending *ass* to me. It doesn't *change* that John sees me as a mere girl incapable of anything besides typing and getting married and having babies. And
it doesn't *change* that they hired that cross-eyed *lug* Conrad Simpson—a mouth
breather who probably still has to sound words out and count on his fingers …"

This edgy diatribe packs a punch—it delivers information about Maggie's backstory as well as attitude.

But be careful. Dialogue freighted with information can sound stagy and artificial, as in this excerpt I made up to demonstrate the point:

"Here's something right up your alley, Digby," Prothero said, jabbing his finger
at a newspaper article. "You know all about poisons. Wasn't your brother killed
eating poisonous mushrooms? I heard that's why you became an expert and
wrote that definitive pamphlet for the Poison Control Center."

Digby scanned the story. "Dr. Willem Banks. Died of strychnine poisoning.
Isn't he that old codger who lives in that huge mansion I wanted to buy a few
years back? Maybe one of my three sisters knew him."

Yes, we get tons of backstory, in all its glory, wedged into wooden dialogue. Never
force words into characters' mouths like this. Use dialogue to convey backstory
only when it feels natural and works dramatically.

NOW YOU TRY: PUT BACKSTORY INTO NARRATION OR DIALOGUE 22.1

Jot down some aspects of your character's life history or professional background that you want to convey to the reader early on in your novel.

1.

2.

3.

WRITE IT AS NARRATION.	WRITE IT AS DIALOGUE BETWEEN TWO CHARACTERS.

⊕ Download a printable version of this worksheet at www.writersdigest.com/writing-and-selling-your-mystery-novel-revised.

BACKSTORY STRATEGY: FICTIONAL DOCUMENTS

Another way to deliver backstory is through fictional documents—wills, newspaper articles, photographs, letters, school yearbooks, and so on. You can reproduce the document or have one of the characters summarize what's in it.

For example, your main character might receive a letter from an old friend, reminiscing about when they were in school together, asking after the main character's family, and reminding the character that the friend once saved his life. Now the friend is calling in his chits and asking for a favor. The letter effectively moves the story along while delivering information about the main character's past.

It's a commonly held belief that readers skip over the fictional documents in mystery novels to get to whatever is happening in the scene. I have no idea if this is true, but I've heard it often enough that I offer these words of caution: Keep those fictional documents short, and don't put anything the reader really needs to know in a fictional document and nowhere else.

BACKSTORY STRATEGY: MEMORIES

Use a memory to tell backstory in a dramatic way. In this an example from Luiz Alfredo Garcia-Roza's *A Window in Copacabana*, Inspector Espinosa remembers his grandmother.

> He dedicated the following two hours to examining a book that, along with a few hundred others, he'd inherited from his grandmother. Every once in a while his grandmother had felt the need to purge some of the thousands of books piled in two rooms of her apartment, and these were destined for her grandson, who also inherited her habit of stockpiling books. Their styles were different: hers were anarchic piles, his orderly stacks against the wall. They shared a disdain for shelving.

The act of examining a book that belonged to his grandmother triggers the memory. This memory is not essential to the plot but gives the reader insight into Espinosa's character, revealing a contemplative, literate side to this tough police inspector. The "orderly stacks" suggest an orderly mind, and a "disdain for shelving" suggests a man who lives alone and feels no need to conform to conventions.

Here are some examples of memory triggers:

- **WHAT A CHARACTER SAYS:** *He sounded just like Red, my mentor at the police academy who …*
- **HOW A CHARACTER LOOKS:** *She had that same look on her face as my first wife right before she slapped me with divorce papers.*
- **A DREAM:** *I dreamed I was back in elementary school, fourth grade, Mrs. Joffey standing there, glaring at me bug-eyed, like I had the IQ of a frog.*
- **AN OBJECT:** *Whenever I saw that photograph, I thought of Joe and the day we …*
- **A SONG:** *That was our song. I remember the first time …*

Memories conveyed in a sentence to a few paragraphs, strategically sprinkled throughout your novel, enable you to reveal layer after layer of your characters' backstories.

BACKSTORY STRATEGY: EXTENDED FLASHBACK

You can also insert an extended flashback—a scene within a scene—to deliver backstory. An extended flashback can show how a character's past experience compels him to behave the way he does in the present. Or it can build understanding of how a situation got to be the way it is now.

Here's how William G. Tapply starts a four-page flashback in the second chapter of *Bitch Creek*:

> An hour before sunup on a June morning almost exactly five years earlier, Calhoun had been creeping along the muddy bank of a little tidal creek that emptied into Casco Bay just north of Portland. A blush of pink had begun to bleed into the pewter sky toward the east. The tide was about halfway out, and the water against the banks lay as flat and dark as a mug of camp coffee. A blanket of fog hung …

A tricky part of writing a flashback is handling the **time-and-space shift**. Notice how Tapply does it simply:

- **THE TIME SHIFT:** *almost exactly five years earlier*
- **THE SPACE SHIFT:** *along the muddy bank of a little tidal creek*

A second tricky part is handling **verb tense**. If the main part of your novel is written in the present tense (*he **pulls** the trigger…*), the solution is simple: Write a flashback in the past tense (*he once **killed** a man …*). But what if the main story is written in the past tense? Logic dictates that the flashback would be written in the past perfect (*he once **had killed** a man …*). Notice that the flashback in the example from *Bitch Creek* begins in the past-perfect tense: *Calhoun **had** been creeping …; A blush of pink **had** begun to bleed …*

Had, had, had … Past perfect quickly gets cumbersome, but the good news is that once you've launched your flashback and oriented the reader by using past perfect a few times, you can revert to past tense, as Tapply does in the excerpt: "The tide **was** about halfway out …"

At the end of a flashback, you once again need to cue the reader that you are returning to the present events of the main story. To show the transition, insert the past perfect a time or two at the end of the flashback; when you're out of the flashback and back in the main story, revert to past tense.

Here's an example of a sentence that signals this transition:

> She **had** never called him. At the time, he **had** thought it was odd. Now he **wasn't** so sure. He **got up** and **headed** …

Keep in mind that an extended flashback interrupts the narrative flow of your main story. Delivered at the wrong time—in the middle of a chase, for instance—a flashback can derail the current action and waste any momentum you've gathered. Delivered at the right dramatic moment, a flashback enhances and deepens your story. Experiment, moving around flashbacks in your novel, to see where they work best.

1. Jot down an event in your character's past that you want to convey dramatically to the reader.

2. Write the flashback as internal dialogue—a memory triggered by something in the present. Write the trigger, then the memory.

3. Write an extended flashback. Remember to orient the reader to the time-and-place shift, shift the verb tense (present to past or past to past perfect), and segue back to the main story at the end.

⬇ Download a printable version of this worksheet at www.writersdigest.com/writing-and-selling-your-mystery-novel-revised.

ON YOUR OWN: LAYERING IN BACKSTORY

1. Read the first three chapters of a popular mystery novel. Make a list of the backstory elements, and notice how the writer chooses to convey each.

2. Each time you layer in some backstory, remember that the stronger and more compelling your front story, the more backstory it can tolerate. Make a conscious decision about how you plan to reveal each layer of backstory:
   - narrator tells all (internal dialogue)
   - dialogue
   - fictional document
   - memories
   - extended flashback

3. Continue writing. Whenever you include backstory, use this checklist to guide your work:

   ____ Be sure this is the dramatically appropriate spot to deliver this layer of backstory.

   ____ Pick the most appropriate method to deliver the backstory (narrator tells all, fictional document, dialogue, memory, or extended flashback).

   ____ Trigger memories with a detail from the present (the sound of a car backfiring triggers the memory of gunshots; the sight of a woman arguing with her husband triggers the memory of arguments with an ex-wife; the smell of cotton candy triggers the memory of a childhood trip to a carnival).

   ____ For flashbacks, orient the reader to the time-and-place shift, shift the verb tense (present to past or past to past perfect), and segue back to the main story at the end.

CHAPTER 23

WRITING THE FINAL CLIMAX

"The best surprise endings don't merely surprise the reader. In addition, they force him to reevaluate everything that has preceded them so that he views the actions and the characters in a different light and has a new perspective on all that he's read."

—Lawrence Block

■■■

Near the end of a mystery novel, the story builds to a dramatic crescendo as the protagonist and the villain face off. Hercule Poirot might have rounded up the suspects and played *whodunit* in the parlor. In modern novels, there's usually a physical fight, a chase, or a cat-and-mouse game with survival at stake.

During the climax, these things usually happen:

- The protagonist hits bottom.
- The protagonist rebounds.
- The villain reveals what happened and the protagonist puts it together.
- The villain is vanquished.

By the end of the final climax, the protagonist and the reader understand the what, how, and why of the crime, and the story is ready to wind down.

THE PROTAGONIST HITS BOTTOM

At the start of the face-off, the protagonist feels like David realizing just how big and dangerous—and possibly invincible—Goliath is. And there's no turning back.

Raise the stakes, and then raise them again. It should feel as if your protagonist has climbed out on a tree limb, a fire's climbing up the trunk, a crocodile is standing on the ground below him salivating, and someone's throwing rocks at him from above. If the character's path is easy, reaching its end won't feel climactic.

Here's how Becky Masterman peppers retired FBI agent Brigid Quinn with woes in the climax of *Rage Against the Dying*. The villain, Emery, has tied her up, taped her mouth, taken her gun, and shot the sheriff, Max, who came looking for her.

> Emery was pissed. He looked at Max bleeding and still on the floor where the .45 had knocked him off his feet. He slipped Max's gun out of his holster stepped over the body to lock the front door, then ran the few quick steps needed to reach me where I lay on the floor, having rolled over on my stomach to ease the agony of my arms taped behind me. I couldn't see him, only hear him as he stepped on my neck and punched the gun into my temple. I felt a spray of his saliva. With the part of me that could drain out and witness myself, I heard myself whimper like a muzzled dog.

Soon after this, Brigid's back spasms and she can barely move. At the same time, she realizes the gasoline she smells is coming from homemade bombs sitting in the next room. It just keeps getting worse—as it should.

This is the moment when the protagonist proves herself. Is she going to wallow in a pit of despond or rally and come back hard to prove herself, prevent any further mayhem, and bring the villain to justice? The story has been driving toward this ultimate test of the protagonist's mettle.

✎ NOW YOU TRY: HITTING BOTTOM 23.1

How does your character hit bottom in the buildup to the final confrontation with the villain? Check the items that apply, and describe them.

___ Injured

_____

___ Ill

_____

___ Exhausted

_____

___ Overmatched physically

_____

___ Blocked

_____

___ Restrained

_____

___ Mentally impaired

_____

___ Afraid

_____

___ Disarmed

_____

⬇ Download a printable version of this worksheet at www.writersdigest.com/
writing-and-selling-your-mystery-novel-revised.

THE PROTAGONIST REBOUNDS

After bottoming out, the protagonist reaches a *turning point* and rebounds. He's
now willing to face whatever consequences await. The turning point is a key moment in the plot when he determines that he's going to face death and outrun past
failures. This is what the protagonist's journey has been all about.

In *Rage Against the Dying*, Brigid gathers her courage and challenges her at-
tacker. "Go ahead and fire that weapon, you motherfucker. Someone is bound
to hear one of the shots and call the cops." He wavers, and she begins to manipulate him to her advantage.

When you write this turning point, be aware of its importance. Your protagonist shifts from being a victim to being the aggressor, from giving up to fight-

ing back. When you write it, *slow down,* open up the moment, and give your protagonist time to gather his thoughts, reason it through, and then make the emotional shift.

THE VILLAIN REVEALS OR THE PROTAGONIST PUTS IT TOGETHER

During the climax, the inner workings of the crime are revealed. Sometimes the protagonist works it out from the clues and confronts the villain. But the villain might also tell the protagonist what happened, boasting and speaking freely in the false belief that the protagonist is about to die anyway.

Here's how it happens in *Rage Against the Dying*:

> "Was it vodka?" I asked.
> "What?"
> "In Lynch's IV bag."
> He put my gun down on the counter and picked up the bottle of Grey Goose. "I figured with all the pain killers he was on, a liter of alcohol going straight to his brain would finish him off but allow me plenty of time to get away from the hospital. How did you know?"
> I started to tell him I saw him posing as a nurse …

This part of the climax is a battle of wits. The villain's confession has to feel earned. Your challenge is to make the reader believe that the protagonist is wily and perceptive enough to get the villain to reveal his secrets.

THE VILLAIN IS VANQUISHED

The climax builds to a face-to-face confrontation in which the protagonist and the villain are willing to pay the ultimate price. Tension builds until, suddenly, something breaks it. In *Rage Against the Dying*:

> We were very still then, he standing about six feet away and able to move quickly, and I on my knees before him. I was out of options and wondered how it would feel to die. We watched one another for a moment, guessing each other's next move, and then were both distracted by the soft but unmistakable sound of a shotgun shell being racked.

You'll have to read the book to find out what happens next; it will surprise you. This exemplary final climax is packed, as it should be, with surprises. Justice is served, though not in a strictly legal sense.

Can you write a villain who gets away with it? Absolutely. Hannibal Lecter survives in Thomas Harris's *Silence of the Lambs*. In my novel *Night Night, Sleep Tight* the villain gets away with it. If a story is loaded with cynicism, the ending can be cynical, too.

There are no hard-and-fast rules except this: The climax should bring the two plotlines—the sleuth's personal journey and the investigation of the crime—to a *satisfying* joint conclusion.

ENDINGS TO AVOID

Here are some endings that will make readers throw the book against the wall:

- **DUH:** This is an ending that's obvious to everyone but the sleuth. This happens when you've telegraphed the ending to the reader (the shadowy figure with bad breath that the sleuth keeps ignoring).
- **OVER THE TOP:** This ending overdoses on violence. The villain holds the sleuth at bay with a machine gun while systematically cutting off the hands and ears of his victims and blowing up houses in a nearby suburb.
- **YOU'VE GOT TO BE KIDDING:** The villain seems incapable of such a crime. (The strangler is an anorexic teenybopper.)
- **SPILL ALL:** The villain, *for no apparent reason*, begins to talk-talk-talk, spilling every detail about the crime.
- **AND THEN I WOKE UP:** This is an ending that suggests that the rest of the book was a dream or didn't really happen.
- **IF ONLY I'D KNOWN:** Yeah, you could have solved it, too, if the narrator hadn't withheld key information.
- **OUT OF SIGHT:** The all-important confrontation takes place offstage.
- **BUT, BUT, BUT:** The ending fails to tie up all the loose ends and explain how and why everything happened.
- **YEAH, RIGHT:** The ending leaves the reader to assume that some key part of what happened was coincidental.

ON YOUR OWN: WRITING THE CLIMAX

1. Write the climax to your novel. Try to include these elements:

- **THE PROTAGONIST HITS BOTTOM.** Pile on the woes.
- **THE PROTAGONIST REBOUNDS.** Open up the turning point from despair to determination.
- **THE VILLAIN REVEALS WHAT HAPPENED, OR THE PROTAGONIST PUTS IT TOGETHER.** Make it logical and believable, and give the sleuth a pivotal role in coaxing the villain to reveal the what, where, how, and why.
- **THE VILLAIN IS VANQUISHED (OR NOT).** Disaster averted. Some form of justice is served.

2. As you write, bring the investigation and your protagonist's journey to a satisfying conclusion. You should be able to answer these questions: Does the protagonist reach his goal? How is the protagonist transformed by solving this crime?

CHAPTER 24

WRITING THE CODA

"Readers don't want to guess the ending, but they don't want
to be so baffled that it annoys them."

—Sue Grafton

■ ■ ■

Mystery novels usually end with a final scene or two of reflection. I call it the
coda. It contains the final resolution or clarification of the plot. Coming after the
book's pull-out-all-the-stops final climax, the coda is like a cleansing breath after vigorous exercise. It's a chance to tie up loose ends. The coda might be nothing more than dialogue between two characters talking about what happened.
It might be an extended internal dialogue in which your main character thinks
about the events of the story. It might include a lighthearted scene between your
protagonist and the love interest. By the end of the coda, all of your plot's puzzle
pieces should fit snugly together.

THE FINAL CODA: AN EXCERPT

Here's part of the ending of Raymond Chandler's *The Big Sleep*, a novel about
pornography and blackmail, and one of the first classics of the hard-boiled genre.
As you read, think about how the main character's introspection puts the story
in perspective and provides a sense of closure.

> I got into my car and drove off down the hill.
>
> What did it matter where you lay once you were dead? In a dirty sump or in
> a marble tower on top of a high hill? You were dead, you were sleeping the big

sleep, you were not bothered by things like that. Oil and water were the same as wind and air to you. You just slept the big sleep, not caring about the nastiness of how you died or where you fell. Me, I was part of the nastiness now. Far more a part of it than Rusty Regan was. But the old man didn't have to be. He could lie quiet in his canopied bed, with his bloodless hands folded on the sheet, waiting. His heart was a brief, uncertain murmur. His thoughts were as gray as ashes. And in a little while he too, like Rusty Regan, would be sleeping the big sleep.

On the way downtown I stopped at a bar and had a couple of double Scotches. They didn't do me any good. All they did was make me think of Silver-Wig, and I never saw her again.

Not much happens here: Detective Philip Marlowe walks out of a house, drives to a bar, and has a couple of drinks. The action itself is irrelevant except to serve as a foil for Marlowe's final bitter reflections. But these poignant paragraphs provide an elegiac coda as Marlowe leaves the story behind figuratively and literally (*I got in my car ...*). He contemplates "the big sleep" to which others have gone and ruminates about the meaning of death (*What did it matter where you lay ...*) and how he's become tainted by what's happened (*I was part of the nastiness now ...*). He stops at a bar and knocks back two double Scotches, presumably to forget, but instead he remembers Silver-Wig, the girl who helped him dodge the big sleep (*... and I never saw her again.*).

PURPOSE OF THE CODA

The final coda should not be a long scene that belabors every point in the story or gives a cumbersome synopsis. It shouldn't introduce new plot strands or new characters. Instead, the coda should bring the protagonist full circle and show the reader how he's been changed by what happened. Here are some of the purposes it can serve:

- **RESOLVE THE MAJOR CONFLICTS.** These include internal conflicts—the dilemmas your main character had to deal with, such as reconciling a past event—as well as external conflicts—the obstacles your protagonist had to overcome to find the killer.
- **ACCOUNT FOR THE FACTS.** This is your last chance to make sure all the important facts are accounted for: why the villain did what he did and who was hiding what secrets.
- **TELL WHAT HAPPENED NEXT.** Clue the reader in on what's happened since the book's climactic action sequence. Did the protagonist survive the wounds

he suffered in the final shoot-out? Has the villain been arraigned? Were the stolen jewels returned to the museum?

- **RESOLVE THE SUBPLOTS …** The coda is a good place to put the finishing touches on any subplots, such as a romance or rivalry between characters.
- **… OR LEAVE A SUBPLOT DANGLING.** You may want to leave a subplot involving your cast of supporting characters unresolved. For example, the detective might be on the brink of connecting with a love interest, or the sleuth might be relegated to desk duty and fighting charges of insubordination at work. Dangling subplots can be carried forward into the next series novel.
- **GET THE SLEUTH'S TAKE ON THE CASE.** Is she satisfied with the outcome? Does she feel justice was served? Does this change her in any fundamental way—does it show that there is hope in this world, or only despair?
- **SAIL OFF INTO THE SUNSET …** The final scene can be a happily-ever-after ending with your characters setting out into a world that's safer because evil has been defeated.
- **… OR LEAVE YOUR HERO OFF BALANCE.** The final scene can leave your protagonist feeling unsettled, with issues to be resolved (in the next book!). Maybe the killer was captured, but the person who put him up to it got away. Maybe your hero did something questionable that he's going to have to live with (killed someone, told lies, put a loved one in mortal danger, slept with the enemy).
- **INJECT A FINAL SHOCKER.** You save a final plot twist for the coda. For example, in one of the final chapters of *Gone Girl,* Nick has left his wife, Amy, and is about to publish a tell-all novel revealing her as a sociopath, when she informs him that she's pregnant with his child. He's stuck. He'll have to stay with her and keep her secrets hidden in order to protect their child.
- **LEAVE THE READER SATISFIED.** The ending need not be a happy one, but it should be satisfying.

FINAL WORDS

The last lines of your book should feel like an ending. One way of doing this is to show your protagonist looking back and looking forward, like the two-faced Janus from Roman mythology, putting the past to rest and moving on. Here are examples of final lines from best-selling mysteries that show the protagonist moving on:

With a deep sigh, George put his car in gear and slowly edged back on to the Scardale road. No matter what the future might hold, it was time to take the first step on the road to burying the past, this time forever. (*A Place of Execution* by Val McDermid)

Overhead, the sky was a brilliant blue. The hot Miami sun warmed hearts and minds and points south. A late-afternoon breeze rattled in the palms and caused the water of Biscayne Bay to gently lap against the boat hull. Life was good in Florida. And okay, so I was going back to working on cars. Truth is, I was pretty happy with it. I was looking forward to working on Hooker's equipment. I'd seen his undercarriage and it was damn sweet. (*Metro Girl* by Janet Evanovich)

She walked away from that building of captive souls. Ahead was her car, and the road home. She did not look back. (*Body Double* by Tess Gerritsen)

Spend time crafting your final sentences. Make them memorable, and leave readers looking forward to your next book.

✎ NOW YOU TRY: WRITE THE FINAL CODA   24.1

A final coda is a workhorse of a scene, so a little housekeeping is needed to make sure it provides a satisfying conclusion to your novel. Make a list of everything you want the ending to accomplish.

ELEMENTS OF A CODA	WHAT YOU WANT YOUR CODA TO INCLUDE
Fills the reader in on what happened since the climactic scene	
Ties up loose ends	
Ends subplots	

Deliberately leaves subplots dangling	
Communicates the protagonist's feelings about the resolution	

⬇ Download a printable version of this worksheet at www.writersdigest.com/writing-and-selling-your-mystery-novel-revised.

🖊 ON YOUR OWN: THE FINAL CODA

1. Decide the backdrop for the coda: What action will take place while your characters reflect on what happened?
2. Write the coda. Use this checklist to guide you:

____ Tell what's happened since the last climactic scene.

____ Summarize the resolution, and communicate the protagonist's feelings about how things turned out.

____ Resolve any loose plot and subplots.

____ Tell what happened since the climactic final scene.

____ Make the final lines sing.

PART III

REVISING

"What's nice about writing is
that nothing's set in stone till it's
finished. It's only then that you
hang yourself out to dry."

—Evan Hunter (a.k.a. Ed McBain)

When I type THE END on a first draft, I celebrate. *Ta-dah!* Strike up the band! Break open the champagne! The hardest part (for me) is over, and the fun is about to begin.

Not everyone shares my enthusiasm for revision. But whether you love it, loathe it, or fall somewhere between those two extremes, there's one thing we can all agree on: No one writes a publishable first draft. Plot and characterization are bound to need fixing; word choice, spelling, and grammar will surely need to be tweaked.

So when you've finished the manuscript, take a moment to pat yourself on the back. Print out the manuscript and set it aside, taking a week or two off to recuperate—you need a break so you'll be able to look at your work with fresh eyes. Then dive into the next phase: revision.

My revision strategy, in a nutshell, is to *take a cleansing breath and then work from large to small.*

1. **BACK UP YOUR MANUSCRIPT.** You should, of course, have been doing this all along, but if you haven't, make a backup copy. You can back up the file to a backup drive on your personal computer, but also back it up to device that's *not* in your house. I e-mail mine to myself and also back it up to cloud storage. If you use a service to put it in the cloud, be sure you understand whether the service will encrypt the file and protect your privacy.

2. **PRINT IT OUT, AND TAKE A BREAK.** You've run the spell-checker, fussed with the margins, and altered the font to see how that changes the page count. One day you love it; the next day all you see are flaws. You know the truth lies somewhere in between. To revise effectively, you need perspective, so print the whole thing out and take a break for a week or two at least. Go fishing, build a birdhouse, take a trip to New Jersey—anything to keep yourself from picking at the manuscript.

3. **PREPARE TO SLASH AND BURN: OPEN THE OUT FILE.** It can be hard to murder your darlings—to delete those cherished words you labored over. So make it easier. Instead of throwing words away, set them aside for safekeeping. If you haven't already done so while you were writing, create an OUT file now where you can paste any words that you cut from your manuscript. If you change your mind later, you'll know where to find them.

4. **FLY HIGH OVER YOUR MANUSCRIPT; IDENTIFY THE BIG CHANGES NEEDED.** Reread the manuscript and, at the same time, give it to a few trust-

ed readers to critique. Compile a list of major revisions needed, such as plot shifts, character adjustments, or slow spots that need firming up.

5. **MAKE THE BIG FIXES.** Rewrite, handling the biggest issues first and working your way down to smaller ones.

6. **FLY LOW OVER YOUR MANUSCRIPT; IDENTIFY THE SMALL CHANGES NEEDED.** Read your revision, and do a careful line edit. Clean up the spelling, grammar, and punctuation; remove redundancies; improve your word choices; tweak dialogue; clarify unintended ambiguities.

7. **START OVER.** Take it from the top! Repeat the entire process until you're certain that the manuscript is as good and as squeaky-clean as you can get it.

How long does revision take? This varies greatly from writer to writer and project to project, but revising a first novel can take as long or longer than it took to write. I wrote my first novel in a year and revised it for three. Really. After ten published novels, I take at least ten months to write and ten weeks to revise, and often I wish I could take longer.

How good is good enough? This is one of the hardest questions to answer. How do you know when a manuscript is finished and you can stop revising? It's a gut feeling, based on your own instincts and feedback from trusted readers. Many writers hire a freelance editor to give their manuscript a thumbs-up or thumbs-down and a final polish. I recommend this, especially if you plan to self-publish.

Is there such a thing as too much revision? There's certainly such a thing as revising the wrong stuff. That's what happens when you hear a writer say, "I rewrote it and sucked the life out of it." The trick is to figure out what's not working and fix it, and to figure out what is working and leave it alone.

The chapters in this section provide advice for how to thoroughly revise your manuscript so it's ready to be launched.

CHAPTER 25

FLYING HIGH

FLYING HIGH

Fixing Plot and Character

"My pencils outlast their erasers."

—Vladimir Nabokov

It's tempting to open up your document and start editing, tweaking word choices and punching up sentences. Sure, you could do that, or you could take a more strategic approach and look first at the big picture. That's not an easy task when we're talking about a 260- to 400-page manuscript.

This chapter suggests ways to *fly high* over your manuscript, focusing on the big fixes needed. After that, read through subsections, focusing on specific aspects that need pulled apart and addressed.

I recommend three techniques for this process:

1. Reread from start to finish, examining the main plot and central character; list the changes you need to think about making.
2. Create a scene-by-scene outline, and analyze the chronology and pacing.
3. Take multiple selective read-throughs, leapfrogging through your manuscript so you can isolate and examine subplots and characters.

REREADING FROM START TO FINISH: EXAMINING THE MAIN PLOT AND MAIN CHARACTER

After you've let your manuscript cool for a few weeks, reread it from start to finish. During the read-through, take notes and keep a running list of suggestions for changes. Pay special attention to these aspects of your novel:

• THE MAIN PLOT

- Does your plot unfold logically and believably, without resorting to coincidence? Would these characters do what your novel has them do?
- Are there at least three major plot twists (turning points where attention is diverted to an innocent suspect or where the murder seems to be something that it isn't)?
- Have you planted all the clues in the story so the solution is plausible?
- Have you camouflaged the clues well and distracted the reader's attention with red herrings so the ending is a surprise?
- Have you played fair with the reader and shared what your point-of-view character knows?
- By the final page, have you explained whodunit, why, and how, and tied up all the loose ends?

• POINT OF VIEW

- Whether you've chosen to write in the first person or third, from single or multiple points of view, have you adhered consistently to your choices?
- Can you strengthen each narrator's voice and make it more consistent throughout the novel?

• THE MAIN CHARACTER

- Have you adequately established why this particular protagonist *needs* to solve this particular crime without resorting to a backstory dump in the first act?
- Have you given your character a sufficiently rich inner life so the reader knows both how she behaves and also what she thinks?
- Are your character's dialogue, inner dialogue, and behavior throughout the book consistent with his personality?
- Does your character actively do the detecting to solve the mystery?
- Have you raised the stakes for the protagonist as the story moves forward?
- Are all the heroics your character undertakes consistent with who she is?
- Near the end, does your character hit the wall? Is he out of options, feeling despair, or certain that there's no way out?
- Is there a satisfying confrontation in which the protagonist defeats the villain?
- By the end, have you resolved your character's inner journey as well as solved the mystery?

- **THE VILLAIN**

  - Have you established a convincing reason why the villain committed the crime(s)?
  - Have you given the villain a sufficiently major role in the novel so that the reader has a shot at guessing his identity?
  - Did you make the villain seem innocent through most of the novel so the revelation of guilt comes as a surprise?
  - Did you lay the groundwork for guilt so the revelation seems plausible?

CREATING A SCENE OUTLINE

A *scene outline* is a useful tool for looking at the big picture. While I'm rereading my manuscript, I put together this outline. For each scene, my outline contains these elements:

- the basic chronology, including when the scene takes place and how much time has elapsed since the start of the novel
- a brief overview of what happens in the scene
- the payoff: what this scene contributes to the plot

Keep your scene outline spare. If you include too much detail, you defeat the purpose of this tool, which is to give you a bird's-eye view of your novel. The example below is the beginning of a scene-by-scene outline for my novel *Never Tell a Lie.*

SCENE OUTLINE FOR *NEVER TELL A LIE*				
CHAPTER	SCENE	DATE AND TIME ELAPSED	DAY/TIME	MAIN PLOT POINTS
1	1	11/1, Day 1	Saturday morning	Yard sale. Ivy (9 months pregnant) gives oddly intense Melinda, whom she knew from high school (also 9 months pregnant), green-glass swan. David takes Melinda inside to see the house.
2	2	Cont'd	Saturday afternoon	Ivy and Jody on the phone. They remember Melinda as odd and needy in high school.

2	3	Cont'd	Saturday evening	Ivy and David take a bath. Her good-luck necklace gets snagged on a towel, and David helps her take it off. She gets green-glass splinter in her foot.
3	4	11/2, Day 2	Sunday early morning	Ivy vacuums attic. Neighbor Mrs. Bindel foists Mr. Vlaskovic's trunk off on her.
4	5	Cont'd	Sunday morning	Ivy and David look in the trunk. Find photos, silver, wedding dress, letters, straitjacket.
4	6	Cont'd	Sunday night	Ivy cleans silver she's keeping from trunk. Sees someone rummaging in the trunk, which is out on the street for garbage pickup. Realizes her good-luck necklace is missing.
5	7	Cont'd	Sunday night	Ivy looks for necklace but can't find it. Tells David she saw someone out at the curb looking in the trunk.

Once you've outlined your entire book, problems with your novel's time line will become more obvious. Here are some aspects to check for:

- **EVERY SCENE EARNS ITS KEEP:** A scene that doesn't *move the story forward* in some significant way may need to be cut or combined with another scene that does.
- **MISSING PIECES:** The outline will show you where pieces of your story are missing. Keep a list of scenes to write or existing scenes that need to be augmented.
- **REPEAT PERFORMANCES:** You've inadvertently delivered the same information twice.
- **CONTINUITY ERRORS:** If you've written a scene that takes place on a Monday, and the next day your character is reading the comics in the Sunday paper, there's a problem.
- **CLUTTERED DAYS:** Be sure you haven't packed twenty hours' worth of events between sunrise and sunset. If you've overfilled time, revise to spread out the events.
- **SNOWING IN SUMMER:** Make sure the weather is right for that time of year and geographic location. If your characters are running around Phoenix in August, be sure they're kvetching about the heat.

- **SUNRISE AND SUNSET:** Check that the sun goes down and comes up when it should. If your character is coming home at 6:30 P.M. in February in the northern hemisphere, it should be dark outside.
- **THE DOMINO EFFECT:** A chronology fix in one scene may require you to adjust the chronology in surrounding scenes.

Use a Scene Outline to Check the Pacing

Pacing is critical to a mystery novel. You want reviewers to proclaim that your story is a page-turner! That doesn't mean that it zooms along at high speed from start to finish. Instead, it needs to be well modulated with ups and downs, and to pick up steam as it reaches the final climax.

As you read your draft, ask yourself: Does the novel bog down in places, or does nonstop action go on for pages and pages, leaving your reader numb? Analyze your scene outline to pinpoint the source of these pacing issues.

✎ NOW YOU TRY: EVALUATE PACING

Get a red, a yellow, and a green highlighting marker. These colors represent the colors in a stoplight: red for stop, yellow for caution, and green for go. Highlight the main plot points in the outline to indicate the intensity of the scene:

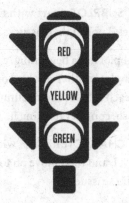

- RED for slower sections that are primarily narrative, basic investigation, and reflection
- YELLOW for rising tension and suspense
- GREEN for action and plot twists

Now lay the pages of your outline on the floor, stand back, and assess your work.

A well-paced novel has rising and falling tension; in other words, scenes with high suspense and action are modulated by scenes of investigation and reflection. Plot twists are spaced out. So you want to see:

- More RED in the first third
- More GREEN in the final third
- A mix of RED, GREEN, and YELLOW throughout

If too many scenes in a row are highlighted with RED, look at ratcheting up the suspense and action so the reader doesn't fall asleep. If you have scene after scene highlighted with YELLOW, you may want to modulate the pace by inserting a scene or two that's primarily reflection. If all your GREEN scenes are bunched together, you should think about restructuring your novel to space them out.

DOING SELECTIVE READ-THROUGHS

Leapfrogging through your manuscript allows you to read and evaluate related passages. It's also a good way to differentiate plot issues from character issues.

Your scene-by-scene outline provides a useful guide for selecting scenes to reread each time through.

- **READ THROUGH BY SUBPLOT.** Start with the largest subplot, and then move on to smaller ones. Look at these issues:

  - Check that each subplot has a beginning, a middle, and an end.
  - Check that each subplot is either resolved or deliberately left unresolved.
  - Consider whether each subplot can be eliminated without damaging the rest of the story. If so, consider deleting it.

- **READ THROUGH BY CHARACTER.** Start with the character that has the largest role in your novel, and then move on to the ones who play more secondary roles. Look at these issues:

  - Is the character consistently portrayed, from hair color to hygiene, dress code to posture?
  - Does the character have a distinctive look and feel? How can you shade the character's dialogue and mannerisms to make her more vivid without creating a cliché?

- Is the character a stereotype? How can you sand the character's edges to make him less of a cliché?
- Does this character change? How can you show the change more effectively?
- Is this character hiding something? Is it too obvious? How can you suggest that more effectively?
- Consider whether the character could be eliminated or combined without damaging the rest of the story.

ON YOUR OWN: FLYING HIGH 25.1

Reread your manuscript, and make a list of changes needed.

1. Create a scene-by-scene outline using this format. Use the outline to check the chronology and pacing of your novel; add to your list of needed revisions.

CHAPTER #	SCENE #	ELAPSED TIME	SEASON/ DAY/TIME	MAIN PLOT POINTS

2. Selectively read through the manuscript, each time looking at a particular subplot or individual characters. Add to your list of needed revisions.
3. Prioritize revisions, starting with big issues that cut across the book and then moving to issues that affect a single chapter or scene.
4. Revise.

CHAPTER 26

FLYING LOW

Polishing Scenes and Sentences

"I cut adjectives, adverbs, and every word which is there just to make an effect. Every sentence which is there just for the sentence."

—Georges Simenon

■ ■ ■

You've made the big changes your manuscript needs. You've written a killer story with twists and turns tuned to perfection. Your protagonist's journey is carefully wrought and fraught. The secrets and surprises are strategically placed. Your characters are as entertaining and interesting as you can make them. Now you're ready to fly low and examine every scene, every paragraph, every sentence, polishing that manuscript to within an inch of its life.

Some final polishing can be done directly in the electronic file. But there's no substitute for reading and editing the printed manuscript. Somehow, errors that slip past on the computer screen seem to pop off the printed page.

Expect to go through your manuscript at least three times during the line-editing phase.

TURNING *TELLS* INTO *SHOWS*

Writers are advised to *show; don't tell*. When the writer uses a generic, bland shorthand to describe a character, they are telling. For instance:

- He was scared.
- She was uneducated and poor.
- It was a typical yuppie apartment.
- He oozed charm.

Use telling details instead. For instance, in *Edge of Dark Water*, Joe R. Lansdale could have said, "Uncle Gene and Daddy didn't look much like brothers, but each of them was pretty gross." Instead, he wrote:

> Uncle Gene was fat as a hog, but without the personality. Still, he was a big man in height and had broad shoulders and arms about the size of a horse's neck. Daddy didn't even look kin to him. He was a skinny peckerwood with a potbelly, and if you ever saw him without a cap it was cause it had rotted off his head. He and Uncle Gene had about eighteen teeth between them, and Daddy had most of them. Mama said it was because they didn't brush their teeth enough and they chewed tobacco. There were times when I looked at their sunken faces and was reminded of an old pumpkin rotting in the field. I know it's a sad thing to be so repulsed by your own kin, but there you have it, straight out and in the open.

Writers also resort to telling when they spell out for the reader what the character feels. You could write, "Janey was uncomfortable in the situation," but it's better to dramatize the situation and show what Janey does and says, and leave the reader to intuit Janey's discomfort.

Summarizing action that would be better dramatized is another kind of telling. If the first act of your novel has your character planning a bank robbery, you don't want to write, "On Saturday he robbed the bank and got away with $5,000 in cash, but one of the tellers recognized him." With all that buildup to the bank robbery, you need to dramatize it.

Sometimes it's okay to tell. Here are a few reasons:

- **TO MAINTAIN A FAST PACE:** Use telling to convey something the reader needs to know without dwelling on it (*We waited for more than an hour for the bus …*).
- **TO AVOID REPEATING SOMETHING YOU'VE ALREADY SHOWN TO THE READER:** If you've dramatized an event, you can summarize it later in the story (*Janey explained what happened, leaving out the part about …*).
- **TO PUNCH A SCENE ENDING AND PROPEL THE STORY FORWARD** (*Then I saw smoke.*)

Look for places in your manuscript where you used generic description, summary, or shorthand to tell the reader about an important character or situation. Decide whether to revise (and show) or leave it as is.

PUMPING UP THE VERBS

Throughout the manuscript, especially in suspense and action scenes, pay special attention to your verb choices.

Vary Physical Reactions

Look out for characters who are forever smiling, frowning, nodding, or shaking their heads. The occasional smile or shake of the head is fine, but the rest of the time, try to come up with more telling and dramatic ways of showing a character's response. Here are three strong examples from Carol O'Connell's *Winter House*:

> "No." She shivered slightly, as if awakening and shaking off dreams. "No, I don't."

> "Was she *insane?*" Bitty's hand flew up to cover her mouth, as if she had just committed a social faux pas, calling attention to an infirmity in front of a cripple.

> "You what?" The vacuum cleaner switched off, and Mrs. Ortega observed a moment of silent disbelief.

Replace Bland Verbs

Some verbs are bland and generic. Whenever you find one anchoring a sentence, consider replacing it with a verb that more vividly shows what's happening.

EXAMPLES OF BLAND VERBS

is	get	have
look	make	move
put	see	take
watch	go	

Here is a sentence with a bland verb and some examples of alternate versions:

BLAND VERB	STRONGER VERSIONS
She *was* in the hall.	She *stood* in the hall.
	She *fidgeted* in the hall.
	She *lounged* in the hall.
	She *lingered* in the hall.
	She *cooled her heels* in the hall.

Pick the Verb That Best Conveys Action and Attitude

When you tweak the verb choice, the action takes on an entirely different meaning. For example, look at this sentence with generic verbs:

> He *got out* of his car and *went* to the front door.

If you want to show a man on a mission:

> He *stepped* from his car and *marched* up the front walk.

If you want to show a drunk coming home from a debauched overnight:

> He *heaved* himself from his car and *stumbled* up the front walk.

On the other hand, if this is a man who's trying to beat the clock:

> He *leapt* from his car and *raced* up the front walk.

Only you know what you're trying to convey. Pick the verbs that show the action and attitude you're aiming for.

Don't Get Carried Away

A word of caution: Don't mangle a perfectly good sentence with an overabundance of creativity. For example, I'd stick with the bland, generic "He got out of his car and went to the front door" rather than this purple alternative:

> He *exploded* from his car and *thundered* up the front walk.

Exploded suggests flying body parts, and *thundered* is a sound, not a quick movement. These are swell verbs, but they don't work in this context.

FERRETING OUT -*ING* VERBS

Action is often stronger when it's conveyed with the active form of the verb. Contrast these sentences:

> He was racing to the car.

> He raced to the car.

With the active verb, *raced,* the sentence feels more direct, the action more active.

To find the –*ing* verbs in your manuscript, use the *Find* feature of your word processor. Enter "ing " (with the trailing blank space), and click FIND to locate –*ing* verbs in the middle of sentences. Enter "ing." (with the trailing period) to locate *-ing* verbs at the end of sentences. Don't remove *every -ing* verb from your manuscript, but look at each one and ask yourself: *Would this sentence be stronger using the active form of the verb?* If so, revise.

WEEDING OUT -LY ADVERBS

Writers sometimes try to pump up bland verbs with *-ly* adverbs (such as *walked quickly, sat lazily,* or *moved painstakingly*). Don't. Here are two ways to revise a verb-adverb combo:

- **REPLACE THE ADVERB WITH A VERB THAT BETTER CONVEYS THE ACTION BEING TAKEN.** *Ambled, marched, shuffled, trundled, staggered, stumbled, goose-stepped*—these can all be used to show how someone walked.
- **REPLACE THE ADVERB WITH MORE DESCRIPTIVE ACTION.** It takes more words, but the dramatic impact is much stronger. For example:

VERB-ADVERB COMBO	REVISION WITH MORE DESCRIPTIVE ACTION
He moved painstakingly.	He grimaced and held his side as he hunched forward and took one step, then another.

To find *-ly* adverbs in your manuscript, use the *Find* feature of your word processor. Enter "ly " (with the trailing blank space), and click FIND to locate adverbs embedded in sentences. Enter "ly." (with the trailing period) to find *-ly* adverbs at the ends of sentences. As each adverb comes up, evaluate whether you want to revise it.

PUMPING UP THE DIALOGUE

Read passages of dialogue *aloud* to identify problem areas:

- **IF IT SOUNDS WOODEN AND ARTIFICIAL:** Revise it. Dialogue should sound like someone talking. Sentence fragments and slang belong in dialogue.
- **IF IT GOES ON FOR TOO LONG:** Cut some of the dialogue and summarize the dull but essential bits.
- **IF CHARACTERS SOUND ALIKE:** Revise to give each character a unique voice. Shape the character's personality through careful word choice and sentence structure as well as content.

- **IF IT SOUNDS FLAT AND UNINTERESTING:** Choose more appropriate words; use more physical presencing (such as a gesture or an action with a prop) to show each character's emotions.
- **IF IT'S UNPRODUCTIVE:** Kill unnecessary chitchat. Get rid of any dialogue that doesn't serve your story. Just because someone would have said it doesn't mean it belongs in the book.

PLAYING WITH ATTRIBUTION AND ACTION THAT ACCOMPANY DIALOGUE

Dialogue is more than the words that appear within quotation marks. There's the attribution (*he said*) and the physical action that goes along with it. Here are some tips for revising those aspects of dialogue:

- **USE *SAID* AND *ASKED*.** These two bland verbs *belong in your manuscript*. *Said* and *asked* invisibly serve up dialogue and should only occasionally be replaced with fancier verbs (*exclaimed, denied, demanded, whispered*).

- **DON'T USE ATTRIBUTIONS UNRELATED TO SPEECH.** What's wrong with this sentence?

    "Help me," she gasped.

Verbs like *gasped, hummed,* or *shuddered* sometimes get stuck in the place of *said*. The problem is, these words don't have anything to do with the act of speaking. A simple fix is to put the spoken words in their own sentence, followed by the non-spoken words (the action) in their own sentence:

    "Help me." She gasped.

Another fix is to relegate the action to its own comma-delimited phrase:

    "Help me," she said, gasping.

- **MAKE SURE THE SPEAKER IS CLEAR.** Whenever you write *he said* or *she said*, it should be crystal clear to the reader who *he* or *she* is. If it isn't, then say who's talking:

    "I don't think so," Linda said.

Or show who's talking with action on the same line alongside the dialogue:

    Linda folded her arms and glared at me. "I don't think so."

- **ELIMINATE ATTRIBUTION WHEREVER POSSIBLE.** Once you get a back-and-forth going between two characters, you don't need *Anne said* or *Linda said* because it's obvious to the reader that the speakers are taking turns.

- **BREAK UP DIALOGUE WITH BITS OF ACTION.** You can alter the dramatic impact of dialogue by breaking it up with movement and physical detail. Below are three versions of identical content. Read them, and consider which is most powerful:

> "Are you going to leave me? Because I need to know now." She stood in the doorway, hands on her hips.

> She stood in the doorway, hands on her hips. "Are you going to leave me? Because I need to know now."

> "Are you going to leave me?" She stood in the doorway, hands on her hips. "Because I need to know now."

I think the last one is the strongest because the reader gets a picture of this woman's stance just before she delivers her ultimatum: *Because I need to know now.* The placement of the action reinforces the words, pumps up the drama, and makes that final line of dialogue seem more confrontational. Play with of bits of dialogue, attribution, and physical presencing in your prose to see what order best dramatizes your story.

NOW YOU TRY: COMBINE DIALOGUE AND ACTION 26.1

DIALOGUE: "Don't move. If you do, I'm going to have to shoot you."
ACTION: The gun trembled as he gripped it with both hands.

Combine the elements and circle the version you feel is most effective.

⬇ Download a printable version of this worksheet at www.writersdigest.com/writing-and-selling-your-mystery-novel-revised.

WEEDING OUT CLICHÉS

A cliché is a phrase that's so overused it feels trite. Unfortunately, even the best word processor won't find these. That's too bad, because my first drafts are riddled with them. I'm forever having characters "batten down the hatches," "eat like a pig," "chomp at the bit," or feel "cool as a cucumber."

If you have a character who's a pompous windbag, then it's fine to let him spout clichés. But strew them in your narrative and you're the one who will seem like a bag of wind.

Clichés often sneak in when you're trying to be eloquent or smart. Inspect the metaphors and similes in your writing for clichés. Then follow these strategies to eliminate them.

Replace Clichés with Fresh, New Images or Metaphors

Here are three examples of some surprising nonclichés from *Citizen Vince* by Jess Walter:

> Game over and Vince is flush, counting a roll of bills as big as a pair of socks.

> Vince can feel his train of thought getting away.

> Regan's kid looks like a bookkeeper approaching middle age, just this side of respectability, even in a coat and tie.

Replace Clichés with More Descriptive Terms

Instead of telling us that a character "ate like a pig," show the gravy stains on his tie, the open-mouthed chewing, the fist-held fork. Show him hunched over the plate and grunting.

STARTING AND FINISHING STRONG

Readers who skim through the middles of scenes land with a thump on the first and last sentences. Initial and final impressions matter. They linger in the reader's mind and are worth your time to fine-tune.

Here are some places to focus your attention:

- **PAGE 1, PARAGRAPH 1**

  - Does your book open with a strong first line?
  - Is the first paragraph strong?
  - Is the first scene strong?

- **START AND END OF EACH SCENE**

  - Does each scene start with a strong opening line and paragraph?
  - Do you establish early in each scene where we are, when it is, and which characters are present?
  - Does each scene feel finished at the end—either with a settled or cliffhanger ending?

- **THE FIRST TIME A SETTING IS INTRODUCED**

  - The first time each interior or exterior setting is used, is it described and brought to life?
  - Is the setting consistent each time your story returns there?

- **THE FIRST TIME A CHARACTER IS INTRODUCED**

  - Is the character's physical presence established and expressed with a few telling details?
  - Is that character's appearance, behavior, and dialogue consistent each time that character reappears?

- **LAST PAGE, LAST PARAGRAPH**

  - Does your book end with a strong final scene?
  - Is the final paragraph strong?
  - Does the final line resonate?

LOOKING FOR TICS

We all have images or actions we overuse. In my prose, I tend to use the word *shrouded* whenever something in a scene is covered or obscured by shadows. In a novel I read not long ago, the writer described several of the female characters—and a dog—as *petite*. Unnecessary words like *just* and *very* may also lard your manuscript.

The better, more striking and unusual an image or turn of phrase, the more the reader will notice when you overuse it. Find your own overused words and expressions and replace them.

STRIVING FOR CONSISTENCY

The devil is in the details, and all details cry out for consistency. Read your manuscript carefully with an eye toward the following:

- **CONTINUITY:** Does a character stand up from a chair and then, two paragraphs later, stand up again? Do two characters drink wine but only one wine glass ends up in the sink? Does the coat a character hung up when entering the house show up folded over the back of a chair when he leaves? Readers notice, and the avid mystery reader will interpret your inconsistency as a clue.
- **GEOGRAPHY:** If you're using real locations, check that the details are correct. Make sure there really is a Starbucks with parking where your characters stop to have coffee.
- **TIME FRAME:** Your time frame should be logical and consistent. A scene that takes place in the morning shouldn't end with car headlights shifting across the living room window. Don't make your character drive an hour to get somewhere that's really four hours away.
- **NAMES:** Be consistent about what each narrator calls each character. Suppose that in scene one, Bill is narrating and says, "Patricia opened the door." From then on, when Bill narrates he should refer to her as "Patricia"—not "Pat," "Patty," "the accountant," or "Miss Vozelle." Other characters should be consistent in how they refer to her as narrators or in dialogue. Her son might call her "Mom," and her mother might call her "Patty-Joe."
- **CONSISTENCY:** Make sure that the places where your characters hang out don't get inadvertently restructured and redecorated between visits, and that a character who's tall and slender in Act I doesn't inexplicably shrink and grow love handles in Act III.

ELIMINATING HEAD HOPPING

Look for point-of-view slips, and clean them up. If you're telling the story from one character's viewpoint, make sure every scene is written with that character as the narrator. If your story has multiple narrators, each scene should be narrated exclusively by one at a time. You can switch narrators, but do so deliberately by inserting a scene break.

FIXING GRAMMAR, SPELLING, AND PUNCTUATION

"Don't publishers fix grammar and spelling mistakes?" an unpublished writer once asked me.

Sure they do. But leave spelling and grammar errors in your manuscript, and it's an invitation for an editor or agent to jump to the conclusion that you can't write your way out of a paper bag. If you're self-publishing, an error-ridden manuscript is the kiss of death.

Your goal should be to produce a manuscript that's grammatically perfect and free of errors in punctuation and spelling before you send it out into the world. Here's how to reach that goal:

- **RUN THE SPELL-CHECKER.** The electronic spell-checker that comes with your word processing program will find and fix obvious typos.
- **RUN THE GRAMMAR CHECKER.** I know the grammar checker is a pain in the behind because it flags all kinds of "problems" that aren't problems at all. For instance, it will want to fix all your sentence fragments, including the ones in your dialogue where you put them deliberately because that's how your characters talk. Run the grammar checker anyway, and skip over the nonproblems. Along the way, find problems you might otherwise miss—like subject-noun agreement, missing punctuation, and repeated words.
- **READ AND EDIT.** Read your manuscript carefully to find the errors your word processing software misses. Take these sentences, for example:

> *It was he last night in Paris. She wanted to walk the Chance Élysées: and after when that, drink a toast two the passed.*

My spelling and grammar checker flags only one error in those two horrendous sentences—*Élysées*—and that's one of the few words that doesn't need to be corrected.

- **HAVE SOMEONE LINE EDIT FOR YOU.** If you're not great at catching spelling and grammatical errors, give the manuscript to someone who is. Have that person mark up a printout, and then make the changes yourself—you'll get a lesson in spelling and grammar. Remember: This is your novel, so you should be the one to decide which changes to make.

Here's a list of things to check for and revise when you're ready to fly low and look at the details.

Weed Out:

____ Spelling, grammar, and punctuation errors

____ Tired, overused verbs

____ Overused images, actions, or turns of phrase

____ Clichés

____ –ing verbs

____ –ly adverbs

____ Wooden, artificial-sounding dialogue

____ Overlong passage of dialogue

____ Unnecessary chitchat

____ Optimal placement of attribution and action with dialogue

____ Unnecessary he said/she said

____ Inconsistencies in time, place, and naming

Polish:

____ Turn tells into shows.

____ Make each major character's dialogue distinctive.

____ Break up dialogue with bits of action.

____ Fine-tune the beginnings and endings of scenes.

____ Describe and establish each setting the first time it appears.

____ Describe and establish each character the first time he or she appears.

____ Keep the point of view from sliding.

CHAPTER 27

SEEKING CRITICISM AND FINDING YOUR OWN FIX

"I hated this book! The writing is so dense it is like trying to read pea soup. The characters were confusing and undeveloped, and the plot ... was there one?"

—an anonymous reader reviews a mystery novel on barnesandnoble.com

■■■

All of us find it hard to hear criticism, especially after having labored for months and poured heart and soul into a manuscript. We want to hear an unqualified "Wow! Your book is more compelling than *Gone Girl* and better written than *The Maltese Falcon*."

Instead we might hear, "Well, I'm not too sure about the ending." Or "Why is your main character so annoying?" Or my favorite: "I don't usually read books like this, so maybe that's why I didn't get it. I mean, why doesn't she just call the police?"

You'll find yourself wanting to interrupt, jump up and down on the table, and explain what you were aiming for. You'll want to yank your gentle reader by the throat and say, "Yeah, right—I'd like to see you try to write a novel."

Worse still, you'll defend your book so loudly that you won't hear what this well-meaning soul, whose only major misstep in life thus far has been to offer to read your manuscript, is trying to tell you. You owe it to yourself, and to anyone who's generous enough to critique your manuscript, to at least listen to and try to understand their feedback.

TAKING CRITICISM

Here are some tips to help you hear what readers are telling you:

- **DON'T INTERRUPT.** To get the most out of a critique, you have to hear and understand what the person is saying. If you keep interrupting, getting defensive, and explaining what you were trying to do, you keep yourself from hearing the criticism. Remember, listening doesn't mean that you have to agree or follow the suggestions the critic offers. You get to decide which criticisms you're going to address and how you're going to address them. *But you owe it to yourself and to your reader to shut up and listen.*
- **ASK CLARIFYING QUESTIONS.** If you're not sure, ask. If your critic says, "I loved the book," ask for specifics of strong sections and favorite elements. If your critic says, "That character seemed flighty," ask for examples. If your reader says, "I didn't understand the ending," ask the critic to summarize how your novel ended so you can see how or why it was misunderstood.
- **TAKE NOTES.** The mind has a wonderful ability to block out pain, so don't assume you'll remember what your critic tells you. Taking notes has an added benefit: It gives you something to do while you're not interrupting. It's odd how comments that seem absurd or infuriating when you first hear them gain validity when you look at them in the cool light of reason, days or even weeks later.

ASKING FOR THE FEEDBACK

You're more likely to get useful comments if you establish advance readers' expectations before giving them your manuscript to critique. For instance, if you want them to line edit, say so. I usually tell advance readers not to sweat the small stuff—though most writers are physically incapable of letting a typo go by without correcting it.

Ask your advance readers to put comments on the manuscript itself and, when they're done, to jot down some high-level reactions, summarizing what they liked and disliked. Then have a good long talk, going through their comments to be sure you understand their reactions.

Here's a list of topics and questions you might discuss with advance readers.

- **OVERALL REACTION:** Best aspects? Weakest aspects?
- **DRAMATIC OPENING:** Did the first scene grab your attention? Did it make you want to keep reading and set up the rest of the story for you?
- **MAIN PLOT:** Is it plausible? Easy to follow? Surprising? Did it hold your interest?
- **SUBPLOTS:** Are they engaging? Plausible? Easy to follow? Do they feel like they belong in the novel? Are they sufficiently resolved at the end?
- **ENDING:** Is the resolution clear? Believable? Surprising?
- **MAIN CHARACTER:** Is the main character believable? Three-dimensional? Sympathetic? Interesting? Did you care about him?
- **VILLAIN:** Does the villain behave logically? Does she seem like a worthy adversary for the main character? Is the motive for the crime(s) clear?
- **OTHER CHARACTERS:** Do they ring true? Hold your interest? Are there any whom you especially liked or found annoying?
- **PACING:** Did the pace keep you reading? What were the slow spots? Were there parts that went by too quickly? Does suspense build? Did it hold your interest throughout?
- **DIALOGUE:** Does each character have a strong, unique voice and sound natural?

Don't settle for yes or no answers. Probe with follow-up questions to get specific feedback on what's working and where problems exist.

 **NOW YOU TRY: GET THE MOST OUT OF THE CRITIQUE**   27.1

Add your own concerns to the list of questions below.

QUESTIONS

1. What did you like or dislike?
2. Is the story holding your interest, or does it bog down in places?
3. Is the story easy to follow or confusing?
4. Did any parts seem implausible? What doesn't make sense?
5. Are there aspects of any of these characters that you especially like or dislike?

6. Were there any characters who didn't ring true? If so, which ones, and how did they seem artificial?

7. Does the story so far seem predictable or surprising?

ADDITIONAL QUESTIONS

8. _____

9. _____

10. _____

11. _____

12. _____

Give the questions and the chapter to a trusted friend or fellow writer. Invite that person to read the material, write her reactions on the manuscript, and think about the questions.

Sit down and discuss the chapter with your reader. Go through the questions. While you're listening, jot down notes about the person's comments along with notes about your personal reactions.

NOTES ON THE CRITIQUE	NOTES ON YOUR REACTION TO THE CRITIQUE

Assess both the critique and your reactions. During the next critique, try to consciously adjust anything you are doing or feeling that might prevent you from getting the most out of the critique.

⬇ Download a printable version of this worksheet at www.writersdigest.com/writing-and-selling-your-mystery-novel-revised.

TRANSLATING COMMENTS INTO REVISIONS

Okay, you've heard the critique. You've got it all written down so that you can consider it rationally. How do you decide what to fix and what to ignore?

There's a scene in one of my all-time favorite mystery novels, *Gaudy Night* by Dorothy L. Sayers, which dramatizes this issue. Harriet Vane has asked Lord Peter Wimsey to read a mystery novel she's writing. She knows something is wrong, but she doesn't know exactly what it is. Peter poses the question she's been dreading:

> "If you ask me," said Wimsey, "it's Wilfrid. I know he marries the girl—but must he be such a mutt? Why does he go and pocket the evidence and tell all those unnecessary lies?"

She defends her hero:

> "I admit that Wilfrid is the world's worst goop. But if he doesn't conceal the handkerchief, where's my plot?"
>
> "Couldn't you make Wilfrid one of those morbidly conscientious people, who have been brought up to think that anything pleasant must be wrong—so that, if he wants to believe the girl an angel of light she is, for that very reason, all the more likely to be guilty. Give him a puritanical father and a hell-fire religion."
>
> "Peter, that's an idea."
>
> "He has, you see, a gloomy conviction that love is sinful in itself, and that he can only purge himself by taking the young woman's sins upon him and wallowing in vicarious suffering ... He'd still be a goop, and a pathological goop, but he would be a bit more consistent."
>
> "Yes—he'd be interesting. But if I give Wilfrid all those violent and lifelike feelings, he'll throw the whole book out of balance."
>
> "You would have to abandon the jig-saw kind of story and write a book about human beings for a change."

This illustrates one of the most difficult questions a reader can ask: Why does a major character do something illogical that's critical to your plot? It's a groaner, because if they ask, you know you have a problem for which there's no simple fix. To make it believable, you may have to alter the character's underlying personality, rework his entire backstory, and integrate the changes into the plot. The revision will cut a huge swath through your book.

Before you slash and burn, corroborate. If you agree with a criticism, then of course you need to address it. If someone else who reads your manuscript mentions the same problem, it should go on your to-do list. If two readers disagree with each other, ask each one to elaborate; the more information you have, the easier it will be to decide whether to address the concern or ignore it.

Next, translate problems into solutions. Here are some examples:

THE READER'S CRITIQUE	THE FIX
Chapter three ends rather abruptly.	Decide whether chapter three should have a cliff-hanger or a settled ending. Then revise the ending so the chapter doesn't feel unfinished.
I knew who did it—I realized Charlie was guilty in the birthday scene.	If the birthday scene is too early for readers to know the villain's identity, then revise the scene. Tone down the clues, and add competing red herrings.
I couldn't tell where this scene takes place.	Establish the setting at the start of the scene.
The wife seemed over the top; no one's *that* evil.	Moderate the wife's dialogue, clothing, mannerisms, and so on to make her more believable and less obviously evil.
Why is your protagonist chasing after the child molester instead of calling the cops?	Establish motivation earlier; add flashbacks showing aspects of Bob's past molestation; establish his distrust of the police; show his growing determination to bring the villain to justice.

THINKING PAST THE OFFERED FIX

Beware of advance readers who bear solutions. An editor once suggested that I rewrite a male main character as a woman. "You write better female characters," she said.

Instead, I tried to figure out what was wrong with the way I'd written my man. I reread my manuscript and realized that every time he found himself in an adversarial situation, he apologized his way out of it. Of course, it's a generalization (true nevertheless), but men are more likely to confront conflict head-on. They're not afraid to get angry or physical when pushed. Apologizing to avoid confrontation is what I tend to do. So rather than revise the character's gender, I rewrote him as a more convincing man.

Carefully consider all the comments you get from readers, but a little red flag should go up whenever someone tells you how to fix your novel. Don't ignore the suggestion, but do try to understand where it's coming from. Ask follow-up questions, and repeat after me: *This is my novel.* You want to know what's working and what's not, and then you can decide yourself what and how to fix.

✏ NOW YOU TRY: FIND YOUR OWN FIX   27.2

Return to the comments you captured during the previous exercise. In the table below, note the reader's main criticisms or suggestions on the left, and note the changes you're going to make on the right.

THE READER'S CRITIQUE	MY FIX

⬇ Download a printable version of this worksheet at www.writersdigest.com/ writing-and-selling-your-mystery-novel-revised.

What Makes a Good Advance Reader?

Who should you ask to critique your manuscript? It's a lot of work to ask of anyone, so you may consider asking a friend or family member to read. Don't. Friends and relatives have feelings about you that will influence what they say about your work. Only an objective, uninvolved reader can give you truly useful feedback, and even then you should be cautious about whom you choose.

A capable critic is someone who's smart, kind, clear thinking, and articulate; someone who reads novels like yours and isn't afraid to tell you the truth. If you're in a good writing group, you're fortunate to have capable critics ready and waiting.

A fellow writer can often frame the strengths and weaknesses of the manuscript in more writerly terms. For example, if the narration is weak, a writer might explain it as a point-of-view issue, whereas the average reader may only be able to tell you that your writing seems tepid.

You need a sufficient number of readers so you can judge whether one reader's reaction is an aberration. On the other hand, you don't want so many that you're overwhelmed with conflicting opinions. I suggest you give your work to at least two readers but not more than four.

A Word About Book Doctors and Freelance Editors

Many writers wonder if it's worthwhile to hire and pay an outside professional editor to bring their book up to snuff. Here are some of the terms you might hear:

- **BOOK DOCTOR:** An independent freelance editor who reads your novel and edits it thoroughly for structure, plot, character development, style, continuity, and so forth.
- **MANUSCRIPT EVALUATION:** The editor reads your entire manuscript and gives you feedback that usually includes strengths, weaknesses, and general suggestions for change.
- **DEVELOPMENTAL EDIT:** The editor reads your novel and notes problems such as structure, pacing, character development, and style. The editor may make revisions or provide you with detailed guidance on how to make the fixes.
- **COPYEDIT:** The editor corrects grammar, spelling, punctuation, usage, and so on. She also catches logical inconsistencies and continuity problems.
- **LINE EDIT:** The editor focuses on the sentences and words, fixing grammar, word choice, punctuation, usage, and spelling.

If you decide to hire someone to edit your book, buyer beware. It's an expensive proposition—running from hundreds of dollars for a basic copyedit to thousands for a thorough developmental edit from an experienced freelance editor. There are scam artists out there, happy to take your money with promises of guaranteed success (there is no such thing).

Hire someone with solid credentials and a good track record. Check out the editor before you commit.

- Ask for a résumé; look for professional editing and/or writing experience.
- Ask for authors the editor has worked with. Call up a few, and chat about their experience with this editor.
- Ask for titles of published books the person has edited; check out the books to see if the editor is thanked on the acknowledgments page.
- Ask to see a sample critique the editor has written. Try to imagine you were the author, and consider whether these comments would be helpful to you.
- Have an extended telephone conversation with the editor. Be sure this is someone with whom you feel comfortable.
- Check for reported problems with this editor on websites like Preditors & Editors (Pred-ed.com) and Science Fiction & Fantasy Writers of America's resource, Writer Beware (www.sfwa.org/other-resources/for-authors/writer-beware). Look for a pattern of complaints, not one squeaky wheel.
- Get a written estimate and contract that defines exactly what the editor will do, the time frame, and the cost.

ON YOUR OWN: SEEKING CRITICISM AND FINDING YOUR OWN FIX

1. Give your manuscript to a few trusted readers.
2. Take notes on their suggestions for changes.
3. Try to hear past their suggested fixes and decide what you think needs to be changed.
4. Sift, prioritize, and make a list of potential revisions.

CHAPTER 28

PREPARING THE FINAL MANUSCRIPT

"When you send something in anything other than Times New Roman 12-point font, I immediately convert to that."

—literary agent Janet Reid, a.k.a. Query Shark

■ ■ ■

You've done everything right. You created a worthy protagonist and wrote a terrific story. You've listened to criticism and revised. You've edited every chapter and polished the words so your prose is squeaky-clean. If your next step is to query agents or editors, you need to prepare a professional-looking, easy-to-read manuscript for submission.

Today, most agents and editors accept manuscripts they've requested as e-mail attachments in a Word or PDF file. To make the best impression, your manuscripts should be formatted the way agents and editors expect.

Begin with a title page, which should contain the title of your book, your name, and your contact information.

MURDER BY THE BOOK

BY VICTOR YABLONSKY

Victor Yablonsky
33 Elm St., Oadale, IL
(011)822-3344 – VictorY@email.net

Here's a checklist for the rest of the manuscript pages:

____ Text: double-spaced, left justified

____ Paragraphs: indent the first line five spaces

____ Margins: 1" to 1.25" on every side

____ Font: Times New Roman, 12 point (You might use other fonts in special circumstances, for instance to set off a text message or show that something is handwritten.)

____ Headers on each page: your name and contact information (phone or e-mail), and the title of the book flush left; page numbers flush right

____ Page numbers: numbered consecutively, not by chapter

____ No footers

____ Remove double spaces (even after a period)

____ Eliminate underlines and bold (use italics for emphasis)

____ Remove tracked changes and comments

____ No copyright notice is necessary; your story is protected under U.S. and International Copyright Laws.

 ON YOUR OWN: REVISE YOUR MANUSCRIPT TO THE PROFESSIONAL STANDARDS

Use the checklist above to format your manuscript to professional standards.

PART IV

PUBLISHING YOUR MYSTERY NOVEL

"Closely akin to the popular delusion … that the construction of the detective story is child's play is an equally unfounded, general belief that the form is a literary gold mine, with financial rewards to the author out of all proportion to the amount of labor involved."

—Howard Haycraft, *Murder for Pleasure: The Life and Times of the Detective Story*

And you thought writing the book was hard. Getting it into the hands of readers is another challenge that requires an entirely different skill set. Now you have to become knowledgeable about the publishing business and make shrewd decisions in support of your book and your writing career.

Over the last decade, publishing has been transformed by the rise of the e-book and the growth of Amazon, the online retailer that now dominates sales of print and digital books. The good news is that crime fiction is surviving the transition nicely, thank you very much. It sells well across all formats, so more publishers are getting in the game and launching new imprints.

One thing hasn't changed: It is still brutally competitive to land a top-tier literary agent and a contract with a solid traditional publishing house. However, with self-publishing, authors no longer need traditional publishers to publish their books.

Traditional or self-publishing? If you're not sure which path is best for you, think about what matters most to you. Prioritize this list, ranking the items from most important (1) to least (7).

____ A higher royalty rate
____ Control over the entire publishing process
____ Speed getting your book to market
____ Low expenses
____ Placement in bookstores
____ Availability in libraries
____ Reviews in trade publications and mainstream media
____ Becoming a *New York Times* best-selling author

The first four items on the list are benefits of self-publishing; the final four are benefits of traditional publishing.

If I were starting over in my career, I'd hedge my bets and pursue both options. I'd finish writing and revising my novel, and query literary agents while I started writing the next one. By the time my next novel was ready to go, I'd know whether traditional publishing had a place for me and whether it was the place I wanted to be.

Here are some terms you need to navigate the turf:

- **TRADITIONAL PUBLISHERS:** Traditional publishers select the books they publish and contract with writers, often through literary agents. They pay

all of the costs associated with bringing a book to market (editing, designing, printing, and distributing.) They pay the writer a royalty for each copy
sold and sometimes an advance against that amount.

- **SMALL INDEPENDENT PUBLISHERS:** Many small presses, referred to as
"independent" because they are not part of larger corporations, publish anywhere from a handful to a couple of dozen books a year. Some follow a traditional publishing business model; others do not.

- **SELF-PUBLISHING (A.K.A. INDIE PUBLISHING):** The author brings the
book to market without going through a publisher. There is no selection process. The author decides which publishing services to use and performs or
contracts out any services needed, like editing, cover design, and printing.

- **VANITY PRESS:** A publisher that requires up-front payment by the author
or a minimum purchase of copies.

- **DIGITAL PUBLISHING:** The published book is an e-book, readable on a computer or e-reader like Kindle, NOOK, iPad, or Kobo. Traditional publishers,
small presses, and self-published authors all have the option to digitally publish. Some mystery imprints are digital only.

- **PRINT-ON-DEMAND (POD):** POD technology enables copies of physical
books to be printed from electronic files and bound on an as-needed basis.
Authors can contract with services that print on demand, though many bookstores will not carry an author's self-published POD books because generally they cannot be returned. Traditional publishers often use POD to keep
print copies of backlist books available. Some brick-and-mortar bookstores
have their own POD printer.

- **DISTRIBUTION CHANNELS:** These are wholesalers that stock and sell print
books and e-books. The largest print book distributors are Ingram and Baker
& Taylor. They wholesale books to booksellers, libraries, and online retailers.
Services that publish and distribute self-published e-books include Amazon
Kindle Direct Publishing, Smashwords, and BookBaby.

- **LITERARY AGENT:** These are professionals who represent authors. They shop
their authors' manuscripts to prospective publishers and negotiate book deals
on their authors' behalves. They take a cut of the author's earnings on the
deals they negotiate, typically 15 percent (20 percent for subrights like foreign translations and film/TV).

- **QUERY:** A letter, often accompanied by a brief synopsis or opening chapter, that pitches a novel to an agent or editor. Most agents and editors want to see a query first, and if it piques their interest, they will request more. Some want to be queried by e-mail, others by snail mail. Typically they post instructions on how to query them on their websites.
- **UNSOLICITED MANUSCRIPTS:** When a *publisher* says it won't consider unsolicited manuscripts, it means it only considers manuscripts submitted by literary agents or by authors from whom one of their editors has requested the manuscript (for instance, from an author who has successfully pitched the book at a writing conference). When a *literary agency* says it won't consider unsolicited manuscripts, it means it expects the author to submit a query first.
- **UNAGENTED SUBMISSIONS:** When a publisher says it won't consider unagented submissions, it means it will only respond to queries sent by literary agents.
- **ADVANCE AND ROYALTIES:** An advance is money a publisher pays a writer after signing the contract but before copies of the book are sold. A royalty is a payment the author receives as each book is sold. Advances must be earned out before additional money is paid to the author.

CHAPTER 29

PLACING YOUR NOVEL WITH A TRADITIONAL PUBLISHER

"Traditional publishing and indie publishing aren't all that different, and I don't think people realize that. Some books and authors are bestsellers, but most aren't. It may be easier to self-publish than it is to traditionally publish, but in all honesty, it's harder to be a bestseller self-publishing than it is with a house."

—Amanda Hocking

■■■

Traditional publishing houses have been publishing mystery novels since 1876, when Harper and Brothers published *The Moonstone* by Wilkie Collins. The Big Five (Penguin Random House, Macmillan, HarperCollins, Hachette, and Simon & Schuster) all have imprints that feature crime fiction, and some have digital-only crime fiction imprints. Amazon's publisher for crime fiction, Thomas & Mercer, functions much like a traditional publisher. Smaller traditional publishers that specialize in crime fiction include Soho, Permanent Press, Midnight Ink, and Seventh Street Books.

NAVIGATING THE PATH TO TRADITIONAL PUBLICATION

The path to traditional publishing begins with a finished, polished manuscript. Really. No, you cannot sell a partial manuscript or a proposal for a first mystery novel to a traditional publisher—not unless you're James Patterson or Beyoncé.

The usual path to traditional publishing starts with a *query*. The author crafts a query letter pitching the novel and sends it (or his literary agent sends it) to an editor at a publishing house. If the editor likes the pitch, he'll request the manuscript. If he likes the manuscript well enough, most editors have to pitch it to their publishing boards before making an offer.

If the author accepts the offer, the author or his agent negotiate the contract that defines such essentials as the following:

- royalty or flat fee
- advance and payment schedule
- delivery date
- publication date
- second-use rights (e-book, audio, translation, etc.)
- free author copies of the book
- review of the cover design
- … and much more

Don't ignore the "and much more." Contracts are long and complicated affairs. Publishers draft boilerplate contracts with terms that benefit them. If you do not have a literary agent negotiating on your behalf, I strongly suggest that you bone up on publishing contracts. The Authors Guild website has a legal services section with postings open to nonmembers. There are also books on the topic. If you can afford it, hire an attorney *who is knowledgeable about intellectual property and book publishing* (not the one who helped you settle an estate or fight a lawsuit).

UNDERSTANDING WHAT TRADITIONAL PUBLISHERS DO

Traditional publishers edit, format, design, produce (in both physical and digital versions), market, distribute, and sell the book. Traditional publishing is notoriously slow. Months can pass from when a manuscript is submitted and accepted or rejected. Then the book's editing and production cycle can take another nine months to two years before the final book is available from retailers. In general, traditionally published books command higher prices than self-published books, but authors get a smaller percentage of the proceeds.

Traditional publishing offers authors and their books better visibility in the marketplace, including reviews in the mainstream media and book industry trade journals like *Kirkus Reviews* and *Publishers Weekly*. Traditionally published books also are more likely to find a spot on the shelf at brick-and-mortar bookstores, making it easier for readers to discover them.

GETTING A LITERARY AGENT

You need a literary agent if you want your book to be considered by most large and medium-sized traditional publishing houses. Their mystery imprints each publish a few debut mystery authors every year, and most of them are picked from manuscripts submitted by literary agents. You may not need a literary agent to be considered by a small press. Most small presses post submission guidelines on their websites.

What a Literary Agent Does for You

Literary agents have become the gatekeepers for traditional publishing. Many agents critique their authors' manuscripts, vetting revisions until they deem a manuscript strong enough to pass muster. A literary agent submits your manuscript to editors she believes, from past experience and track record, are looking for the kind of mystery novel you've written. Then the agent follows up with those editors to make sure your manuscript doesn't get lost in the heaps of submissions. The better your agent's reputation, the more quickly your manuscript is likely to rise to the top of an editor's slush pile and get considered.

However, having a brilliant agent doesn't guarantee a book contract. When your book gets rejected—and most submissions do at least a few times—your agent should tell you the reasons given and send you the rejection letters. Your agent will contact you when an editor expresses interest. She will try to encourage an auction—a bidding war between publishing houses for your novel—and negotiate contract details with your interests at heart. Many agencies have access to an attorney who reviews contracts as needed. Agencies also negotiate foreign language rights and subsidiary rights like audiobooks or a movie option.

All reputable literary agents work strictly on commission. That's the built-in incentive. If your agent doesn't sell your book, he doesn't get paid. Checks from your publisher go to your agent, so you don't get paid until your agent does. Agents take out their agreed-upon commission (typically 15 to 20 percent) from book advances and royalties, and pay authors the remainder.

What a Reputable Literary Agent Should *Not* Do

An agent who charges you for services prior to selling your novel is violating accepted industry practices. Some agents charge for expenses such as photocopying. This is fine if it's been documented and agreed upon up front. But beyond that, if you're being charged for services before you get a book contract—whether they call it a reading fee, a marketing fee, a retainer, or another euphemism—something's fishy.

When in doubt, refer to the Canon of Ethics on the Association of Authors' Representatives (AAR) website.

How to Target Agents Who Are Right for You

Honesty, integrity, chutzpa, smarts, and knowledge of the book business and contract negotiations—those are the basic ingredients of a competent literary agent. There are hundreds of them out there, many of them former editors and publicists with inside knowledge of the publishing business. Some agents have formidable track records. Others are just starting out and hungry to prove themselves.

Finding the right agent for you is a little bit like finding a soul mate, though the match should be between *your writing* and *the agent's taste*. You want an agent who has unvarnished enthusiasm for your work combined with the knowledge of which editors will share that enthusiasm—that's the ticket.

Target agents who represent crime fiction. When I last checked the online database of the Association of Authors' Representatives (AAR), 386 literary agents were listed, and 138 of them represented the mystery genre. To find out which agents are bringing home the bacon, read *Publishers Weekly* or get a free subscription to the online newsletter *Publishers Lunch* and read their weekly Deal Lunch, which reports on recent agent/publisher deals. You can find out more information about specific agents in Writer's Digest Books's annual *Guide to Literary Agents*, which prints profiles submitted by literary agents.

Agents receive an overwhelming number of queries each day from authors, so look for ways to make your query stand out. Here are some tips to help ensure your query is seriously considered:

- **OBTAIN REFERRALS FROM FRIENDS, RELATIVES, AND FELLOW WRITERS.**
  A referral from a friend, colleague, or family member, ideally a published author, editor, or reviewer, is hands down the best way to get your work considered. Ask everyone you know—you'll be surprised to discover that you know people who know literary agents. Network with published writers you meet at mystery conferences, or join the local chapter of Mystery Writers of

America, Sisters in Crime, or the National Writers Union. I have found that most published mystery authors are happy to share their experiences with agents, and you might even get a referral.

- **MEET AGENTS AT WRITING CONFERENCES AND WORKSHOPS.** Agents teach, speak on panels, critique manuscripts, and listen to pitches from writers at many writing conferences and workshops. They are looking for new talent. At mystery conferences like the New England Crime Bake, Sleuthfest, Thrillerfest, and Left Coast Crime you can sign up to pitch your novel to an agent.
- **IDENTIFY AGENTS WHO REPRESENT BOOKS LIKE YOURS.** A little online research (for instance, Google "James Patterson's agent") will quickly turn up the name of the literary agent who represents any well-known author. Or go to the mystery section of a bookstore and pull out every recently published mystery novel that reminds you of your own, or that is written by any author whom you admire. Read the acknowledgments page. Most writers thank their agents. Make a list of which agent represents which author. It's a good bet that any of those agents are worth querying.

✎ NOW YOU TRY: CREATE AN ACTION PLAN TO TARGET AGENTS   29.1

1. In the first column, compile a list of ten to thirty potential agents.

AGENT/ AGENCY	REASON YOU PICKED THIS AGENT	CURRENTLY TAKING QUERIES?	COMPLAINTS	MEMBER OF AAR?	CONTACT INFORMATION

2. Write down why you picked each agent:
   - name of the friend, relative, colleague, or other writer who referred you
   - date and event where you met the agent
   - published mystery author this agent represents
   - the great deal this agent recently negotiated
3. Cut one: Check with the agency's website and eliminate any that are currently not taking queries.
4. Cut two: Notice whether any agency on your list has had complaints against it, and if so, do you see a pattern? Websites with useful information for identifying agents with sketchy reputations include *Preditors & Editors* and *Writer Beware* (hosted by Science Fiction and Fantasy Writers of America).
5. Check to see if the agent is a member of the Association of Authors' Representatives (www.aar-online.org/). While there are good agents who are not AAR members, it may be something to consider when you prioritize.
6. Sort: Prioritize your list, from most desirable to least.

⬇ Download a printable version of this worksheet at www.writersdigest.com/writing-and-selling-your-mystery-novel-revised.

WRITING THE QUERY

Wouldn't it be nice if you could attach your manuscript to an e-mail, shoot it over to a list of agents and editors, and instantly get a yes? Unfortunately, the publishing world doesn't work that way. Most agents and editors like to be *queried* first—which is a fancy way of saying they want to hear the elevator pitch of your novel so they can decide if it's worth their while to read it.

Check the agent's website to see if she has specific requirements for queries. An agent will usually say, for instance, whether she wants to be queried by snail mail or e-mail, and whether she wants a pitch only or pages, too. A typical query includes:

- a letter, customized for each agent
- a synopsis or the first ten pages of the manuscript

Never send your entire manuscript unless an editor or agent has specifically asked for it. An agent is more likely to respond to your query if you demonstrate some knowledge of who she is, so never send a boilerplate query letter that begins *Dear Agent*.

Anatomy of a Query Letter

The query letter should be short, no more than one printed page. Agents tell me they prefer direct, business-like letters that convey the concepts of your novel so enticingly that they simply *must* see your complete manuscript posthaste. The query is 100 percent marketing, somewhat like the copy on a book jacket, and its only purpose is to make an agent or editor want to read your book.

---

(1) Subject: Debut mystery by Las Vegas magician, referred by Max Flash

(2) Dear Mr. Jones:

(3) I am enclosing the first ten pages of *Jiggery Pokery*, a mystery novel, in the hope that you will want to see the manuscript and help me find a publisher for it.

(4) *Jiggery Pokery* is a suspense thriller that takes place in Las Vegas and features Melinda Starr, private investigator. Starr is the daughter of a master magician and uses the skills she learned as her father's assistant to hunt down a serial killer who picks his victims with the help of a roulette wheel.

(5) I know you have represented my friend, Max Flash. Max suggested that I query you. (6) My book, too, takes readers to the world of the professional magician, and though it is more hard-boiled and less occult, it should appeal to a similar audience.

(7) I am a professional magician with a considerable following in North America and Europe. I have written more than a dozen nonfiction articles on magic and have a monthly column in *Magic* magazine. This is my first novel.

Thanks very much for your time. (8) I have included the first ten pages and look forward to hearing from you. (9) Please let me know if I can send you the manuscript to evaluate.

Sincerely,
Siegfried Shazam
23 Piltdown Lane
Paramus, New Jersey 03333
(10) Phone: 002-444-5555
Website: sshazamagician.com
E-mail: sshazam@isp-server.com
Twitter: sshazamagic

---

1. The subject is all-important to distinguish your query.
2. Address the query to a specific agent.
3. Get right down to business and say why you are writing.
4. Give the book title, genre, and a one-paragraph synopsis.
5. Include a personal connection if you have one.
6. Say why this agent is right for this novel, what kind of mystery you've written, and the target audience.
7. Include any aspects of your personal background that are relevant and will help sell the book. If it's your debut novel, say so.
8. Mention that you've enclosed the opening pages or a synopsis—whatever the agent has requested in her submission guidelines.
9. Close with: Can I send you my manuscript?
10. Below your signature, place your contact information, website, and social media platforms that will support your marketability as an author.

Keep in mind that the lion's share of queries is screened by publishing interns or junior staffers. Your *subject line* is paramount.

Here's some extra ammunition to use if you've got it. Let the agent know if:

- an author, editor, or other mutual acquaintance suggested you send your manuscript to this person
- you have anything in common with this person (attended the same college, grew up in the same town in Minnesota, both used to work in advertising)
- you met this person at a conference, bookstore, party ... wherever
- you heard this person speak somewhere, or you read something this person wrote; comment on some idea you took away from his remarks
- established, respected writers or media personalities have read and liked your manuscript and agreed that you can convey their enthusiasm
- this will be your first published novel; publishers and agents are looking for undiscovered talent
- you've been published before (self- or traditionally) and sold an impressive number of books; say how many and over what time period
- you or your book are in some way comparable to a best-selling author or novel; cite the comparison, but avoid hyperbole

Finally, make sure your query is flawless—no spelling, grammar, or punctuation errors, no clunky sentences or awkward transitions. Triple-check that you have spelled the agent's name correctly.

WRITING THE SYNOPSIS

The synopsis for querying agents and editors is much shorter and less detailed than the before-the-fact synopsis you may have written while planning your novel. Some writers, me included, find this short synopsis harder to write than the novel. You have only a page or two to get it right, and the future of your beloved novel hangs in the balance. The synopsis has to be informative, but it cannot be boring. It has to make your novel sound fabulous, but it can't be puffed up with self-praise.

Say it with me: *The synopsis is a marketing pitch.* Remember, this is *not* a blueprint of the book or a summary of everything in it. It should be as specific as possible, including details that make your book unique.

To get a feel for how to write a synopsis that pitches your mystery novel, visit an online bookstore and read publishers' descriptions of mystery novels. Here are three excerpts from publishers' descriptions of mystery novels:

> Convicted murderer Melvin Mars is counting down the last hours before his execution—for the violent killing of his parents twenty years earlier—when he's granted an unexpected reprieve. Another man has confessed to the crime. Amos Decker, newly hired on an FBI special task force, takes an interest in Mars's case after discovering the striking similarities to his own life. (*The Last Mile* by David Baldacci, Grand Central Publishing)

> Chief Inspector Armand Gamache of the Sûreté du Québec and his team of investigators are called in to the scene of a suspicious death in a rural village south of Montreal. Jane Neal, a local fixture in the tiny hamlet of Three Pines, just north of the U.S. border, has been found dead in the woods. The locals are certain it's a tragic hunting accident and nothing more, but Gamache smells something foul in these remote woods, and is soon certain that Jane Neal died at the hands of someone much more sinister than a careless bowhunter. *Still Life* introduces series hero Inspector Gamache, who commands his forces with integrity and quiet courage. (*Still Life* by Louise Penny, Minotaur Books)

> On a hillside near the cozy Irish village of Glennkill, the members of the flock gather around their shepherd, George, whose body lies pinned to the ground with a spade. George has cared for the sheep, reading them a plethora of books every night. The daily exposure to literature has made them far savvier about the workings of the human mind than your average sheep. Led by Miss Maple, the smartest sheep in Glennkill (and possibly the world), they set out to find George's killer. (*Three Bags Full* by Leonie Swann, Doubleday)

Your synopsis can be up to two pages long, single-spaced. Like publisher synopses, yours should introduce the main characters, establish the setting, and summarize your story including your opening gambit and some of the plot twists. You don't have to reveal the ending.

Here's the first page of the synopsis for my novel *Come and Find Me*.

> For two years, Diana has been a recluse. The thirty-five-year-old computer security expert rarely leaves her modest suburban ranch house in a Boston suburb, not since she returned from Switzerland. There, in the shadow of the Eiger, she and her partner in life and in work, Daniel Spector, had been climbing the icy face of Waterfall Pitch. She was securing her own footing in the frozen cascade of water when Daniel slipped. Diana is haunted by the sound of his cry echoing across the gorge and by the image of his body frozen and wedged somewhere in an icy crevasse, suspended there forever because of that one moment when she looked away.
>
> She and Daniel had been part of a group of hackers. Most of them were idealists whose goals were to expose security flaws and shake software companies, businesses, and government agencies out of their complacency. For some, the goal was to prove how smart and superior they were. But one after the other, fellow hackers peeled away. Some went to the dark side to make their fortunes by creating serious mayhem. Others went legit, taking high-level security jobs. Diana and Daniel, along with Daniel's best friend, Jake, were about to open a security consulting company and get paid to ferret out security flaws and protect systems from predatory hackers. The trip had been to celebrate their impending transition.
>
> Diana returned home devastated. She broke all the mirrors in her house, unable to bear the sight of her own reflection. For months she remained housebound, turning her home into a fortress ringed with invisible electronic security fences. Redundant satellite, fiber optic, cable, and DSL feeds ensured that the Internet, her link to the outside, never goes down. Whatever she needed from the outside she had delivered, and her only visitors were her sister, Ashley, and Jake.
>
> When Diana's sister goes missing, Diana is forced out of her protective crouch. She …

A synopsis offers a *fast-forward overview* of your book. Here are some techniques to borrow from these examples in writing your synopsis:

- Write in the present tense.
- Summarize your main characters.
- Describe the setting and context.
- For once, it's okay to tell and not show; dramatizing takes too long.

- Summarize the plot, hitting the major plot twists.
- Communicate your protagonist's motivation and key challenges.
- Don't try to explain every character and plot point.

SENDING OUT QUERIES

Sending out queries and waiting for responses can be nerve-wracking, and it only gets worse after rejections start coming in. Try to disconnect from the whole process emotionally. Think of it as a marketing campaign for which you're the hired help—because as surely as there are death and taxes, you will get rejections. This race goes to the persistent.

Make a plan, and keep track. Send e-mail queries to four or five of your top choices. Each time you get a rejection, send out a query to the next agent on your list. If it's been four weeks and you haven't gotten a response, send a follow-up e-mail. If after eight weeks you still haven't heard, forget about that agent and send out the next query.

QUERYING A SMALL PRESS

Just like a major publishing house, a small press enters into a contract with the author, edits and publishes the book, markets and handles distribution, and pays the author royalties. Generally speaking, a small press offers a smaller advance and has smaller print runs than larger publishing houses.

Most small presses post their submission guidelines on their websites. Some small presses accept unagented queries.

Targeting small presses requires due diligence. There are plenty of scam artists who dangle the promise of a book contract while their only goal is to take your money. So research the reputation of any small press before you query:

- Make sure it has a track record for selling books like yours.
- Look at some of its finished books. Do they look professionally designed and presented? Is the text clean and copyedited?
- Google the name of the press with the words "publishing scam."
- Check out the publisher on the *Preditors & Editors* website or in *Writer Beware* on the Science Fiction & Fantasy Writers of America website.
- Look at the track record of some of the house's published books. (Use Amazon's "Sales Rank" feature.)

A red flag should pop up if you submit your manuscript and the editor starts talking about reading fees, publishing fees, a fee for cover art, or a fee to list your book on Amazon. You should also be suspicious if the editor suggests an unusually high list price for the book.

Ask about their distribution channels. It will be easier to get your book into bookstores and libraries if the small press sells its books through a major distributor such as Ingram Content Group or Baker & Taylor, Inc.

If you sell your manuscript to a small press without the help of a literary agent, I strongly recommend you either hire an attorney who knows how to evaluate a publishing contract or do the research required to evaluate and negotiate it yourself. You want to be sure your best interests are represented across the range of important issues, including how royalties are computed and reversion of rights (a.k.a. what happens when your book goes out of print or the small press goes belly-up).

NOW YOU TRY: PREPARE TO APPROACH SMALL PRESSES 29.2

1. Decide if you want to be published by a small press.
2. Compile a list of small presses to target—fill in the first column below:

SMALL PRESS	REASON YOU PICKED THIS PUBLISHER	AUTHOR COMPLAINTS	THEIR BEST-SELLING AUTHORS	CONTACT INFORMATION

3. Check the reputation of each publisher on your list by consulting the Preditors & Editors website (pred-ed.com). Try to distinguish between a few disgruntled authors and a pattern of poor business practices. Eliminate any publishers with consistently reported problems.

4. Check out each publisher on your list in *Novel & Short Story Writer's Market*, published by Writer's Digest Books. Based on what you glean, add this publisher's contact information or eliminate it from the list.

5. Search Amazon for mysteries published by each publisher, and note their sales rank. Search *inside* some of its books to see if they are professionally presented and edited. Decide whether this publisher seems like the company you want to keep.

6. Sort. Prioritize your list from the most desirable small presses and independent publishers to the least.

7. For your final choices, visit the publisher's website and prepare a query package that meets their specifications for submissions.

⬇ Download a printable version of this worksheet at www.writersdigest.com/writing-and-selling-your-mystery-novel-revised.

HANDLING REJECTION

Expect rejection. You'll have agents who say, "No thank you," to your query letter; you'll have editors who ask to see a chapter (shout for joy!) and then ask for the manuscript (cross all fingers and toes), and then send a letter saying sorry. An editor may even hold on to your book for months as your hopes mount, only to reject it.

Remind yourself how competitive this business is. A good agent already has a full plate of clients vying for attention. Each editor has slots for only a few new authors in a given year.

Most often, the rejection says something boilerplate and generic, like these examples from my very own pile of rejections:

"I am sorry to say that I don't have the requisite enthusiasm to take on the project and represent it properly."

"The market is very tight right now, and I am being highly selective about the new properties which I am taking on."

"I'm afraid I don't think I'd be able to sell it. The writing is good, but the storyline didn't work for me."

But you may get a rejection that goes on at some length about your novel's strengths and weaknesses. Cherish these, because agents and editors rarely take time to say anything unless they see potential. If you start to see a pattern—for example, if several rejection letters say your main character isn't strong enough, or if one points to a weakness in your plot and you agree, stop! Consider revising the manuscript to address the problems before sending it out to more agents and editors, and exhausting all of your top choices. Once you've been rejected by an agent or editor, you don't get a do-over.

Even if an editor loves your manuscript, few editors can make yes-or-no decisions unilaterally. The editor usually has to convince other editors, as well as sales and marketing departments, that your book is terrific *and* that there's a strong market for it. Book publishing is a business. A decision to publish a book is not a reward for literary quality; it's a gamble for financial gain.

With each rejection, feel your skin thickening as your ego grows calluses—you'll need them. Pick yourself up, dust yourself off, and send out a new query. The next one could be the one that clicks.

A FINAL WORD

If your mystery novel is a good one *and* luck is with you, it will find a publisher. When that happens, break out the champagne. Celebrate!

Then start writing the next book before you get sucked into the vortex of promoting the one you just sold.

ON YOUR OWN: PUT TOGETHER A QUERY

1. Research the agents and publishers you intend to query; prioritize them.
2. Write a tailored query for each of the first five agents or publishers on your list. Use this checklist to guide you:

   ____ Address this specific agent or editor by name.

   ____ In the subject line, lead with what distinguishes this query from the pack.

   ____ Say why you are writing.

   ____ Include your book title, genre, and a one-paragraph synopsis.

   ____ Specify the kind of mystery and the target audience.

   ____ Say why you think this particular literary agent is right for your novel.

____ Include aspects of your personal background that are relevant and will help sell the book.

____ Include the opening pages or a synopsis—whatever the agent has requested in her submission guidelines.

____ Share any personal connection you have to the agent, including a reminder of where you met this agent or editor, or who referred you.

____ Mention praise for your work from a published writer who has agreed to let you use the quote.

____ Tell the agent or publisher if this is your debut novel.

____ Close with Can I send you my manuscript?

____ Below the signature, place your contact information, website, and social media platforms that will support your marketability as an author.

____ Check for spelling, grammar, and punctuation errors; revise clunky sentences and awkward transitions.

3. Prepare a second batch of five queries that are ready to go out when you receive a rejection.

CHAPTER 30

SELF-PUBLISHING YOUR NOVEL

"My biggest word of advice to any new future writers thinking about diving into self-publishing: Edit."

—Amanda Hocking

■ ■ ■

Self-published authors are their own publishers. All of the publishing tasks taken on and paid for by a traditional publishing house—editing, formatting, cover design, distribution, marketing, order fulfillment, and so on—fall to self-published authors or the freelancers they hire.

Self-publishing is fast and gives the author complete control over the finished product. Though self-published e-books tend to be priced lower than traditionally published books, the author takes a higher percentage of the revenue. Rates vary, but in a typical scenario the author's royalty rate for an e-book published with a traditional publisher might be 25 percent; if self-published, that same e-book might return 65 percent to the author.

Here's what mystery author Libby Fischer Hellmann, a "hybrid author" who self-publishes some of her novels and publishes others with a traditional press, has to say about being an indie author:

> I am running a small business now, and I am very much aware of the bottom line. Most of my profit goes back into the business with additional marketing and promotion. That, in itself, is an overwhelming task, and it has taken valu-

able time away from my writing. I hire editors, copyeditors, and cover design-ers. I have a webmistress, a social media manager, and a street team. I also have four foreign translations that require a different type of promotion. Running a business also means figuring out what project should be indie published versus traditionally published.

This chapter provides an overview of self-publishing—a snapshot that comes with this caveat: The publishing business is changing rapidly. For authors who choose to pursue this route, I recommend that you research the options and services available when you are ready to go to press. Resources include Jane Friedman's informative blog (janefriedman.com), which offers the latest information for self-published authors. Also refer to the online forum and author advice center hosted by ALLi, the Alliance of Independent Authors (selfpublishingadvice.org). Writer Beware (www.sfwa.org/other-resources/for-authors/writer-beware), hosted by the Science Fiction & Fantasy Writers of America, devotes an entire section to self-publishing.

SELF-PUBLISHING: CONTROLLING IT ALL

A self-published author makes a host of key decisions about the published book. These include the format (print, digital) it will take, compatibility with which e-readers, the distribution channels, the sale price, and the type and breadth of marketing.

Some of the tasks a self-published author will need to perform (or hire out) include:

- editing and proofreading
- converting and formatting the text
- designing the book layout and cover
- promoting

This can seem overwhelming. Tools to support indie authors are evolving, and an entire cottage industry of services has sprung up to help authors who want to off-load some of the work.

Editing

Professional editing is the single most valuable investment indie authors can make in their self-published books. Hire a freelance editor when you have made the manuscript as literate and compelling and clean as you can get it.

Here are the levels of editing offered by professionals:

- **CONTENT EDITING:** This type of editing looks at the big picture, critiquing the overall effectiveness of the storytelling, characterization, pacing, and narrative voice.
- **COPYEDITING:** This service edits sentences and paragraphs for clarity and flow, and corrects grammar, punctuation, and spelling.
- **PROOFREADING:** This is the final edit, the essential nitpicking to check the formatted manuscript for typos and spacing glitches.

One of the best ways to find a good freelance editor is through word of mouth. Ask indie authors whose work you admire, and browse KBoards (Kindle discussion boards) at kboards.com, for recommendations.

Converting and Formatting Text for E-books

To generate a clean, professional-looking book, most publishing services (like Smashwords, CreateSpace, or Amazon Kindle Direct Publishing) require that you *unformat* your Word file first. Follow the guidelines provided by whatever service you are using. After that, the book will need to be formatted and styled.

These are the most typical e-book formats:

- **EPUB:** The standard format for e-books, this works on most devices.
- **MOBI:** This is Amazon Kindle's proprietary format.
- **PDF:** This format is fine for displaying on a computer but problematic on some e-readers.

Designing the Book Cover

Your book's cover is the only thing many potential readers will ever see, and the version they will most likely encounter is no larger than a thumbnail. It needs to be eye-catching, and the title should be readable even at this small size. At a glance, it should look like a mystery novel (not a romance or a textbook).

Entire books are written about book cover design, and if you want to design your own I encourage you to read one. You don't want your book cover to look cheesy or amateurish. Remember: Your cover is your book's first, and possibly only, visual handshake with potential readers.

NOW YOU TRY: ASSESS BOOK COVERS

1. Go to Amazon and browse through the Kindle Store for high-ranking and best-selling mystery novels. Copy the thumbnails of the covers that catch

your eye, and paste them into a file. Copy the thumbnails of the covers you like least, and paste them into a separate file. You now have a gallery of the best and the worst. Notice what the best ones have in common, particularly in contrast to the worst. Look at:

- color
- text size and font for the title
- text size, font, and placement for the author's name
- blurb placement (or the absence of blurbs)
- image
- overall look and feel

2. Browse Amazon's romance and fantasy novels in the Kindle Store. Notice how these covers convey *romance* or *fantasy* instead of *mystery*.

DISTRIBUTING YOUR BOOK

It's up to you whether to distribute your book through a single channel or through multiple ones. For instance, if you want it to sell exclusively on Amazon to Kindle readers, use Kindle Direct Publishing. If you want your book to be available to folks who read on Kindles, Nooks, iPads, and Kobos, go with a distributor like Smashwords, BookBaby, or Draft2Digital. If you want to sell a print version, you can hire a print-on-demand (POD) service like CreateSpace, Lulu, or Lightning Source.

If cost is not an issue, you can hire a company to take care of everything—converting, formatting, POD, distribution, and marketing your manuscript—for a fee. For instance, Lulu offers full-service publishing packages. Shop around and be sure to read each company's customer reviews.

Do your research and compare costs and services of the different providers. Think about which aspects of the publishing process you want to do yourself. Learn all that you can about your audience so you know which e-readers are right for them. And make room in your day for promoting and marketing your newly published mystery novel while you're writing the next one.

APPENDIX OF RESOURCES FOR MYSTERY WRITERS

MYSTERY WRITER GROUPS

Writing is a solitary activity, but many organizations provide the writer with support and encouragement from like-minded souls. Here are some organizations that can be helpful for creating community:

- **SISTERS IN CRIME (SINC) WWW.SISTERSINCRIME.ORG:** Sisters in Crime is a supportive organization for published and unpublished mystery writers. Founded in 1986 by a group of women mystery writers, including *New York Times* bestseller Sara Paretsky, its mission is to combat discrimination against women in the mystery field and to promote their professional advancement. SinC has a special chapter for unpublished writers (GUPPIES), an Internet chapter, and local chapters worldwide.
- **MYSTERY WRITERS OF AMERICA (MWA) WWW.MYSTERYWRITERS.ORG:** Mystery Writers of America is a nonprofit professional organization of mystery and crime writers. MWA awards the prestigious annual Edgar Awards. Unpublished authors can join as Affiliate Members. MWA publishes an Approved Publisher List on their website that contains publishers whose authors qualify for "active status" membership. MWA has local chapters.
- **INTERNATIONAL THRILLER WRITERS (ITW) THRILLERWRITERS.ORG:** Established to recognize and promote the thriller genre, the International Thriller Writers is an honorary society of authors of both fiction and nonfiction who write thrillers, including murder mystery, detective, suspense, horror, supernatural, action, espionage, true crime, war, and adventure. ITW sponsors the annual Thrillerfest conference in New York City. Mystery au-

thors can apply for Active membership if they are commercially published writers and Associate membership if they are industry professionals, non-commercially published writers, or others.

MYSTERY CONFERENCES

Many conferences held annually in the United States focus on crime fiction. Some are primarily for fans. Others focus on writing and provide panels and workshops on craft, and pitch sessions with agents and editors. Mystery conferences are great places to meet writers and readers, and to learn about crime fiction and the publishing business.

The largest fan conference is Bouchercon, which takes place in a different location each fall. Other large conferences for fans and readers are Thrillerfest, which focuses on thrillers; Malice Domestic, which focuses on traditional mysteries and cozies; Left Coast Crime; and Florida's Sleuthfest. Smaller conferences with an emphasis on writing mysteries include Book Passage's intimate Mystery Writers Conference, the New England Crime Bake, and Magna Cum Murder.

ANNUAL MYSTERY CONFERENCES: A SNAPSHOT VIEW				
CONFERENCE	FOUNDED	LOCATION	WHEN	AUDIENCE
Bouchercon	1970	North America; location changes annually	Fall	Fans, writers, editors
Book Passage Mystery Writers Conference	1994	Corte Madera, California	Summer	Writers
California Crime Writers Conference	2011	Los Angeles, California	Biannual	Writers
Deadly Ink	2000	New Brunswick, New Jersey	Summer	Fans, writers
Killer Nashville	2006	Nashville, Tennessee	August	Writers
Left Coast Crime	1991	Western North America; location changes annually	Winter	Fans, writers
Magna Cum Murder	1993	Muncie, Indiana	October	Fans, writers
Malice Domestic	1989	Bethesda, Maryland	April	Fans, writers
New England Crime Bake	2002	Boston, Massachusetts	November	Writers
Sleuthfest	1994	Orlando, Florida	March	Writers, fans
Thrillerfest	2006	New York, New York	July	Writers, fans
Writers' Police Academy	2009	Green Bay, Wisconsin	August	Writers

SOURCES FOR RESEARCHING LITERARY AGENTS AND PUBLISHERS

Here are some sources for sleuthing out the track records and reputations of literary agents and publishers:

- **ASSOCIATION OF AUTHORS' REPRESENTATIVE (AAR) (AARONLINE. ORG:)** AAR is a nonprofit professional organization for agents. The website hosts a member database and posts the ethical standards by which members agree to abide.
- *GUIDE TO LITERARY AGENTS* **(WRITER'S DIGEST BOOKS):** This annually updated volume provides a comprehensive listing of literary agents, with specific information on what they want and how they want it. It also includes useful tips and interviews with insiders.
- **LITERARY MARKET PLACE (INFORMATION TODAY, INC.):** Known as the LMP, this two-volume reference is available in public libraries. It lists publishers along with the genres they represent, the number of books they published the previous year, contact names, and how to get in touch with them.
- *NOVEL & SHORT STORY WRITER'S MARKET* **(WRITER'S DIGEST BOOKS):** Find the latest information about the market for mystery fiction in this annually updated volume. Pinpoint which book publishers are looking for mystery novels, and find lists of major houses as well as small and independent presses.
- **PREDITORS & EDITORS (PRED-ED.COM):** This independent website provides all kinds of information for authors. It reports dishonest agents, shoddy publishing practices, contest scams, book doctors who fleece unwitting authors, and poorly run writing workshops.
- **PUBLISHERS LUNCH/DEAL LUNCH (LUNCH.PUBLISHERSMARKET PLACE.COM):** Subscriptions are free to this online newsletter, which reports the latest news in the publishing business. The weekly Deal Lunch reports on recent agent/publisher deals.
- **WRITER BEWARE (WWW.SFWA.ORG/OTHER-RESOURCES/FOR-AUTHORS/WRITER-BEWARE):** This is part of the Science Fiction and Fantasy Writers of America website and provides information about fraudulent agents, scams, copyright, electronic rights, and so on.

INDEX

WRITING & SELLING YOUR MYSTERY NOVEL